Deposit Insurance in China

I0894803

This book examines and compares the rationale, design, and implementation of deposit insurance in the US, the UK, and China, with the aim of finding an effective solution for China's nascent deposit insurance scheme by learning from the US and UK models.

Deposit insurance, a pillar of the financial safety net that protects insured deposits and serves as a guarantee against losses on insured accounts, has become increasingly important in bank resolution. Using a comparative and interdisciplinary approach, this book examines the legal and regulatory issues surrounding deposit insurance schemes in three jurisdictions – the US, the UK, and China. It offers a timely analysis of the operating mechanisms and implications of deposit insurance during the global financial crisis. It also provides an in-depth doctrinal analysis of the US, the UK, and China's deposit insurance laws. Based on these discussions, the author proposes suggestions for reforming China's deposit insurance system and practice.

The title will appeal to scholars and students of banking and banking law as well as legal and financial practitioners in the fields of commercial law and banking and financial regulation.

Ningyao Ye is currently Assistant Professor in Financial Law at the School of Juris Master, China University of Political Science and Law. His research interests include international financial law, banking law, and capital market regulation.

Deposit Insurance in China

Lessons from the US and UK Experience

Ningyao Ye

Routledge
Taylor & Francis Group
LONDON AND NEW YORK

First published 2025
by Routledge
4 Park Square, Milton Park, Abingdon, Oxon OX14 4RN

and by Routledge
605 Third Avenue, New York, NY 10158

Routledge is an imprint of the Taylor & Francis Group, an informa business

British Library Cataloguing-in-Publication Data
A catalogue record for this book is available from the British Library

ISBN: 978-1-041-00945-0 (hbk)
ISBN: 978-1-041-01036-4 (pbk)
ISBN: 978-1-003-61275-9 (ebk)

DOI: 10.4324/9781003612759

Typeset in Times New Roman
by Deanta Global Publishing Services, Chennai, India

This book is dedicated to my wife, my son, my parents, my supervisors and my dear friends.

谨以此书献给我的妻子，我的儿子,我的父母, 我的导师及我的朋友。

Contents

Figures

Tables

Abbreviations

ABC	Agricultural Bank of China
BCBS	Basel Committee on Banking Supervision
BCM	Bank of Communication
BIF	Bank Insurance Fund
BIS	Bank for International Settlements
BOC	Bank of China
CBRC	China Banking Regulatory Commission
CCB	China Construction Bank
CCP	China Communist Party
DIF	Deposit Insurance Fund
DIFMC	Deposit Insurance Fund Management Corporation
DRR	Designated Reserve Ratio
EU	European Union
FCA	Financial Conduct Authority
FDIC	Federal Deposit Insurance Corporation
FPC	Financial Policy Committee
FSA	Financial Services Authority
FSB	Financial Stability Board
FSCS	Financial Services Compensation Scheme
FSDC	Financial Stability and Development Committee
FSF	Financial Stability Forum
FSOC	Financial Stability Oversight Council
GDP	Gross Domestic Product
GFC	Global Financial Crisis
HKSE	Hong Kong Stock Exchange
IADI	International Association of Deposit Insurers
IMF	International Monetary Fund
LOLR	Lender of Last Resort
NFRA	National Financial Regulatory Administration
NPL	Non-Performing Loan
OCC	Office of the Comptroller of the Currency
OTC	Office of Thrift Supervision
PBOC	People's Bank of China
PRA	Prudential Regulation Authority

SAIF	Savings Association Insurance Fund
SCV	Single Customer View
UK	United Kingdom
US	United States

Preface

This book investigates legal and regulatory issues regarding deposit insurance schemes and banking regulation in three jurisdictions – the United States (US), the United Kingdom (UK), and China – from a comparative, interdisciplinary, and transnational perspective, with specific suggestions and recommendations for unresolved Chinese problems and practice in regard to deposit insurance.

The book principally explores the rationales, designs, and country specifics of deposit insurance among the US, the UK, and China and attempts to find an effective solution for China's nascent deposit insurance scheme by comparing and drawing lessons from the US and the UK models. After the global financial crisis (GFC), an increasing number of countries have realised the important functions of deposit insurance, which is an essential component of the financial safety net and is considered an ex-post resolution mechanism dealing with bank failures. During the GFC in 2008, both the US and the UK encountered various problems in their financial markets, while their deposit insurance schemes with different patterns played distinct functions and roles in resolving problematic banks, such as the Northern Rock run, which became the first UK bank run in 150 years. China, as an emerging country with the second-largest economy globally, which just deviated from a centrally planned economy and stepped into a new era on the free market, also has initiated its deposit insurance scheme in 2015. China has witnessed the further opening-up of the banking sector as privately owned banks and locally registered foreign banks started their businesses to attract Chinese depositors. In fact, unlike the US which has a very sound deposit insurance system, both China and the UK have an urgent need to strengthen their deposit insurance schemes.

Against this backdrop, the book aims to examine three countries' deposit insurance schemes and respond to four underlying questions: first, how deposit insurance works and what good practices can be used to build an effective deposit insurance scheme; second, how deposit insurance and banking regulation work in the US, what features contribute to the US's deposit insurance scheme, and what improvements to deposit insurance were implemented after the global financial crisis; third, how deposit insurance and banking regulation work in the UK, what characteristics contribute to the UK's deposit insurance scheme, and what progress has been made since the global financial crisis; fourth, how the banking sector in China is transitioning to a more market-based sector, what impacts the implicit deposit insurance scheme had on the Chinese banking sector, what problems were exposed under the implicit deposit insurance scheme, what features contribute to China's deposit insurance scheme, and whether the current legal and regulatory framework is effective and efficient in running a deposit insurance scheme. In responding to these questions, this book provides suggestions and recommendations for China's policymakers regarding how to build an effective deposit insurance scheme based on country specifics. I also thank the editors at Sweet & Maxwell for their permission to reproduce the following article in this book:

Ningyao Ye, 'The Reform of Deposit Insurance after the Global Financial Crisis: How the FDIC Evolved from a Deposit Insurer to the Saviour of Banks?' (2020) 3 *Journal of Business Law*, 219, 240.

1 Introduction

1.1 Research Background

In modern financial markets, the banking industry always plays an essential role in countries' policy objectives, economic growth, and financial stability simply because one insolvent bank may lead to a 'domino effect' in the whole financial system. Therefore, banking instability has become a severe issue that significantly threatens financial markets. Consequently, in order to maintain financial stability and public confidence, deposit insurance, regarded by many as a vital part of the financial sector safety net and an ex-post resolution measure dealing with bank failures, has emerged and become increasingly important for achieving financial stability and public confidence. At present, more than 100 countries have installed deposit insurance schemes, while many countries have gained experience from the recent global financial crisis (GFC) and realised the importance of having an effective deposit insurance system.[1] In particular, building up an effective deposit insurance system has increasingly drawn attention from many international financial organisations at an international level and a universal consensus of good practices for establishing effective deposit insurance schemes has been gradually reached.[2]

Deposit insurance, which provides protection for insured deposits and interests, can be deemed as a guarantee against losses of insured accounts, unlike other private insurance driven by profit.[3] There are two principal functions designated to deposit insurance. First, deposit insurance is designed to maintain financial stability by eliminating the threat of bank runs and promoting public confidence. Second, deposit insurance safeguards ordinary depositors who stand at a disadvantaged position under bank failures. Additionally, a noteworthy function of deposit insurance is to promote competition between small and large banks.[4] Nevertheless, to achieve those functions, a well-managed and well-designed deposit insurance system is required. Garcia indicates that a well-designed deposit insurance system could eliminate bank runs by reassuring depositors and maintaining the stability of the banking system, while a well-designed deposit insurance system is also required to be incentive-compatible in order to avoid moral hazard, adverse selection, and agency problems.[5] Simultaneously, as stressed by the Financial Stability Forum (FSF), a well-designed deposit insurance system, as a crucial part of the financial safety net, is also supported and bolstered by sound prudential regulation

DOI: 10.4324/9781003612759-1

and supervision, good corporate governance, sound accounting standards, and the enforcement of effective laws.[6]

Deposit insurance has been divided into two types – explicit deposit insurance and implicit deposit insurance. In brief, an implicit deposit insurance scheme means that there is no formal arrangement for deposit protection, so the government has the discretion to decide whether or not to protect depositors' savings, and, most of the time, the funding source for reimbursing depositors depends on the government's financial capability, especially the availability of public funds. On the contrary, an explicit deposit insurance scheme would be accompanied by an integrated legal system, a straightforward deposit insurance law, or an enabling law contained in general financial services law, which illustrates rules governing the system.[7] So far, explicit deposit insurance has become common sense on an international scale.

Under the Core Principles for Effective Deposit Insurance Systems released by the Basel Committee on Banking Supervision (BCBS) and the International Association of Deposit Insurers (IADI), it is clear that explicit deposit insurance is preferable to implicit deposit insurance.[8] Accordingly, many countries and jurisdictions have transitioned from implicit deposit insurance or blanket guarantees to explicit deposit insurance. It is equally fair to say that explicit deposit insurance naturally has some advantages over implicit deposit insurance, which provides a high degree of certainty for depositors and financial markets by setting a clear scope of obligations for associated authorities, a structured process for dealing with bank failures, and a funding mechanism covering the costs of bank failures.[9] However, economically speaking, explicit deposit insurance, normally bringing high costs of protecting deposits, such as 100 percent coverage and operational costs, has been deemed by policymakers as an expensive and bold mechanism.[10]

Unfortunately, Hoelscher has noted that both explicit and implicit deposit insurance may create moral hazard as an intrinsic feature.[11] MacDonald has written that 'moral hazard refers to the adverse effects, from the point of view of the insurer, that insurance may have on the insuree's behaviour'.[12] It can be seen that eliminating moral hazard is one of the most challenging parts of implementing effective deposit insurance.

With the existence of deposit insurance, it has been suggested that bank managers, who have a general understanding of government bail-out plans, are believed to take excessive risks, thereby jeopardising market discipline and increasing the possibility of moral hazard. Recent crises have demonstrated that governments have usually provided generous liquidity and capital support for banks which have been classified as too big to fail. Taking the UK as an example, Royal Bank of Scotland, Lloyds, and HBOS, three large banks in the UK whose collapses occurred by 2008, were injected with £37 billion by the UK government.[13] However, Helfer, a former Chairman and Chief Executive Officer of the Federal Deposit Insurance Corporation (FDIC), points out that providing support clearly involves moral hazard even for troubled but solvent banks; she also has found that the most effective measure for warding off moral hazard is to encourage market discipline to punish imprudent behaviours by allowing severely collapsed banks to go bankrupt and imposing strict restrictions on troubled but solvent banks.[14]

With respect to ordinary depositors, as mentioned by Campbell and Cartwright, the responsibilities of depositors, such as the incentives of monitoring the performance of banks and the assessment of risk level, have been relieved.[15] Simultaneously, large depositors, creditors, and shareholders, who are in a better position for monitoring banks and possess vigorous lobbying power in policy-making processes compared to ordinary depositors, are not willing to contribute and jeopardise moral hazard. Notably, without explicit rules of accountability, even regulators and deposit insurers are possibly associated with moral hazard.

There are three additional agency problems in conjunction with moral hazard as well. First, it is not unusual for politicians to impose a burden on deposit insurers through their administrative powers. Second, the board of directors of privately-run deposit insurance is normally composed of representatives from each member bank, which triggers regulatory capture. The third issue is the effective cooperation between different financial authorities.

To address those problems, many international organisations have issued research explaining the importance of good practices against moral hazard. Usually, adopting an explicit limited coverage deposit insurance scheme is a reasonable approach. Before setting out the scope of coverage, it is noteworthy that policymakers should ponder what kind of financial institutions and financial instruments should be covered by the deposit insurance scheme. In reality, extending coverage to all types of deposits and depositors has exacerbated the level of moral hazard since it violates the primary objective of deposit insurance. As mentioned by both the FSF and the IADI, explicit deposit insurance is preferable, and deposits should be defined precisely in relevant laws and contracts.[16] Moreover, depositors who have the capability to monitor the performance of banks and exert market discipline might be excluded from the scope of deposit insurance.[17] Fundamentally, the scope of deposit insurance coverage is determined by various country specifics. More significantly, a straightforward and integrated legal system is needed because financial stability is maintained by all participants of the financial sector safety net, not merely by the deposit insurance agency.

Although China has transitioned from implicit deposit insurance to explicit deposit insurance since May 2015, it is still at a crossroads. Therefore, this thesis compares deposit insurance schemes between the United States (US), the UK, and China, from a comparative, interdisciplinary, and transnational perspective, in order to provide critical suggestions for prospective improvements to China's deposit insurance system.

The earliest record of deposit insurance in the US was in 1829 in the state of New York. Subsequently, from 1829 to 1917, 14 states, at the state level, adopted deposit insurance schemes to protect depositors from economic disruptions and losses. Eventually, by the early 1930s, all schemes had ceased due to the lack of workable and sustainable mechanisms.[18] Having witnessed the increasing number of bank failures in the US between 1886 and 1933, Congress proposed approximately 150 deposit insurance plans.[19] Finally, in 1933, the market panic and lack of confidence in the US meant that the financial sector had reached the verge of collapse. In order to restore financial stability and market confidence, the FDIC was created by the Banking Act of 1933.[20] The FDIC, to date, is still playing a leading role and is a pioneer around the world.

Significantly, the FDIC has multiple functions in US banking regulation. First of all, the FDIC is a federal primary regulator for state non-member banks and state-chartered thrift institutions.[21] Second, deposits of insured banks and thrift institutions have been protected by the Deposit Insurance Fund (DIF). Prior to 2006, the FDIC had managed and operated the Bank Insurance Fund (BIF) and the Savings Association Insurance Fund (SAIF) respectively. After the implementation of the Federal Deposit Insurance Reform Act of 2005, which took effect in 2006, the assets and liabilities of the BIF and the SAIF merged and transferred into the new Deposit Insurance Fund (DIF).[22] Third, in fact, the FDIC acts as a receiver or conservator to resolve failed or failing insured depository institutions. After the GFC, the Dodd-Frank Wall Street Reform and Consumer Protection Act (the Dodd-Frank Act) assigned a significant role to the FDIC in regard to resolving failures of large, complex, and systemically important financial institutions (SIFIs).[23]

Notably, the FDIC is capable of examining the condition of insured banks and taking prompt corrective action, since the Federal Deposit Insurance Corporation Improvement Act of 1991 (FDICIA) conferred the authority of resolving troubled insured depository institutions to the FDIC, aimed at constraining the threat of bank failures.[24] In addition, the FDIC was officially created as an independent agency from the US government, but the members of the board of directors are appointed by the US President with advice and approval from the Senate. Needless to say, maintaining an independent operation away from the government is preferable for deposit insurers in performing functions effectively.[25]

The UK had not had a formal deposit insurance scheme until 1982.[26] In the past, large banks that were unwilling to accept the introduction of deposit insurance argued that healthy and safe banks had to subsidise risky and small banks, especially when facing flat-rate premiums.[27] By 1982, the formal deposit insurance scheme was introduced as an outcome of increasing concerns over depositor protection, whereas the scope of this scheme was barely extended to individuals and companies on a basis of co-insurance.[28] Nevertheless, at the same time, UK building societies provided informal deposit insurance for depositors in consideration of financial stability, as they had experienced rapid growth since 1970.[29] By 1986, UK building societies were officially included in the UK's formal deposit insurance scheme. With the Deposit Insurance Schemes Directive and the Financial Services and Markets Act 2000 (FSMA) coming into effect, the Financial Services Compensation Scheme (FSCS), an independent deposit insurer in the UK, was created to pay out insured depositors.[30]

Unlike the FDIC with its broad mandates, the FSCS adopts a 'pay box' model, indicating that the FSCS is only responsible for assessing and paying out compensation to claimants in relation to financial services offered by Financial Conduct Authority (FCA) authorised financial firms and the Prudential Regulation Authority (PRA) authorised financial firms in light of relevant rules.[31] After 2008, in the wake of the collapse of Northern Rock, co-insurance was scratched from the FSCS, and the UK coverage limit has been raised to £85,000.[32] Nonetheless, compared with the FDIC in the US, public awareness and public trust towards the FSCS are relatively low, which was mirrored by long queues of panicking depositors outside every branch of Northern Rock.[33] Furthermore, even though the FSCS may have the latest information regarding troubled banks, it does not have the authority to implement prompt corrective action to resolve troubled banks. By drawing lessons from the GFC, the FSCS has deployed a new funding mechanism since April 2008, which is regarded as a hybrid fundraising approach that combines ex-ante and ex-post funding arrangements in consideration of flexibility and fund adequacy. A threshold demonstrating the maximum amounts of premiums that can be annually levied by the FSCS from each sub-scheme is calculated by the PRA and the FCA.[34]

Deposit insurance has made great efforts to maintain financial stability in both the US and the UK, whereas it is a novel idea in China. To date, China has become the second largest economic entity and the largest emerging market in the banking industry.[35] Indeed, like the US and the UK, China's economy was also proportionally dampened by the global financial crisis. However, China's banking industry illustrated strong resistance to the damage of the crisis and still remained resilient. There were two justifications explaining this circumstance. First, state-owned commercial banks were the leading force in China's banking market. Second, during the crisis, the Chinese government was believed to have exceptional financial capability to provide a blanket guarantee or bail out.

China has been undergoing financial reform since the 'Reform and Open Policy' proposed by Deng Xiaoping in 1978. At the present stage, China aims to overhaul its banking system in pursuit of a more diverse, competitive, and open banking market with various banks, since foreign capital is apparently becoming an essential force that cannot be neglected in China's banking market and the market shares of medium and small-sized banks are gradually rising. As of the end of 2014, there was further opening in China's banking system, as totally private-owned banks were allowed to start financial services but had to afford risk and losses by themselves. By the end of 2019, 17 private-owned banks had been granted banking licences by the National Financial Regulatory Administration (NFRA) to provide banking services, especially accepting deposits from the public.[36] After 2010, China's banking regulatory framework has been promoted constantly through the adoption of international standards and participation in relevant international organisations, such as the Basel Committee, the World Bank, and the IMF. Eventually, since 1 May 2015, China has launched a formal deposit insurance scheme, following the global trend.

China has proposed and regarded a deposit insurance scheme as a vital advance in financial reform since the issuance of the 'Decision of the State Council on Reform of the Financial System' in 1993.[37] However, due to vigorous lobbying from state-owned commercial banks, the official announcement of the Deposit Insurance Regulation was delayed to 2015.[38] Looking into China's contemporary banking reform, the key issue is the marketisation of state-owned commercial banks, simply because their high level of non-performing loans has been a 'time bomb' for China's economy and the Chinese government, leading to critical concern over China's financial stability. China's banking system has been administered by the Chinese government for years, leading to a closed and conservative banking sector in China and the fragility of China's banking system. In 1999, the State Council decided to establish four fully state-owned asset management companies. The primary objective of these asset management companies was to transfer non-performing loans from the state-owned commercial banks and remove bad loans from balance sheets.[39] Accordingly, the Ministry of Finance (MOF) and People's Bank of China (PBOC) had provided liquidity and additional funds separately for asset management companies to acquire non-performing loans. By the end of 2006, as stated by the CBRC, the recovery rate of cash and the recovery rate of assets were 20 percent and 24 percent respectively.[40] Therefore, it is fair to say that the government and taxpayers have, in fact, borne the massive costs of non-performing loans triggered by state-owned commercial banks' imprudent behaviours, which pushed China's banking system to the verge of collapse.

Indeed, along with progressive banking reforms on building up a market-oriented banking system and facilitating interest rate liberalisation, it is to be said that a deposit insurance scheme is also needed for China's current banking market in pursuit of economic growth and feasible reform. Currently, the Financial Stability Bureau of the PBOC has been temporarily appointed as China's deposit insurer by the State Council. China's coverage limit is RMB 500,000, and deposit insurance premium rates are no more than 0.016 percent.[41] By the end of 2023, China's deposit insurance fund had accumulated RMB 81.01 billion.[42] However, very little official guidance and reports on the governance and the mandates of China's deposit insurer have been released yet, thus the mandates and the operating mechanism of the Financial Stability Bureau of the PBOC in managing China's deposit insurance scheme are mysterious and ambiguous. In academia, despite many articles analysing deposit insurance schemes with respect to the UK and the US, only a few researchers explore China's first deposit insurance system.

All in all, compared with the established deposit insurance systems in the US and the UK, deposit insurance in China is totally new and different and is still being tested. Additionally, the ultimate goal of China's banking reform is to build a culture of market orientation and the liberalisation of interest rates, transitioning from state-owned to privatised and modern banks. Therefore, with the deepening of economic reform, Chinese policymakers regarding deposit insurance should formulate a special resolution to cope with the unique situation which has occurred in China's banking system and should carefully consider the political, economic, and cultural specifics of China. Simultaneously, useful and practical experiences and lessons learnt from the US and the UK, which have advanced banking markets, should be followed.

1.2 The Scope of This Book

1.2.1 Deposit Insurance in the Context of Financial Regulation

The banking industry in the modern world has become a non-substitutive role in economic growth and social stability. Therefore, deposit insurance has been invented to prevent bank runs, protect depositors, and facilitate public confidence.[43] Unlike other profit-driven private insurance, deposit insurance, in this research, belongs to the financial sector safety net that consists of prudential regulation, the lender of last resort, and deposit insurance. It is noteworthy that this research is focused on how the US, the UK, and China utilise deposit insurance as a prerequisite resolution against bank collapses, rather than blanket guarantees and bail out supported by the government, from a comparative, interdisciplinary, and transnational angle. In this context, China, as a newcomer in deposit insurance, should learn from the UK and the US's experiences in setting up effective deposit insurance schemes in two different models based on their country specifics after the global financial crisis, in terms of building up an integrated and effective banking regulation through the start of deposit insurance.

1.2.2 Regulation

'Regulation' in this thesis is widely utilised and defined.[44] In this context, it refers to government control over deposit insurance, including the decision-making of relevant policies, legislation, quasi-legal tools, and dynamic regulation and supervision implemented by related financial authorities. Two points should be noted in this research. First, when it comes to deposit insurance, discussions on bank insolvency will be inevitable; however, bank insolvency is very unique and totally different from normal business insolvency as there is a special resolution dealing with bank insolvency. Thus, this research will not explore China's enterprise insolvency law.[45] Second, this research concentrates on the effective practice of relevant regulations, operating mechanisms, and institutional design, rather than taking a theoretical perspective.

1.3 Research Objectives

This book attempts to study deposit insurance in the US, UK, and China from transnational, historical, legal, and regulatory perspectives. This book attempts to do the following:

- To explore the nature, rationale, good practices, and how deposit insurance impacts banking stability with positive and negative effects;
- To investigate features, operating mechanisms, and the institutional design of deposit insurance in the US and its development after the global financial crisis;
- To probe into the characteristics, operating mechanisms, and institutional design of the UK deposit insurance scheme, to find out how it operates, what advantages it has, and how it should be optimised;
- To discover China's first deposit insurance scheme based on previous research on the US and the UK's post-crisis regulatory frameworks of deposit insurance;
- To find out how China can learn from the UK and the US's experiences, on the basis of comparative, interdisciplinary, and transnational study.

1.4 Research Methodologies

1.4.1 Doctrinal Legal Research

This research is mainly based on library resources; thus, the primary approach applied in this thesis is doctrinal research, providing an integrated and critical explanation of guidance, rules, principles, legal frameworks, and standards.[46] Doctrinal research plays a vital role in this study and will be repeatedly used throughout all chapters. Moreover, this methodology will be employed to emphasise deposit insurance laws, regulations, and institutional structures in the US, the UK, and China, with several applicable doctrines arising from other countries. Doctrinal research usually works on a theoretical basis, where relevant laws correspond to relevant questions. It involves analysing the doctrine, its developments and methods. In this thesis, doctrinal research will be used to answer questions such as 'what' or 'how' to identify relevant laws and regulations related to deposit insurance. This research will critically and coherently analyse and revisit laws and regulations at the national level, core principles, and standards at the international level, which incorporate financial regulation, relevant banking laws, relevant deposit insurance laws or regulations, insolvency laws, and institutional structures throughout all chapters. Furthermore, by examining and utilising other scholars' articles, official reports, and statistics from governments, regulators, and deposit insurers, this research will critically evaluate the applicability and compliance of deposit insurance and anticipate future developments and reforms. Additionally, this study's doctrinal research is based on a broad range of sources, not merely legal doctrines, as deposit insurance is highly regarded as a cross-departmental and interdisciplinary system. Thus, economic factors, country specifics, and public awareness will also be considered.

1.4.2 Comparative Legal Research

Comparative legal research is regarded as another crucial research method in this thesis. Comparative study is concerned with the similarities and differences of a specific area through comparing different legal systems and jurisdictions.[47] One beneficial advantage of comparative legal research is that it provides more solutions to potential regulatory developments. By comparing different jurisdictions and legal systems, scholars can study some practical issues from special viewpoints; and there are more chances for scholars to find an appropriate choice for their own theoretical systems. Therefore, for adoption, reform, and modification of law, comparative legal research is a better choice.

In this thesis, comparative legal research is concerned with two objectives. First, comparing similarities and differences between three very different models of deposit insurance in the US, the UK, and China after the global financial crisis; second, providing suggestions for China's long-awaited deposit insurance system by learning from the experiences and lessons of the US and the UK.

Unlike other components of banking regulation, deposit insurance is a controversial and heated issue. Additionally, the differences between these three jurisdictions on deposit insurance are expected, as there are no universally agreed-upon standards in deposit insurance. This results in countries deciding to start their deposit insurance schemes based on macroeconomic conditions, political environment, and legal systems. Deposit insurance in developed countries is experienced and integrated. However, deposit insurance is a two-fold system for developing countries. A well-designed and well-managed deposit insurance system, of course, could bring good results, but an inappropriate system would bring problems for developing countries. Furthermore, major differences between the US, the UK, and China stem from their different economic conditions, political environments, and historical and cultural backgrounds. Despite China having released the deposit insurance regulation and learning some experience from the US and the UK, compared with these two long-developed countries, the practices of deposit insurance in China are still under experimentation. This comparative study will try to identify differences in the practices of deposit insurance between the US, the UK, and China by examining legal systems, institutional structures, and operational mechanisms. By and large, this comparative legal research will summarise the similarities and differences between the three countries in order to give recommendations to China's long-awaited deposit insurance scheme, as well as the marketisation and liberalisation of China's banking industry.

1.4.3 Case Study

Case study, in this research, concentrates on individuals and small groups rather than all participants or the entire system. Case study is usually is applied to social science and politics. In this thesis, case study is a secondary approach and is applied in Chapters 3, 4, and 5. Notably, the cases in this research are about bank failures during the global financial crisis and Chinese banking instability. The research will illustrate several landmark cases of bank failures from the UK and the US, such as Northern Rock and Lehman Brothers, aimed at reflecting the increasing importance of deposit insurance since the global financial crisis. Furthermore, there are several important cases demonstrating why China needs deposit insurance. This thesis attempts to prove the necessity and functions of deposit insurance through these cases, as well as to point out flaws and particular issues in the US, the UK, and China's deposit insurance schemes. Participants of the case study in this research will be the selected banks whose collapses have impacted deposit insurance. The data collection is based on media and official reports from each deposit insurer and government.

1.5 Originality

Despite deposit insurance drawing much attention in China, very few academic papers in conjunction with China's first deposit insurance scheme have been published in English literature so far. Deposit insurance and its regulation, at the present stage, are essential for countries all over the world. However, the majority of academic articles in this area concentrate on deposit insurance schemes in developed countries, like the US and the UK, rather than developing countries like

China. There is no research focusing on the similarities and differences between the US, the UK, and China, especially how China can learn from the US and the UK's experience. Therefore, this thesis attempts to fill the gap in the existing research, starting a comparative study on deposit insurance schemes among the US, the UK, and China. When it comes to China's first deposit insurance scheme, the academic research in this regard is extremely limited as China has just set up a deposit insurance scheme amid a low-key image since May 2015. Unlike the UK and the US, which have a long history of running deposit insurance schemes, deposit insurance in China is a novel term and quite a new system, so very few scholars have written articles exploring China's deposit insurance scheme. It is noteworthy that this research is the first work to probe into China's first deposit insurance scheme, and to comprehensively study the practical situation of China, including the macroeconomic condition, regulatory framework, political environment, and legal system, by comparing it with the US and the UK. Without taking these factors into consideration, it is difficult to discuss critically and find an effective solution. Therefore, the originality of this research is to find out the applicable and feasible solution for China to build up an effective deposit insurance scheme by drawing from drawing international standards and recommendations from international organisations, and the experience from the US and the UK.

This research has practical implications as well. After the GFC, all countries have paid unprecedented attention to maintaining financial stability and optimising their financial safety nets, as they realise how important the banking industry is. The US, the UK, and China, as three important financial hubs, are facing multiple challenges from the banking industry, especially regarding how to safeguard depositors and resolve 'too big to fail' banks. Indeed, the reform of deposit insurance and its regulatory architecture needs adequate theoretical support. As a result, this research aims to benefit the US, the UK, and China's financial safety nets by providing practical recommendations and suggestions for policymakers.

1.6 Structure of the Book

This book consists of seven chapters. After this introductory chapter, Chapter 2, titled 'The Good Practices of Deposit Insurance: How to Build an Effective Deposit Insurance System', attempts to identify good practices of deposit insurance that might positively affect promoting bank stability and containing moral hazard. This chapter presents the discussion based on suggestions and recommendations proposed by international organisations (such as the IADI, the IMF, and the FSB). This chapter also discusses moral hazard, which is the intrinsic feature within deposit insurance that gives incentives to each participant to take excessive risks. Therefore, following suggestions and recommendations made by international organisations and scholars, this chapter aims to verify the good practices of deposit insurance and how they can restrict moral hazard and promote financial stability. In the end, this chapter also summarises the main characteristics and good practices of deposit insurance and lays a coherent foundation for the following chapters regarding the research.

Chapter 3, titled 'Deposit Insurance in the US: Experience, Country Specific, Institutional Structure and Reform', attempts to revisit and analyse the working mechanism of the FDIC as a multi-functional regulatory agency from the law and finance perspective. The focus concentrates on the FDIC's shifting role from a deposit insurer to a comprehensive troubleshooter for failing banks. First, this chapter provides a brief overview of the historical development of US deposit insurance, revealing the significant developments of US deposit insurance from a retrospective perspective. Next, this chapter examines the importance of deposit insurance in US banking regulation. Third, this chapter elaborates on the rationales of the FDIC, demonstrating how deposit insurance works in the US. Finally, this chapter seeks to explore the post-crisis reform of the FDIC, in terms of how the FDIC resolves large troubled banks.

Chapter 4, titled 'Deposit Insurance in the UK: Experience, Country Specific, Institutional Structure and Reform', seeks to reconsider and analyse the operating mechanism of the FSCS as a classical pay box model based on IADI's classification. The focal point in this chapter concentrates on the FSCS's significant reforms since the Northern Rock run during the global financial crisis and suggestions for future reforms of the FSCS. First, this chapter provides a historical overview of the deposit protection scheme in the UK, illustrating the historical developments of the UK deposit insurance scheme. Second, it stresses the designs and characteristics of the FSCS and attempts to find drawbacks under the present scheme. Next, this chapter discusses the lessons learnt from the Northern Rock run, which was a landmark case showing how bank runs occurred during the global financial crisis. Finally, it provides discussion in relation to the future reforms of the FSCS.

Chapter 5, titled 'Deposit Insurance in China: Experience, Country Specific, Institutional Structure and Reform', seeks to rethink and analyse the working mechanism of China's deposit insurance scheme. This chapter discusses and identifies the reasons why China needs deposit insurance, the major developments and characteristics of China's deposit insurance scheme, and the weaknesses of China's deposit insurance scheme. For this purpose, this chapter first provides a retrospective review of the history of banking regulation and deposit insurance in China, giving a clear understanding of China's struggling progress in developing its deposit insurance scheme and banking regulation. Then, the chapter analyses the current banking regulatory structure in China. Third, this chapter examines the features of implicit deposit insurance in China, with three selected cases demonstrating how the Chinese government resolved troubled banks under the implicit deposit insurance scheme. Finally, this chapter examines the characteristics of China's first deposit insurance scheme and explores impacts brought by this deposit insurance scheme on the banking sector.

Chapter 6, entitled 'Suggestions and Recommendations for China's Deposit Insurance Scheme: From a Comparative Perspective', attempts to provide suggestions and recommendations for future reforms on China's deposit insurance scheme, from a comparative study by comprehensively comparing China with the UK and the US. This study aims to investigate how China transitions its deposit insurance scheme from the UK's pay box model to the US's risk-minimiser model.

Its objective is to provide a comprehensive and comparative study explaining how the UK and the US influenced China's financial regulation and deposit insurance, from institutional architecture to relevant laws and regulations. The remainder of this chapter seeks to suggest a roadmap for prospective reforms of China's deposit insurance by drawing lessons from the FSCS and the FDIC. This chapter examines to what extent the relevant reforms and features can fulfil the function of China's deposit insurance scheme.

Chapter 7 is a chapter concluding and summarising the main findings in this research with a final remark. It concludes how this research has answered the research questions and fulfilled the objectives of the research through its chapters. This chapter also points out the limitations of this thesis and makes recommendations for future scholars to further study in this area.

Notes

1 Financial Stability Board (FSB), 'Thematic Review on Deposit Insurance Systems Peer Review Report' (8 February 2012) < http://www.fsb.org/wp-content/uploads/r_120208.pdf?page_moved=1> accessed 11 August 2024.

2 Many significant international financial organisations publish important guidance, including: International Association of Deposit Insurers (IADI) and Basel Committee on Banking Supervision (BCBS), 'Core Principles for Effective Deposit Insurance Systems' (June 2009), Financial Stability Forum (FSF), 'Guidance for Developing Effective Deposit Insurance Systems' (September 2001). Many international financial institutions, like International Monetary Fund (IMF) and the World Bank, have published a number of working papers for deposit insurance guidance.

3 R. Mark Williamson, 'Regulatory Theory and Deposit Insurance Reform' (1994) 42 *Cleveland State Law Review* 114.

4 Asli Demirgüç-Kunt, Edward Kane, and Luc Laeven, 'Deposit Insurance Design and Implementation: Policy Lessons from Research and Practice' in Asli Demirgüç-Kunt (eds), *Deposit Insurance around the World: Issues of Design and Implementation* (MIT Press 2008) 8.

5 Gillian G. H. Garcia, 'Deposit Insurance Actual and Good Practices: Good Practice for Deposit Insurance' (2000) International Monetary Fund, Occasional Paper No. 197, 4.

6 Financial Stability Forum, 'Guidance for Developing Effective Deposit Insurance Systems' (Financial Stability Forum, September 2001) <http://www.fsb.org/wp-content/uploads/r_0109b.pdf> accessed 19 August 2019.

7 For instance, the US has the Federal Deposit Insurance (FDIC) Act of 1933, and Canada has the Canada Deposit Insurance Corporation (CDIC) Act of 1967. In the UK, the enabling law is contained in the Financial Service and Markets (FSMA) Act 2000.

8 IADI, 'IADI Core Principles for Effective Deposit Insurance Systems' (International Association of Deposit Insurers, November 2014) <http://www.iadi.org/en/assets/File/Core%20Principles/cprevised2014nov.pdf> accessed 3 September 2024.

9 Andrew Campbell and Paula Moffatt, 'UK Depositor Protection in the Aftermath of the Banking Crisis' (2010) 25 *Journal of International Banking Law and Regulation*, 488.

10 Dalvinder Singh and John Raymond LaBrosse, 'Northern Rock, Depositors and Deposit Insurance Coverage: Some Critical Reflections' (2010) 2 *Journal of Business Law*, 56.

11 David S. Hoelscher, Michael W. Taylor, and Ulrich H. Klueh, 'The Design and Implementation of Deposit Insurance' (2006) International Monetary Fund, Occasional Paper No. 251, 26.

12 Ronald MacDonald, 'Deposit Insurance' (1996) Bank of England, Handbooks in Central Banking No. 9.

13 Peter T. Larsen, 'UK Launches £37 Billion Bank Rescue' *Financial Times* (London, 13 October 2008) < https://www.ft.com/content/83bc2cea-98ef-11dd-9d48-000077b07658> accessed 25 December 2019.
14 Ricki T. Helfer 'What Deposit Insurance Can and Cannot Do' (1999) 36 *Finance and Development*, 24.
15 Andrew Campbell and Peter Cartwright, 'Co-insurance and Moral Hazard: Some Reflections on Deposit Protection in the UK and USA' (2003) 5 *Journal of International Banking*, 10.
16 Financial Stability Forum, 'Guidance for Developing Effective Deposit Insurance Systems' (Financial Stability Board, September 2001) <http://www.fsb.org/wp-content/uploads/r_0109b.pdf> accessed 19 December 2019 and IADI, 'Core Principles for Effective Deposit Insurance Systems' (n8).
17 Andrew Campbell and Peter Cartwright, 'The Protection of Bank Depositors: New Developments' (1999) 22 *Amicus Curiae*, 26.
18 These states include New York, Vermont, Indiana, Michigan, Ohio, Iowa, Texas, Oklahoma, Kansas, Nebraska, Mississippi, South Dakota, North Dakota, and Washington.
19 Federal Deposit Insurance Corporation (FDIC), 'The First Fifty years – A History of the FDIC 1933–1983' (FDIC, Washington DC, 1984) < https://www.fdic.gov/bank/analytical/firstfifty/> accessed 17 September 2024.
20 *Ibid.*
21 Mark Jickling and Edward V. Murphy, 'Who Regulates Whom? An Overview of US Financial Supervision' (Congressional Research Service, 2017) <https://fas.org/sgp/crs/misc/R44918.pdf> accessed 2 September 2024.
22 Pub. L. 109-171, § 2102.
23 Sheila C. Bair, 'FDIC Chair Describes New Resolution Authority' (2010) 29 *American Bankruptcy Institute Journal*, 10.
24 See 12 USC, § 1820, § 3305 and Pub. L. 102-242, § 2241.
25 IADI, 'Governance of Deposit Insurance Systems Guidance Paper' (International Association of Deposit Insurers, 6 May 2009)<http://www.iadi.org/en/assets/File/Papers/Approved%20Guidance%20Papers/Governance%20Final%20Guidance%20Paper%206_May_2009.pdf> accessed 16 July 2024.
26 Andrew Campbell and Peter Cartwright, 'Co-insurance and Moral Hazard: Some Reflections on Deposit Protection in the UK and USA' (n15), 11.
27 Sherman J. Maisel, 'Supervisory Issues' in Edward P. M. Gardener (ed.) *UK Banking Supervision: Evolution, Practice and Issues* (Allen & Unwin, London, 1986), 60, 78.
28 *Ibid.*
29 John Grady and Martin Weale, *British Banking, 1960–85* (Palgrave Macmillan 1986) 76.
30 Directive 94/19/EEC.
31 FSMA 2000, s 213 (3) (a).
32 Coverage also includes investments and home finance, which have limits up to £50,000.
33 Dalvinder Singh and John Raymond LaBrosse, 'Northern Rock, Depositors and Deposit Insurance Coverage: Some Critical Reflections' (2010) 2 *Journal of Business Law*, 56.
34 FCA, 'Reviewing the Funding of the Financial Services Compensation Scheme' (December 2016) <https://www.fca.org.uk/publication/consultation/cp16-42.pdf> accessed 28 December 2019. Simultaneously, the threshold can be checked at the official website of the FSCS.
35 David Barboza, 'China Passes Japan as Second-Largest Economy' *The New York Times* (2010, New York) <http://www.nytimes.com/2010/08/16/business/global/16yuan.html?pagewanted=all&_r=0> accessed 30 December 2023.
36 Jamil Anderlini, 'China Opens Door to Private Banks' *Financial Times* (2014, London) < https://www.ft.com/content/7096239e-a8e0-11e3-bf0c-00144feab7de?mhq5j=e2> accessed 1 July 2024.

37 Jianing Wei, *The Research of Deposit Insurance and Financial Safety Net* (China Economic Publishing House 2014) 1.

38 *Ibid.*

39 Four asset management companies are responsible for four major state-owned banks: Great Wall for Agricultural Bank of China, Huarong for Industrial and Commercial Bank of China, Cinda for China Construction Bank, and China Orient for Bank of China.

40 CBRC, '2006 Statistics of Asset Management Companies in China' (2006) <http://www.cbrc.gov.cn/chinese/home/docView/2456.html> accessed 5 November 2019. The first round bailout of non-performing loans started from 1998 and ended in 2006.

41 PBOC, 'Basic Knowledge of China's Deposit Insurance' (July 2015) <http://www.pbc.gov.cn/jinrongwendingju/146766/2165207/2813774/index.html> accessed 6 December 2023.

42 PBOC, 'Statistics of the Deposit Insurance Fund' (March 2024) <http://www.pbc.gov.cn/jinrongwendingju/146766/2165207/5318126/index.html> accessed 5 July 2024.

43 Charles W. Calomiris and Matthew Jaremski, 'Deposit Insurance: Theories and Facts' (2016) the National Bureau of Economic Research, Working Paper No. 22223.

44 Robert Baldwin, Martin Cave, and Martin Lodge, *Understanding Regulation: Theory, Strategy, and Practice* (2nd edition, Oxford University Press 2013) 3.

45 China has a complete bankruptcy system based on the Enterprise Bankruptcy Law 2007. However, China has not yet had bank insolvency law so far. Accordingly, the CBRC says that Chinese bank insolvency law is underway.

46 Terry Hutchinson, 'Doctrinal Research' in Dawn Watkins and Mandy Burton (eds), *Research Methods in Law* (Routledge 2013) 9.

47 Konrad Zweigert and Hein Kotz, *An Introduction to Comparative Law* (3rd edition, Oxford University Press 1988) 2.

2 The Good Practices of Deposit Insurance

How to Build an Effective Deposit Insurance System

2.1 Introduction

After lessons learnt from the GFC, deposit insurance, at the present stage, is becoming an increasingly essential constituent of the financial sector safety net that safeguards financial stability and consolidates banking regulation. In light of statistics released by the IADI, so far more than 100 countries have established explicit deposit insurance schemes in recent decades.[1]

Many international organisations, like the IADI, the Financial Stability Board (FSB), the World Bank, and the International Monetary Fund (IMF), have published numerous pieces of research that attempt to find practical and theoretical principles and suggestions for countries to build up their deposit insurance schemes with straightforward objectives and specific features of deposit insurance.[2]

In order to establish a well-designed deposit insurance scheme, all deposit insurers and relevant financial authorities should better consider the good practices tabled by these international financial organisations, as well as absorb them into their own deposit insurance schemes. Simultaneously, a well-designed deposit insurance scheme, regarded as an ex-post banking resolution under the financial safety net, can perfectly fit into an entire financial regulatory framework. For example, a well-designed deposit insurance scheme plays a significant role in striking a balance between moral hazard and market discipline, which, to some extent, may constrain contagious risks. Besides, the fundraising mechanism of deposit insurance is another key issue for having an effective deposit insurance scheme.

This chapter seeks to find out good practices and specific features of deposit insurance that help countries build up effective deposit insurance schemes. Many scholars, from both the financial and legal sector, have also discussed good practices of deposit insurance, in order to facilitate the resilience of deposit insurance. Therefore, the purpose of this chapter is to explore good practices for building an effective deposit insurance scheme, to provide well-designed features for deposit insurers and supervisors, and to introduce critical developments to current deposit insurance theories.

DOI: 10.4324/9781003612759-2

2.2 Rationale and Objectives of Deposit Insurance

In theory, when it comes to regulation, public interest theory (market failure theory) and capture theory (private interest theory) are usually used to conduct analysis on regulatory policies. Viewed from the public interest theory, which underlines that regulation should benefit the public first, deposit insurance can be regarded as a social welfare measure to protect ordinary and unsophisticated depositors, as well as to promote financial stability.[3] However, from the insight of private interest theory, which, according to Stigler and Posner, argues that regulatory bodies and politicians are captured by particular groups, deposit insurance is expected to subsidise bankers and speculators who pursue risky investment portfolios from the contributions of healthy banks.[4] Therefore, deposit insurance should be designed with principal and precise objectives.

Generally, maintaining financial stability and protecting depositors are two principal objectives of deposit insurance.[5] At the present stage, the banking market is extremely interconnected, as one bank failure could lead to a domino effect for the entire banking market, devastating financial stability. Along with this contagious feature, when a bank encounters a liquidity shortage, low public confidence may trigger a severe bank run, accelerating the process of the bank failure that threatens financial stability. For the sake of financial stability, deposit insurance has been created to promote public confidence and reduce the possibility of market panics and bank runs.[6]

Depositor protection is the other principal objective of deposit insurance. In reality, due to information asymmetry, depositors are usually unable to access key information relevant to their host banks, such as balance sheets, financial statements, and risk management.[7] Even if depositors had the most accurate and recent information available, most of them would be incapable of understanding such information because of a lack of professional knowledge. Therefore, deposit insurance is focused on serving to safeguard ordinary and unsophisticated depositors who stand in a disadvantaged position.

However, based on private interest theory, deposit insurance that covers depositors' losses can be utilised by politicians to achieve political purposes, in terms of maintaining political stability or obtaining support from voters.[8] In addition, the failures of 'too big to fail' banks have been a headache for all governments around the world, because the losses of giant amounts of savings deposited in 'too big to fail' banks would lead to social instability and chaos, potentially overturning a regime. Therefore, even with a deposit insurance scheme in effect, the government, in consideration of political factors, would seek to keep problematic 'too big to fail' banks alive by offering massive government bailouts or blanket guarantees. Therefore, apart from maintaining financial stability and protecting depositors, it is said that deposit insurance is driven by political purposes.

Nevertheless, the argument about 'which objective should be privileged' has drawn attention from academia.[9] Accordingly, the justification of giving priority to financial stability is that deposit insurance, as a crucial part of the financial sector safety net, is created to eliminate market panics and contagious risks rendered by low market confidence.[10] However, most scholars have reached a consensus that these two principal objectives are parallel and reconcilable. Owing to the existence of information asymmetry that adversely impacts the free flow of information, depositors are often unable to access the key information and data of host banks. As a consequence, some financially sound banks might be negatively affected by market rumours followed by panic withdrawals.[11] In response to such situations, facilitating depositor protection as a direct and effective measure devoted to promoting financial stability could play a more effective role in jeopardising market panics and the possibility of bank runs. It is noteworthy that a well-designed deposit insurance scheme not only can protect small depositors who are likely to be disadvantaged under bank failures, but can also eliminate bank runs by restoring financial stability.[12]

Besides, it is important to note that deposit insurance has additional objectives with respect to promoting competition between small and large banks and resolving financially nonviable banks through coordination with other financial authorities and an integrated regulatory framework.[13] However, although a well-designed and functional deposit insurance scheme can contribute to preventing bank runs and enhancing public confidence, there is, to date, no empirical case proving that systemic risks have been effectively halted merely by the existence of deposit insurance, which, however, would be blocked by effective and efficient cooperation and coordination between all participants of the financial safety net.[14]

The Financial Stability Forum (FSF), now replaced by the FSB, has emphasised the importance of situational analysis and the feasibility of implementing achievable objectives of deposit insurance. Policymakers in each country are advised to take situational analyses into account on a flexible basis. These analyses include:

- Economic factors, the general framework of the banking system, and public acceptance level and expectations;
- The state of legal, prudential regulatory, supervisory, accounting, and disclosure regimes.[15]

Currently, many countries have transitioned from implicit deposit insurance schemes to explicit deposit insurance schemes because there is convincing evidence demonstrating that explicit deposit insurance schemes have overwhelming advantages over implicit deposit insurance schemes.[16] As noted by Campbell and Moffatt, after adopting an explicit deposit insurance scheme, the public will have a clear understanding of deposit insurers' responsibilities and payout procedures in accordance with relative laws and regulations.[17] Furthermore, explicit deposit insurance, as described by Williamson, is a guarantee for depositors against losses.[18] Thus, it is fair to say that a well-designed and transparent deposit insurance law or regulation is requisite to serving public interest and financial stability. However, economically speaking, explicit deposit insurance that produces high costs of protecting depositors and maintaining financial stability, like 100 percent coverage and compensation, has been regarded as an expensive and controversial mechanism from policymakers' perspective.[19]

Needless to say, strengthening deposit insurance's role in prudential regulation is favoured by most deposit insurers that have broad mandates, particularly in implementing prompt corrective action and timely banking resolutions.[20] Importantly, to fulfil the function of deposit insurance, relevant standards, such as accountability, coverage, risk assessment, and corporate governance, etc., should be updated periodically in order to adapt to the volatile financial markets, thereby facilitating the resilience of deposit insurance.[21]

2.3 The Mandates of Deposit Insurance

2.3.1 Privately Run Deposit Insurance Schemes and Government-Run Deposit Insurance Schemes

At present, there are generally two mainstream models governing deposit insurance schemes. One is the privately run model, where a deposit insurance scheme is operated by member banks or peers with private funding, and the other is the government-run model with government backing and public funding. In light of Garcia's survey, government-run deposit insurance schemes have been highly recommended, and the majority of countries have chosen government-run deposit insurance schemes in lieu of blanket guarantees, whereas country specifics still play a decisive role.[22]

In fact, government-run deposit insurance schemes have several advantages over privately run deposit insurance schemes. First, a government-run deposit insurance scheme enables the deposit insurer to exercise its powers and responsibilities directly through its administrative powers granted by relevant laws and regulations, especially in accomplishing its mission to protect depositors who might represent public interests. Second, with government backing, deposit insurers become financially capable of tackling systemic risks or severe problems arising from banking markets, which might maintain financial stability by underpinning market confidence.[23]

However, the main disadvantage of a government-run system is obvious, as political intervention that interrupts the regular operation of deposit insurers may frequently occur in pursuit of macroeconomic objectives and social stability, which, however, reversely impacts the effectiveness of deposit insurance. Regarding privately run deposit insurance schemes, Garcia found that although a privately run deposit insurance scheme might reduce the expenses of each member bank, it is hard for a privately run deposit insurance scheme to deal with large bank failures due to the lack of credibility, administrative powers, and financing resources.[24] Along with Garcia's findings, Diamond and Dybvig point out that government-run deposit insurers naturally have advantages over private insurers as privately run deposit insurance systems lack adequate resources in terms of funding resources, administrative resources, and human resources.[25] Therefore, as discussed above, government-run systems might be practical and preferable for most countries rather than privately run systems.

2.3.2 *Should Deposit Insurers Be Equipped with Narrow Mandates or with Broad Mandates?*

The mandates of deposit insurers have been classified as narrow mandates or broad mandates, which depend on the scope of powers and obligations.[26] When it comes to deposit insurers with narrow mandates, they are defined as a paybox model, and their main responsibilities are merely designated to manage the deposit insurance fund safely and to compensate insured depositors rapidly when a bank collapses.[27] In addition, some deposit insurers with narrow mandates are required to extend their obligations in terms of setting deposit insurance premium rates and collecting premiums regularly. It is reasonable to say that, to fulfil their functions, deposit insurers with narrow mandates have to set up effective communication with relevant financial supervisors to receive precise information associated with deposit insurance, as well as report information about problematic banks to relevant financial regulatory bodies.

Regarding deposit insurers with broad mandates, their obligations are not confined to the fundamental scope discussed above. Basically, deposit insurers with broad mandates are assigned wide obligations to monitor the performance of the banking sector in order to estimate potential failures and take prompt corrective actions, such as closing and liquidating troubled banks or carrying out faster payouts. It is noteworthy that deposit insurers with broad mandates have to shoulder the responsibilities of prudential regulation and bank resolution, for example, determining deposit insurance premium rates based on the assessment of banks' soundness and risk management, and closing or liquidating failing banks in light of relevant laws or regulations. In addition, some deposit insurers with broad mandates can even provide financial assistance to problematic banks for the sake of maintaining financial stability and minimising depositors' panics.[28]

By and large, whether a deposit insurer operates with narrow mandates or broad mandates, well-defined deposit insurance laws or regulations are consistently required to ensure that deposit insurers are capable of undertaking their responsibilities, powers, and discretion. In response to systemic risks of banking collapses that trigger contagions in the banking sector, deposit insurers sometimes may be assigned with additional obligations and powers to restructure or close troubled banks, to restore financial stability. Finally, all forms of deposit insurers should independently conduct their responsibilities, so as to help deposit insurers dodge political interferences.[29]

2.3.3 *Institutional Structure*

Regarding the institutional structure of deposit insurance schemes, a choice for deposit insurers, whether deposit insurers should be an independent and autonomous financial authority or assigned to an existing legal entity such as the central bank, has been considered for years.[30] More importantly, the institutional structure or organisational structure of a deposit insurer is subject to its mandates enacted in the relevant deposit insurance law or regulation, as institutional structure is vital for the deposit insurer to achieve its objectives.[31]

Nevertheless, the FSB stresses that assigning the functions of deposit insurance to existing financial authorities enables deposit insurers to draw on staff and skills from experienced authorities, for example, the central bank.[32] Clearly, this measure can save the costs pertaining to operation, administration, and human resources arising from running a deposit insurance scheme. Another advantage of this method is that information sharing between the deposit insurance department and other departments will be enhanced. When a deposit insurer becomes a subsidiary of a larger financial regulator, sharing information between the deposit insurance department and other departments within the larger financial regulator will be more convenient, efficient, and time-saving.

However, the principal disadvantage of this approach is clear, as it is difficult for a larger financial regulator to separate its other responsibilities and interests from deposit insurance, resulting in conflicts of policies.[33] During the GFC, financial supervisors all over the world proposed a series of bank resolutions under intense political pressure; however, most of the resolutions focused more focused on accommodating macro perspectives with respect to public interest and macroeconomic objectives.[34] Establishing an independent deposit insurance scheme is a practical way to mitigate regulatory forbearance, as financial regulatory bodies are unwilling to close troubled banks due to the fear of criticism and damage of reputation.[35] Therefore, to fulfil the functions of deposit insurance efficiently, it is ideal for deposit insurers to retain an independent role with a separate legal personality.

Although administering a deposit insurance scheme through a separate agency is preferable, developing countries that are just step into this area have to assign the administration of deposit insurance to an experienced financial regulatory body because of the shortage of experienced staff and skills.[36] Most importantly, it is clear that a deposit insurer should be clearly defined in relevant laws and regulations, regardless of being an independent agency or not.[37] Besides, policymakers have to ponder how to build up effective coordination and communication between deposit insurers and other financial safety net participants.

2.4 Interrelationships between Deposit Insurance and Other Participants of Financial Regulation

2.4.1 Prudential Regulation, Supervision, and Resolution

Financial regulatory bodies not only have an obligation to implement enforceable rules to promote risk management, good governance, and capital adequacy, but they also have to carry out prompt corrective action or structured early intervention and resolutions to cope with risks in a timely manner.[38] Particularly, financial regulatory bodies are responsible for implementing prompt corrective action to resolve troubled banks in order to minimise losses of troubled banks before they become undercapitalised. As a result, prompt corrective action that can immediately correct risky financial institutions so as to relieve the burden on deposit insurance schemes should be introduced to work with deposit insurance. In accordance with a study by Benston and Kaufman, prompt corrective action has been perceived as an efficient resolution mechanism promoting the efficiency and resilience of the banking sector.[39]

Besides, the effectiveness of a deposit insurance scheme can be facilitated by setting capital requirements like capital adequacy ratios or capital reserves that compel insured institutions to cut non-performing assets and non-performing liabilities. Moreover, the shareholders and managers of undercapitalised banks also should be prohibited from receiving dividends and subsidies to promote financial viability of undercapitalised banks.[40] Ring-fencing, which aims to protect deposits from ordinary depositors and small businesses by separating retail banking from universal banks, is an emerging approach that assists prudential regulation in reducing the likelihood of bank failures and the losses of depositors. However, implementing ring-fencing, of course, will generate adverse effects on profit-driven banks, because traditional banking services and functions have been significantly scratched.[41]

It is necessary to integrate prompt corrective action into prudential regulation, which can ensure that financial supervisors have an obligation and the power to correct or close problematic banks before they become insolvent.[42] Any delays in closure or liquidation can give rise to increasing costs of bank insolvency, simply because the bankers of troubled banks are likely to recklessly gamble in pursuit of recovery, for example, promising depositors high interest and high returns, which ultimately put pressure on deposit insurance schemes. Therefore, deposit insurers with broad mandates should promptly propose the resolution of failed banks, collaborating with relevant financial regulators in finding incentive-compatible measures for closing or liquidating insolvent banks.

2.4.2 Banking Resolution for Resolving Troubled Banks

All countries are expected to erect an integrated and effective legal framework dealing with troubled banks, increasing banking recovery rates. At present, there are three basic resolution mechanisms for coping with troubled banks. In light of the guidance paper released by the FSB, they are: liquidation and reimbursement; purchase and assumption transactions; and open-bank financial assistance.[43]

Liquidation and reimbursement is a basic and easier measure for dealing with troubled banks under a deposit insurance scheme, referring to the idea that deposit insurers or financial regulators will take responsibility to liquidate or close troubled banks and then reimburse insured depositors by paying insured deposits directly or transferring insured depositors to another surviving bank.[44] This method is usually applied to a troubled bank that has no franchise value to be acquired or recovered. Theoretically, promptly paying off insured depositors is a straightforward and effective way to maintain financial stability, especially when encountering a contingent systemic crisis.[45] However, this method is more disruptive compared with the other two methods, because depositors, in the situation where they get paid through deposit insurance schemes, have to seek new host banks, and the availability of credit is decreased due to the reduction of banks and capital.[46]

The second approach, namely purchase and assumption transactions that require a healthy financial institution to assume some or all obligations and liabilities of a failed bank and purchase some or all its assets, has been largely applied by the FDIC.[47] Smart acquirers prefer to purchase performing loans and other good-quality assets, and the remainder has been disposed of by receivers or liquidators.[48] This approach also includes bridge bank and other interim arrangements, seeking to avoid further deterioration and provide enough time for deposit insurers or receivers to look for potential acquirers. Another advantage of this approach is that acquirers usually get transactions done by utilising their own funds, not public funds, particularly during the stable period. However, the only disadvantage of this method is that, during financial turbulence, healthier banks are financially incapable of purchasing assets from troubled banks due to the shortage of capital and incentives, especially when such circumstances occur in developing countries. Faced with the other two methods, purchase and assumption is less disruptive and less costly.[49]

Third, open-bank financial assistance as a resolution mechanism attempts to provide troubled banks with extra capital arising from public funds, which, however, is usually utilised by banks perceived as 'too big to fail' banks.[50] Nevertheless, this approach has engendered a series of problems in relation to issues such as fairness, adverse selection, and moral hazard. One considerable disadvantage of using this approach is that public funds are possibly injected to keep problematic banks afloat. Apart from capital injection, through using this method, deposit insurers might take control of capital and senior management within troubled banks, as well as the removal of managers and directors.[51] Therefore, ideally, making use of private capital to resolve troubled banks is a preferable option rather than using public funds, and the use of public funds should be restricted to further prevent systemic risks.[52] Nonetheless, if a single bank failure may lead to a significant threat against financial stability or national economies, the open-bank assistance, perhaps, is considered to be a proper approach for dealing with troubled banks.[53]

2.4.3 Ring-Fencing Regulatory Structure

Ring-fencing has been regarded as an emerging regulatory mechanism in response to problems arising in financial sectors.[54] The purpose of implementing ring-fencing is to legally deconstruct large financial groups or universal banks, reallocating and dodging risks through the following measures:

- Separating risky assets;
- Avoiding engagement in risky activities or investing in risky assets;
- Bankruptcy remote.[55]

In the banking sector, ring-fencing requires the retail bank, incorporated in a universal bank, to become a legally separated entity so as to avoid risks triggered by investment activities. The Glass-Steagall Act was a pioneering banking act with the purpose of regulating ring-fencing activities in response to banking collapses during the Great Depression. Ring-fencing, in theory, requires universal banks to strip their deposit-taking activities from risky investment activities and reallocate riskier investment activities into different entities. However, even under ring-fencing, these entities are still prone to being exposed to systemic risks, and the change to ring-fencing has led to the instability of banking operations.[56] Although it was not difficult to implement the Glass-Steagall Act after the Great Depression, during the 1990s, the implementation of the Glass-Steagall Act was inefficient and ineffective, leaving US banks at a disadvantage in competition with foreign banks.[57] Finally, the Glass-Steagall Act was repealed by Congress in 1999.[58]

The UK, in December 2013, drafted a legislation for ring-fencing based on the Vickers Report, which came into effect on 1 January 2019.[59] The Vickers Report is highly similar to the Glass-Steagall Act, which argues that retail banking activities are designed to be legally isolated and insulated from risky investments and services. Simultaneously, the implementation of ring-fencing is expected to reduce over-reliance on government guarantees, deposit insurance, and taxpayers. Furthermore, as noted by Campbell and Moffatt, the Vickers Report points out the location of the fence and the height of the fence; banks are merely able to participate in ring-fencing activities with the permission authorised by the regulators, and ring-fenced banks should separately and legally operate within the groups on a standalone basis.[60]

Faced with the Glass-Steagall Act, the Vickers Report has proposed two new developments. One is the protection of the payment system, including private-run payment systems, and the other is the projected costs of implementing ring-fencing. However, both the Glass-Steagall Act and the Vickers Report have placed domestic banks at a disadvantaged position, as they have to face many restrictions when competing with foreign banks.

After the GFC, Paul Volcker suggested that deposit-taking institutions should be strictly restricted from engaging in riskier activities, simply because deposits are federally guaranteed.[61] As a result, this suggestion has become the Volcker Rule, enacted in the Dodd-Frank Wall Street Reform and Consumer Protection Act (Dodd-Frank). This Act has imposed restrictions on the underlying banking activities:

- Participating in proprietary trading;
- Acquiring or retaining any equity, partnership, or other ownership interest in order to support a hedge fund or private equity.[62]

Another provision of ring-fencing is the Lincoln Amendment, which aims to require universal banks to reallocate derivative trading businesses into separate nonbank affiliates.[63] Under this provision, the FDIC and the Federal Reserve no longer provide direct financial assistance to systemically important financial institutions.[64] However, in fact, the effectiveness and the implementation of the Volcker Rule and the Lincoln Amendment have been weakened by many exceptions and variances.[65] It is understandable that both UK and US regulators have faced vigorous lobbying from the financial industries, especially the banking industries, thereby impairing the effectiveness of ring-fencing rules. Not surprisingly, the Dodd-Frank Act is an existing example.[66]

As an emerging solution addressing systemic risks, ring-fencing has made contributions to financial stability by minimising panics and creating modularity. For instance, ring-fencing can help financial markets avoid public panic, one of the major triggers for bank collapses, by eliminating adverse selection and safeguarding depositors' savings. Furthermore, contemporary financial markets are more complex than they used to be, and financial derivatives are becoming increasingly complicated for unsophisticated customers. Therefore, clarity and security in financial markets have been essential for maintaining financial stability and safeguarding customers. Thus, establishing ring-fencing is considered to be a preferable approach to addressing these problems, as it has created modularity to decrease ambiguity and mutual interventions between different departments within the same financial groups. For instance, it reduces the 'domino effect' and contagions arising from risky investments taken by different departments.[67] Ideally, with the development of a ring-fencing regulatory structure, in the future, ring-fencing authorities might be placed in a better position to manage deposit insurance rather than having it administered by an independent deposit insurer. At the present stage, ring-fencing, as a novel idea, lacks good practices, and it is uncertain what regulatory functions ring-fencing can fulfil.

2.5 Moral Hazard in Deposit Insurance Systems

There are significant discussions relating to the existence of moral hazard, which is deemed intrinsic to deposit insurance systems.[68] MacDonald has said that 'in the literal sense, moral hazard refers to the adverse effects, from the point of view of the insurer, that insurance may have on the insuree's behaviour'.[69] In particular, moral hazard might be introduced by various causes. Taking the US savings and loan crisis in 1980 as an example, a generous deposit insurance scheme, financial liberalisation, and regulatory failure were the major reasons leading to moral hazard.[70] Focussing on deposit insurance, a generous deposit insurance scheme incentivises financial participants who are covered by the scheme to introduce moral hazard.[71]

Regarding insured banks, which generally get more benefits from deposit insurance systems than other parties, it is important to note that they are the principal force reshaping market discipline and containing moral hazard. In addition, deposit insurance schemes, aimed at protecting deposits, offer an incentive that encourages managers and bankers of insured banks to utilise insured deposits in an imprudent way and invest insured deposits in high-risk but high-profit investment portfolios, because risks are ultimately conveyed to deposit insurers.[72] During past financial crises, many governments had a strong will to rescue banks regarded as 'too big to fail' through direct capital injection and liquidity assistance.[73] Nevertheless, Helfer, the former Chair of the FDIC, has found that the government seeking to provide financial support to financial institutions, including troubled but solvent banks, clearly involves moral hazard.[74] Simultaneously, she also adds that the most efficient approach to dealing with moral hazard is to allow the financial markets and participants to discipline imprudent behaviours taken by financial institutions, letting them fail or imposing necessary costs on these imprudent financial institutions, despite 'too big to fail' banks.[75]

With respect to depositors, deposit insurance relieves their responsibility to monitor banks' performance, enabling them to pay less attention to banks' risk management, risk control, and portfolios.[76] As a consequence, deposits simply flow to depository institutions that offer higher interest rates and high returns. However, without an explicit deposit insurance scheme, uncertainty would make depositors confused regarding what kind of financial products will be covered and by how much deposits will be repaid. On the contrary, Demirgüç-Kunt and Detragiache have noted that this uncertainty introduces a positive impact, as depositors are incentivised to monitor banks' performance when they face ambiguous coverage.[77] Unlike private insurance repaying losses for certain risks, deposit insurance is perceived as a guarantee to minimise the losses of depositors.[78] McCoy underlines that explicit deposit insurance reimburses depositors regardless of any types of deposits or reasons behind bank failures, so that deposit insurance discourages depositors from monitoring banks, leading to undue risks.[79]

In addition, large depositors, creditors, and shareholders, who engage in vigorous lobbying to persuade governments to provide greater protection for their interests, are also unwilling to monitor the performance of banks. In such a situation, despite large depositors, creditors, and shareholders being in a better position to monitor the banks' performance, they usually have no intention of taking over responsibilities for overseeing the latest circumstances of banks due to potential government guarantees or the existence of deposit insurance. Therefore, the coverage of deposit insurance should be limited in order to incentivise creditors, shareholders, and senior management to bear the losses produced by their imprudent behaviours. The 'least cost' test introduced by the FDIC is an effective and efficient measure to decrease the likelihood of moral hazard among deposit insurance systems, aimed at strengthening market discipline and incentive-compatible regulation.[80] Moreover, moral hazard is also is related to regulators and deposit insurers involved in deposit insurance schemes when there is a lack of accountability.[81]

2.5.1 Mitigating Moral Hazard

Moral hazard has led to serious concerns over the legitimacy of deposit insurance, as deposit insurance has been doubted for producing poor incentives and high costs to stop systemic risks which introduce contagions in the whole financial system.[82] Apparently, moral hazard is a very controversial topic in contemporary deposit insurance schemes, as it is hard to strike a balance between all participants. For example, under risk-based premiums, risky banks that must pay higher deposit insurance premiums than well-capitalised banks are likely to bet on risky but profitable investment portfolios so as to prolong their operation and repay deposits, whereas well-capitalised banks make less contribution to the deposit insurance fund.[83] By and large, to minimise moral hazard, deposit insurance should be optimised to enable all financial participants to behave in a prudent manner that consolidates the financial safety net and eliminates moral hazard.[84]

2.5.1.1 Setting Up an Explicit and Transparent Deposit Insurance System

Clearly, deposit insurance needs to have an explicit definition in relevant laws and regulations, and, then, public awareness should be strengthened to facilitate the profile and reputation of deposit insurance schemes, given the Northern Rock case in the UK during the GFC. Importantly, although most depositors may not have professional knowledge about finance, it is better to enact rules in relevant laws and regulations that require banks to disclose their risk management and level in consideration of public interest. Besides, the classification of financial derivatives, especially deposits, seeking to offer more certainty about the coverage of deposit insurance and bank resolution, should be accurately and clearly defined in relevant laws and contracts, which can help deposit insurers and policymakers formulate a precise scope of deposit protection for both insured depositors and insured institutions.[85] Most importantly, with a clear and accurate legal definition of deposits, depositors would have a clear understanding of whether their deposits are insured or not.[86]

Furthermore, for the sake of prompt corrective action and efficient bank resolution, financial regulators are responsible for promptly capturing precise information either from examinations of financial institutions or markets. Similarly, a deposit insurer with broad mandates, regarded as the risk minimiser model, also has to capture accurate and updated information regarding the latest performance of the banking industry, so that the deposit insurer can propose prompt plans of reimbursement, resolution, and liquidation in case of sudden bank collapses. Additionally, a deposit insurer, responsible for setting a reasonable coverage limit, should incorporate the distribution of deposits into its analysis on its coverage limit from the macro level, not just based on average amounts of deposits. Therefore, codifying relevant regulations, laws, or memorandums to set up an effective connecting mechanism that shares information timely between deposit insurers and other financial regulators appears to be an efficient measure promoting information disclosure and transparency.[87] Notably, in the Northern Rock case, transparency and information disclosure were disastrous, and depositors were unaware of the existence of the UK deposit protection scheme, resulting in severe bank runs outside each branch of Northern Rock. Thus, it can be identified that transparency and information disclosure play a significant role in preventing bank runs and panics.[88]

2.5.1.2 Establishing Limited Deposit Insurance Coverage

In light of the IADI's Core Principle 8, there are four specific features of deposit insurance coverage: (1) limited and credible; (2) covering the large majority of depositors; (3) exposing certain amounts of deposits to market discipline; and (4) consistent with the deposit insurance's objectives and particular features.[89] However, setting a limited coverage, aimed at eliminating moral hazard through exercising market discipline, is one of the most challenging missions for running an effective deposit insurance scheme.[90]

Notably, to carry out an effective coverage limit, it is important to verify which financial institutions and financial derivatives would be covered. Clearly, financial institutions that take deposits from the public are necessary. As for other financial instruments, the IADI lists the following types of deposits, principals, and interests that should be covered:

- Deposit of all types, including demand, savings, and time deposits, that are denominated in domestic currency;
- Promissory notes that are issued by members of the deposit insurance system or defined as deposits by relevant laws and regulations;
- Both principal and any accrued interest that has not already been added to the principal would be covered.[91]

With regard to foreign currency deposits, whether to cover them under deposit insurance is mainly based on country specifics. If domestic currency deposits have a monopoly on most transactions, deposit insurers need not expand the coverage to foreign currencies. However, when foreign currency deposits become the principal currency in the majority of domestic transactions, deposit insurers should include that foreign currency in the coverage of deposit insurance to maintain financial stability. Ideally, reimbursements are better repaid in the domestic currency. However, if necessary, deposit insurers seeking to cover deposits in the form of foreign currencies are responsible for ensuring that member institutions already have already had sound and well-managed foreign exchange systems to offset foreign-exchange fluctuations.[92]

Besides, in accordance with the guidance released by the IADI, there are some specific types of deposits that might be excluded from deposit protection, as follows:

- Interbank deposits;
- Deposits of government departments and of regional, provincial, and municipal governments, and other public bodies;
- Deposits of individuals who are regarded as responsible for the deterioration of an institution, including deposits belonging to the directors, managers, large shareholders, and auditors of banks;
- Deposits that carry excessive interest rates;
- Bearer deposits.[93]

In addition, deposit insurance coverage should exclude larger depositors and unsecured creditors, thereby exposing them to market discipline and motivating them to pay more attention to the bank's performance.[94] As a result, banks have to face increasing pressure and monitoring from large depositors and unsecured creditors on their riskier investment portfolios, which might urge them to remain sound in line with financial regulators' objectives. In reality, as noted by Campbell and

Moffatt, small or unsophisticated depositors are generally incapable of exercising market discipline and assessing risks in particular banks due to information asymmetry and the lack of professional knowledge.[95]

The IADI also adds four specific limitations to explain why it is hard for small depositors and unsophisticated depositors to discipline imprudent behaviours: first, it is unrealistic to ensure that small and unsophisticated depositors are able to receive the latest information in relation to the performance of banks; second, unlike corporate depositors, larger depositors, and creditors, small and unsophisticated depositors may not have the requisite professional knowledge and skills needed to understand financial reports like quarterly reports, monthly reports, and other official reports of banks; third, during a crisis, the costs of changing banks can be expensive for ordinary depositors, as without government backing those depositors will usually be placed at a disadvantaged position against large banks; fourth, in practice, by distributing savings in multiple individual accounts or joint accounts with different banks, it is noteworthy that small depositors can easily keep account balances below the threshold of coverage.[96]

Regarding large depositors and creditors, they should become a major force, excluded from deposit insurance schemes, to monitor bank performance. Large depositors and creditors usually have a deeper relationship and cooperation with the banks. For example, some corporate depositors cooperate with banks on issuing new financial derivatives; hence they have access to the latest and most accurate information regarding the financial condition of banks. Therefore, large depositors and creditors should be encouraged to pay attention to bank performance by not including them in deposit insurance schemes. However, although large depositors and creditors can have useful information and analyse the information, they have to pay significant costs for changing banks, and when host banks become problematic, they cannot withdraw deposits as flexibly as ordinary depositors.[97] This is to say, large depositors and creditors also have difficulties in protecting their deposits, so all expectations of exerting market discipline cannot be put on them.

With regard to the amount of deposit insurance coverage, the IMF suggests that the amount of deposit insurance coverage ought to be approximately one or two times per capita Gross Domestic Product (GDP). However, in practice, the scope of deposit insurance coverage is deliberately decided by the distribution of deposits and the average amount of most small depositors.[98] According to suggestions made by the IADI, the limit of deposit insurance coverage should be set to cover the majority of depositors, but the total value of insured deposits should be limited within a rational range that incentivises large depositors to monitor bank performance.[99] An appropriate scope of coverage can strike a balance between small depositors and larger depositors in terms of decreasing bank runs and promoting market discipline. Both the IADI and the IMF assert that, from a macro perspective, sound coverage is consistent with the objectives of deposit insurance and the financial safety net.[100] In essence, the scope of deposit insurance coverage should be designed on an *ad hoc* basis in response to ever-increasing innovative derivatives and inflation, although high costs may result from periodic adjustments in terms of strengthening public awareness and carrying out periodic reports. Simultaneously, to set a reasonable and fair scope of deposit insurance coverage that benefits both domestic banks and foreign banks, international competitiveness is suggested to be taken into consideration.

However, there is a question about whether universally unified standards of deposit insurance coverage exist. In the current situation where countries have totally different economies, it is hard to unify standards globally because of huge wealth gaps between developed countries and developing countries. One approach to determine the limit of deposit insurance coverage is to apply the ratio of the coverage level compared to per capita GDP. However, as shown in Table 2.1, though the IMF has provided a standard for coverage, most countries do not follow this standard, as it seems to be out of date. As shown in Table 2.1, a majority of developed countries have adopted a ratio of less than four. The lower ratio indicates that costs of banking systems are relatively reasonable and the possibility of a financial crisis has been decreased.

In light of Table 2.1, for some developing countries, in order to improve financial stability, they have put forward a higher ratio which might trigger more losses during a crisis, rather than developed countries with a lower ratio.[101] Thus, compared with banks registered in developed countries, banks incorporated in developing countries are more willing to invest in riskier portfolios and assets because governments in developing countries generally provide generous deposit insurance coverage. This may raise the probability of triggering moral hazard due to the high coverage provided to depositors and banks.[102] As a consequence, this circumstance where developing countries, on the contrary, have generous deposit insurance coverage illustrates that deposit insurance in developing countries may encounter more difficulties in preventing moral hazard. Therefore, developing countries indeed need some suggestions or recommendations to set a rational and reasonable deposit insurance coverage in consideration of developed countries' experience.

Table 2.1 Coverage, GDP, and Ratios in Different Countries

Jurisdiction	*Coverage Level (US Dollar)*	*Per Capita GDP in 2023 (US Dollar)*	*Ratio (Coverage Level/Per Capita GDP)*
France	111,685.30	44,460.82	2.51
Germany	111,685.30	52,745.76	2.12
Italy	111,685.30	38,373.17	2.91
Spain	111,685.30	32,676.98	3.42
Switzerland	101,220.00	99,994.94	1.01
United Kingdom	113,710.11	48,866.60	2.74
United States	250,000.00	81,695.19	3.06
Australia	185,389.00	64,711.77	2.86
China	71,315.50	12,614.06	5.65
Canada	73,030.00	53,371.70	1.37
Mexico	160,000.00	13,926.11	11.49
Indonesia	150,048.00	4,940.55	30.37

Source: the latest data released by the World Bank and each deposit insurer. Ratios are calculated by the author.

2.5.2 Co-insurance

The principal goal of co-insurance is to require banks and depositors to share losses arising from bank failures, indicating that depositors have to bear proportional losses of bank failure, even losses caused by bankers' misconduct. Accordingly, it attempts to incentivise depositors to maintain market discipline and monitor banks' performance. Despite strengthening market discipline, it is very controversial to describe the advantages and disadvantages of co-insurance.

On one hand, without imposing incentives and responsibilities, depositors, as human beings, may deposit their savings in riskier banks which promise higher interest with higher returns regardless of excessive risks taken by banks, resulting in adverse effects on market discipline and financial stability.[103] Furthermore, 100 percent deposit insurance coverage merely imposes a burden on financial regulatory bodies and deposit insurers, as they ultimately have to shoulder all responsibilities and compensate losses, leading to moral hazard by not compelling bankers and depositors to exert market discipline. Under 100 percent deposit insurance coverage, the managers of banks may utilise insured deposits to invest in high-risk but high-profit investment portfolios in pursuit of high bonuses and dividends as deposit insurance schemes would ultimately recover losses, while depositors are assured to purchase riskier financial derivatives without any hesitation because of the existence of 100 percent coverage.

However, on the other hand, owing to information asymmetry, ordinary and unsophisticated depositors that lack access to sufficient and updated information associated with their host banks find it difficult to make precise decisions and monitor bank performance, while banking regulators, who are capable of capturing and judging key information in a prompt way, are obligated to monitor banks instead of depositors.[104] Apart from information asymmetry, despite having access to the latest information, without professional knowledge and experience, depositors are incapable of making rational decisions. Therefore, it is unrealistic to expect ordinary and unsophisticated depositors to probe into bank management, so financial regulators and supervisors are responsible for taking action against troubled institutions and granting priority to small and unsophisticated depositors. In addition, without transparency, unsophisticated depositors are prone to being affected by market rumours, which lead to bank runs and market panics.[105]

The collapse of Northern Rock in the GFC was a landmark case demonstrating how market rumours accelerate the failure of a bank. In this case, uncertainty, poor design of deposit insurance coverage, and market rumours led to the first UK bank run since 1878, resulting in significant adverse effects on the UK retail banking sector.[106] During the Northern Rock run, the UK had adopted coinsurance, with 100 percent deposit insurance coverage for the first £2,000 and 90 percent deposit insurance coverage for the next £33,000.[107] However, in reality, the UK government ultimately bailed out Northern Rock in order to maintain public confidence and financial stability. As a consequence, coinsurance has been abandoned. Arguably, although market discipline is, in essence, a key player in maintaining financial stability, public confidence indeed is needed to preserve financial stability as well. Therefore, co-insurance might be utilised by large depositors as they usually have professional skills and experience, and 100 percent deposit insurance coverage can be applied to small depositors or unsophisticated depositors to safeguard their hard-earned money.

At present, most countries have transitioned to high-level but limited 100 percent protection, which represents the popular trend around the world, revealing that co-insurance no longer plays an important role in deposit protection.[108]

2.5.3 Risk-Based Premiums

The mechanism of risk-based premiums represents the newest development in deposit insurance.[109] This mechanism incentivises banks to concentrate on capital adequacy and avoid taking excessive risks, as well-capitalised institutions pay lower premiums than financial institutions that take excessive risks. In theory, this mechanism purports to reduce the cross-subsidy and moral hazard in the banking market, as riskier institutions that take excessive risks have to pay higher deposit insurance premiums, regarded as punishments, rather than sound financial institutions.

However, limitations on the mechanism of risk-based premiums are also clear and controversial. In particular, well-capitalised depository institutions that benefit the most from financial stability, under this mechanism, do not need to make greater contributions to the deposit insurance funds, whilst riskier institutions that have an urgent need for capital support are incapable of affording higher premiums.[110] Inevitably, riskier banks may attempt to prolong their lives by attracting deposits by promising high interest and high returns.

Besides, time lag is another limitation affecting the effectiveness of risk-based premiums. Generally, this mechanism is effective in capturing known risks rather than new and innovative risks because the future of financial markets is very difficult to anticipate and assess. As a consequence, insured institutions, particularly riskier institutions, might be inspired to bet on new risky investment activities in pursuit of high returns.[111]

Therefore, to reflect risks precisely, this mechanism needs to collaborate with other mechanisms to establish an integrated risk assessment regime.[112] As for experienced countries that already have specific experience and skilled staff, it is convenient for them to set up a functional risk-based premium assessment. However, for newcomers, simplicity is best, so they should be patient while developing their own deposit insurance schemes.

The US has been playing a leading role in performing risk-based premium assessment. The Federal Deposit Insurance Corporation Improvement Act (FDICIA) 1991 first introduced the concept and the rationale for calculating premiums based on the risk level and CAMELS ratings.[113] So far, a growing number of countries have adopted risk-based premium assessment in their deposit insurance schemes.[114]

2.5.4 Mitigating Outside Interference

Currently, three main urgent issues relating to outside interference on deposit insurers still exist in conjunction with moral hazard. These issues are political interference, regulatory capture, and cross-departmental coordination.

The first problem refers to political interference. It is common that, in a government-run deposit insurance system, politicians get involved in banking regulation and adversely impact deposit insurers' management and decision-making through their political and administrative powers. To mitigate such situations, the best approach is to build a straightforward, transparent, and integrated regulatory framework committed to insulating political interference and politicians, which imposes restrictions and sanctions on politicians for their imprudent behaviours.

The second problem is directed at regulatory capture, a situation in which deposit insurers become more focused on bankers' interests rather than depositors' and taxpayers' interests. Nevertheless, this situation usually occurs in privately run deposit insurance systems.[115] Therefore, privately run deposit insurance systems are suggested to be transitioned to government-run systems or to let officials concentrate on public interests by not allowing banks to play a dominant role on the board of directors in privately run deposit insurance systems.

The third problem is the absence of cross-departmental coordination. It is common that, in some countries, different functions are distributed to different financial authorities, which makes information sharing more time-consuming. Typically, in developing countries, owing to the shortage of experienced staff and skills, central banks, the policymakers of monetary policy, generally take over the responsibility for running deposit insurance systems. Therefore, a clear clarification of objectives and functions among deposit insurers and other financial regulatory bodies is a prerequisite and more crucial than institutional location. Most importantly, a highly independent deposit insurer is still desirable.[116]

2.5.5 Improving the Credibility of Deposit Insurers

2.5.5.1 Independence

While independence is not a big problem troubling privately run deposit insurance systems, it is a major challenge for government-run deposit insurance systems. Ideally, a deposit insurer should play an independent role between politics, monetary policy, and financial supervisors, and run a deposit insurance scheme in light of relevant laws and regulations. In particular, the board of directors of deposit insurers should be formulated in a flexible manner and retain an odd number in order to reach of a majority.

Furthermore, governments have an obligation to nominate board members in accordance with relevant laws and regulations, ensuring the integrity of the board. Members of the board should be required to focus on public interest rather than bankers' interests and political interests. The IADI has issued guidance for board formation, recommending that several posts on the board should normally be normally occupied by leaders arising from financial supervisory authorities and the ministry of finance; each central bank should occupy a vacancy, and the remainder should be nominated outside the government in order to maintain political independence and operational independence.[117]

Obviously, board members have a responsibility to eliminate conflicts of interest, in terms of cutting ties with insured banks. Nevertheless, bankers are likely to be nominated as consultants for deposit insurers, whose suggestions are targeted at broadening the horizon of policy-making. Furthermore, the deposit insurance laws or regulations are supposed to detail the 'fit and proper' principles and authorise staff with immunity and protection for the implementation of their obligations.[118]

2.5.5.2 *Accountability and Legal Protection*

Although a government-run deposit insurer needs to be free from political interference and vigorous lobbying, it is accountable to the government, public, and bankers for its actions and decisions. Generally, a deposit insurer is accountable to the ministry of finance, as it usually provides start-up funding for running a deposit insurance system. Furthermore, a deposit insurer is responsible for releasing the latest information and issuing warnings to the public and banks. For the sake of transparency, a deposit insurer has a duty to release its financial statements via annual reports and annual audits.

Nevertheless, it is noteworthy that legal protection or immunity dedicated to keeping financial supervisors away from unnecessary legal allegations when they perform their duties is needed to ensure that financial supervisors can act in good faith.[119] Although financial supervisors are expected to prevent and resolve bank failures through carrying out various punishments such as fines, penalties, and revocation of licences, etc., financial supervisors are always criticised for implementing these sanctions unsuccessfully when troubled banks become insolvent. Sometimes, financial supervisors even have to face legal action against their behaviours that trigger adverse effects or delay of corrective action.[120]

For deposit insurers with broad mandates who are responsible for taking timely and prompt action against troubled banks, legal immunity aimed at protecting individual staff involved in such actions is necessary. Therefore, legal protection for individual staff when they carry out their obligations should be formally written into relevant laws or regulations.[121] In order to ensure that supervisors act in good faith, clear and detailed statutory provisions are required to be well defined. Particularly, two situations justify legal immunity and should be taken into consideration: first, deposit insurance law or regulation should provide statutory immunity to deposit insurers and individual staff against unnecessary lawsuits that accuse them of performing their duties in good faith;[122] and, second, legal protection principally helps financial authorities or individual supervisors avoid the cost of lawsuits against their actions while exerting their duties in good faith.[123]

However, so far, a universally unified approach for statutory protection of financial supervisors and individual staff has not yet been introduced due to the existence of two legal systems – common law and civil law. As concluded by Campbell, common law systems tend to provide a high level of protection to both deposit insurers and individual staff who act on behalf of financial authorities, whereas civil law systems prefer to stand by the rights of citizens who can prove that financial authorities are liable for their losses.[124]

2.6 Avoiding Adverse Selection

2.6.1 Establishing Compulsory Membership

According to Principle 7 of the IADI's Core Principles, the membership of a deposit insurance system is compulsory for all deposit-taking banks whose locations are placed in the country, including state-owned commercial banks and other depository financial institutions supervised by prudential regulation.[125]

When considering the financial viability of deposit insurance, all depository financial institutions that benefit from deposit insurance should automatically become members of deposit insurance schemes and contribute to the costs of running these schemes. Nevertheless, the principal argument concerning compulsory membership is that it may lead to cross-subsidisation between sound banks and weak banks, as sound banks have to undertake more responsibilities and costs for maintaining a workable deposit insurance scheme. However, all members, especially large and complex financial institutions, are expected to benefit from strengthened financial stability amid gradually increasing public confidence in the financial markets. Importantly, compulsory membership could impose legal obligations and pressure on banks when depositors are aware of basic knowledge regarding deposit insurance.[126]

The membership of deposit insurance is suggested to cover all deposit-taking institutions, including state-owned commercial banks, in consideration of enhancing competition.[127] Therefore, state-owned commercial banks, as members of deposit insurance schemes, have to contribute deposit insurance premiums like other deposit-taking institutions, despite having government guarantees.[128] Furthermore, state-owned commercial banks have to abide by the same supervision and coverage as other financial institutions. Thus, in some countries, banking laws or regulations are advised to integrate state-owned commercial banks into prudential regulation. Alongside the recommendations discussed above, full government guarantees should be scrapped.

With regard to foreign financial institutions, foreign bank branches, subsidiaries, and offshore businesses, the issue of whether these institutions are allowed to join membership has been concerned, as some countries' deposit insurance systems exclude these institutions from their deposit insurance schemes, while some nations expand membership to these institutions in pursuit of competitive banking markets.

2.7 Funding of Deposit Insurance

2.7.1 Ex-ante Funding Mechanism or Ex-post Funding Mechanism?

The deposit insurance fund can be accumulated either from levying on an ex-ante basis or charging ex-post levies on surviving institutions after a crisis or a failure. In addition, hybrid funding mechanisms that combine ex-ante funding mechanisms and ex-post funding mechanisms appear to be a new alternative mechanism for dealing with deposit insurance funds.

At present, the popular option is to apply an ex-ante funding mechanism in a deposit insurance scheme. In light of the survey released by the IADI, the ratio of deposit insurance schemes adopting ex-ante funding mechanisms has gradually risen from 83 percent to 90 percent.[129] In theory, ex-ante funding mechanisms, aimed at covering prospective losses and expenses of bank failures, require deposit insurers to collect deposit insurance premiums and manage the deposit insurance fund before a financial crisis actually occurs. Therefore, a deposit insurance scheme equipped with an ex-ante funding system, in comparison with ex-post funding mechanisms, facilitates the reliability of faster payouts so as to reduce the chances of bank runs and market panic, thereby promoting public confidence and maintaining financial stability.[130]

Besides, levying ex-ante premiums, deemed as a buffer against losses of bank failures, is supposed to spread losses and costs of running a deposit insurance scheme over time. In other words, the ex-ante funding mechanisms can be regarded as a hedge against prospective losses of bank failures. Apart from loss sharing, ex-ante funding mechanisms are more equitable than ex-post funding mechanisms, because all members have to make contributions, through paying premiums and submitting information, to underpin deposit insurance systems, whereas in ex-post funding systems deposit insurers are merely able to levy premiums from surviving banks.

However, unfortunately, ex-ante funding mechanisms still have several drawbacks. Typically, start-up funds of deposit insurance schemes and ongoing deposit insurance premiums might cut the profits of member institutions as, even without bank failures, they have to pay premiums to sustain deposit insurance schemes.[131] Simultaneously, without a specified restriction enacted in relevant laws and regulations, insured banks may attempt to spread the costs of deposit insurance premiums to depositors.

In contrast, ex-post funding mechanisms, as elaborated by Hoelscher, operate in 'loss-sharing' or 'mutual guarantee' models.[132] Usually, deposit insurers determine to levy deposit insurance premiums after bank failures or financial crises. Furthermore, ex-post funding mechanisms might be more comfortable for insured institutions because fewer premiums would be charged during stable period so that they have more availability of capital for investment activities in the financial markets. Another benefit of adopting an ex-post funding system is that it incentivises banks, especially the majority of large banks, to monitor peers mutually.

However, compared with ex-ante funding mechanisms, ex-post mechanisms give rise to uncertainty. Since the accumulation of the deposit insurance funds merely starts after crises or bank failures, faster payouts become more doubtful and unrealistic. Furthermore, fairness can be in doubt under ex-post funding mechanisms, as sound and surviving banks have to pay higher prices for covering depositor compensation and bank resolution mechanisms, but failed banks are incapable of contributing premiums to the deposit insurance funds. As a consequence, under a volatile economic climate, such situations where deposit insurance premiums are only levied from sound and surviving banks may exacerbate the financial viability of surviving banks and lead to distrust towards deposit insurance schemes.[133] Nonetheless, ex-post funding systems, as summarised by Garcia, are normally run by private deposit insurers who have insufficient resources and specified obligations.[134]

However, the recent GFC demonstrates that ex-ante systems are incapable of dealing with large failures and ex-post levies are still required to sustain deposit insurance schemes.[135] As a result, hybrid funding systems that combine ex-ante funding mechanisms and ex-post funding mechanisms are considered to be an alternative mechanism.[136]

2.7.2 Determining the Target Deposit Insurance Fund

At present, there are two different measures used to set the target level of the deposit insurance funds. The first, which is labelled flat rate premiums, purports to charge insured banks a steady premium rate over a long time, without any upper or lower limits. The second, which sets a planned limit, aims to charge flexible deposit insurance premiums in accordance with the planned limit and practical situations.[137]

Regarding the first approach, although a fixed rate brings about certainty to member banks, the flexibility of the deposit insurance funds is jeopardised when encountering volatile markets. Faced with the inadequacy of deposit insurance funds, deposit insurers are usually entirely backed by the government or other financial regulatory bodies rather than themselves. Therefore, policymakers should consider setting a target for deposit insurance funds in response to unknown risks or sudden crises. As for the second approach, it is more reflective of the financial markets and risk exposures of individual member institutions, as member institutions are suggested to pay steady premiums in a good economic environment but differentiated premiums in an economic downturn.[138]

Furthermore, deposit insurers with broad mandates, like the FDIC, are responsible for determining the target level of the deposit insurance funds in order to cope with any financial distress that may happen in the future. More specifically, underlying factors should be taken into account in reaching a reasonable target. These factors are:

- The composition of member banks (number, size, lines of business);
- The liabilities of member banks and the exposure of the deposit insurer;
- The probability of failures and the characteristics of losses;
- The potential default rates of member institutions under the macroeconomic conditions;
- The state of the supervisory and regulatory regime;
- The resolution approaches and the resolution powers of the deposit insurer;
- The availability and adequacy of liquidity funding.[139]

2.7.3 Collecting and Managing Deposit Insurance Premiums

Member institutions are required to pay deposit insurance premiums periodically based on the premium rates and the total value of their insured deposits. Ideally, deposit insurers can directly collect premiums from member institutions to cover operating expenses and accumulate funds to the target level. In practice, different countries have different upper limits or lower limits on the accumulation of deposit insurance premiums, and the upper or lower limits should be determined based on the percentage of insured deposits to total deposits.[140] Furthermore, procedures should be detailed in relevant deposit insurance laws or regulations, coupled with rules regarding returning premiums when premiums accumulate to the target level. Normally, premiums, regarded as operating expenses of insured banks, are legally tax-exempt. Insured institutions that benefit most from financial stability and deposit insurance are obligated to pay premiums in a timely manner.

Considering capital inadequacy and liquidity shortages, deposit insurers have to adopt conservative investment strategies to manage fund resources. In light of the IADI's guidance, deposit insurers can only can make use of the deposit insurance funds by investing in investing the safest assets in the financial markets, such as short-term government securities, treasury bonds, and deposits. Deposit insurers should be restricted from seeking highly profitable and liquid investment portfolios, such as foreign exchange markets.[141] In addition, deposit insurers should avoid maintaining deposit insurance funds in a single insured bank, because one-off withdrawals may not only trigger a liquidity crunch in that bank but also might lead to a liquidity shortage in domestic interbank markets.

2.7.4 Government Guarantees

Seeking government guarantees is a subordinate choice for deposit insurers, as when there is a healthy economic environment with a well-managed deposit insurer, government guarantees are never considered. When encountering capital inadequacy, deposit insurers might seek capital support from the ministry of finance or the central bank without any collateral, and governments are willing to assist deposit insurers to ensure financial stability. Nevertheless, once deposit insurers determine to borrow from the markets, they would do better to get prior approval from the ministry of finance, and so would other participants of the financial safety net.[142]

However, King claimed that, without sufficient deposit insurance funds, government guarantees are eventually inevitably utilised for coping with troubled banks, which would deteriorate moral hazard.[143] Theoretically, government guarantees are generally regarded as the last resort for resolving 'too big to fail' banks because of their massive influence on financial stability.[144] Nevertheless, during the recent global financial crisis, despite calls for allowing 'too big to fail' banks to fail, banks whose failures had negatively affected financial stability usually received guarantees from governments. Northern Rock, which was neither a systemically significant bank nor an international bank, was a landmark case illustrating how a bank gets bailed out.

Moreover, as stressed by the IADI, a single bank failure would trigger weak public confidence, criticism of prudential supervision, and regulatory capture of bankers, leading to blanket guarantees in favour of the financial markets.[145]

Accordingly, the IADI's statistics demonstrate that, during the recent global financial crisis, 19 member countries had temporarily utilised blanket guarantees; 22 member countries had raised deposit insurance coverage on a permanent basis; and 7 member countries had temporarily raised coverage level.[146] Therefore, it is admitted that faced with a severe crisis, deposit insurance is not capable of sustaining financial stability, and government guarantees are still supplementary for maintaining financial stability.[147] However, Ayadi emphasises that, after the market chaos is contained, government guarantees should be removed from the markets as soon as possible, and then substituted by deposit insurance.[148] Therefore, it is fair to say that without an effective and well-designed deposit insurance scheme, government guarantees are still needed to maintain financial stability.[149]

2.8 Conclusion

Although the majority of countries have reached a consensus to establish deposit insurance systems in consideration of financial stability and depositor protection, establishing an effective and well-designed deposit insurance system is much more complicated. An effective deposit insurance scheme should not only set out realistic objectives but also needs to exploit good practices. However, there is no one-size-fits-all model for building an effective deposit insurance scheme; thus, policymakers should consider designing good practices of deposit insurance based on country specifics.

How to minimise moral hazard has been a headache troubling policymakers, as moral hazard is an intrinsic feature of deposit insurance. The only way to minimise moral hazard is to build up an effective and well-designed deposit insurance system with good practices, which could either maintain financial stability or protect depositors by not exacerbating moral hazard or market discipline. Therefore, good practices suggested by academics and international financial organisations should be taken into consideration to the maximum limit of moral hazard.

In the meantime, in order to maintain financial stability, deposit insurance, as one major component of the financial safety net, also needs to set up effective collaboration and coordination with other participants of the financial safety net, in terms of banking supervision, prudential regulation, and lender of last resort. In addition, new mechanisms in financial regulation, like ring-fencing, also help deposit insurance maintain financial stability and protect depositors. Most importantly, an effective deposit insurance scheme with good practices should strike a balance among deposit insurers, depositors, and banks, the major participants involved in deposit insurance.

Notes

1 IADI official website brings together data of explicit deposit insurance. The data is available at <https://www.iadi.org/about-iadi/who-we-are/> accessed 10 July 2024.

2 Many international organisations have issued core principles and standards on deposit insurance, like 'Core Principles of Effective Deposit Insurance' by the Basel Committee on Banking Supervision and the International Association of Deposit Insurers.

3 Michael Hantke-Domas, 'The Public Interest Theory of Regulation: Non-Existence or Misinterpretation?' (2003) 15 *European Journal of Law and Economics,* 165, 167.
4 George J. Stigler, 'The Theory of Economic Regulation' (1971) 2 *The Bell Journal of Economics and Management Science*, 3, 21. And see Richard A. Posner, 'Theories of Economic Regulation' (1974) 5 *The Bell Journal of Economics and Management Science*, 335, 343.
5 IADI, 'IADI Core Principles for Effective Deposit Insurance Systems' (International Association of Deposit Insurers, November 2014) <http://www.iadi.org/en/assets/File/Core%20Principles/cprevised2014nov.pdf> accessed 3 November 2023.
6 Deniz Anginer and Asli Demirgüç-Kunt, 'Bank Runs and Moral Hazard: A Review of Deposit Insurance' (World Bank, 2018) <http://documents.worldbank.org/curated/en/548031537377082747/pdf/WPS8589.pdf> accessed 20 December 2023.
7 Ronald MacDonald, 'Deposit Insurance' (Bank of England 1996) <http://www.bankofengland.co.uk/education/Documents/ccbs/handbooks/pdf/ccbshb09.pdf> accessed 10 November 2023.
8 Frances Rosenbluth and Ross Schaap, 'The Domestic Politics of Banking Regulation' (2003) 57 *International Organisation*, 307, 336.
9 Gerald P. O'Driscoll, Jr., 'Deposit Insurance in Theory and Practice' (1988) 7 *Cato Journal*, 661, 681.
10 Ronald MacDonald, 'Deposit Insurance'. (n7)
11 Varadarajan V. Chari and Ravi Jagannathan, 'Banking Panics, Information, and Rational Expectations Equilibrium' (1988) 43 *Journal of Finance*, 751.
12 Andrew Campbell and Paula Moffatt, 'Protecting Bank Depositors after Cyprus' (2013) 1 *Nottingham Insolvency and Business Law eJournal,* 27, 50.
13 John Raymond LaBrosse and David G. Mayes, 'Promoting Financial Stability through Effective Depositor Protection: The Case for Explicit Limited Deposit Insurance' in Andrew Campbell, John Raymond Labrosse David G. Mayes and Dalvinder Singh (eds), *Deposit Insurance* (Palgrave Macmillan 2007) 11.
14 Asli Demirgüç-Kunt and Enrica Detragiache, 'Does Deposit Insurance Increase Banking System Stability? An Empirical Investigation' (2002) 49 *Journal of Monetary Economics*, 1378.
15 Financial Stability Forum, 'Guidance for Developing Effective Deposit Insurance Systems' (Financial Stability Board, September 2001) <http://www.fsb.org/wp-content/uploads/r_0109b.pdf> accessed 19 December 2023.
16 Geoffery P. Miller, 'Deposit Insurance for Economies in Transition' (1997) 2 *Yearbook of International Financial and Economic Law*, 103.
17 Andrew Campbell and Paula Moffatt, 'UK Depositor Protection in the Aftermath of the Banking Crisis' (2010) 25 *Journal of International Banking Law and Regulation*, 488.
18 R. Mark Williamson, 'Regulatory Theory and Deposit Insurance Reform' (1994) 42 *Cleveland State Law Review*, 105,114.
19 Dalvinder Singh and John Raymond LaBrosse, 'Northern Rock, Depositors and Deposit Insurance Coverage: Some Critical Reflections' (2010) 2 *Journal of Business Law*, 56.
20 Financial Stability Forum, 'Guidance for Developing Effective Deposit Insurance Systems' (n15).
21 Ronald MacDonald, 'Deposit Insurance' (n7).
22 Gillian G. H. Garcia 'A Survey of Deposit Insurance Practices' (1999) International Monetary Fund, Working Paper WP/99/54.
23 Gillian G. H. Garcia 'Deposit Insurance Actual and Good Practices: Good Practice for Deposit Insurance' (2000) International Monetary Fund, Occasional Paper No. 197, 4.
24 *Ibid.*
25 Douglas W. Diamond and Philip H. Dybvig, 'Bank Runs, Deposit Insurance, and Liquidity' (1983) 91 *The Journal of Political Economy*, 401, 416.

26 The mandates can be classified into four categories: 'pay box' mandate, 'pay box plus' mandate, 'loss minimiser' mandate, and 'risk minimiser' mandate. In the 'pay box' model, the deposit insurance just pays out when the institution fails. Responsibilities increase from 'pay box' model to the 'risk minimiser' model.
27 IADI, 'IADI Core Principles for Effective Deposit Insurance Systems' (n5).
28 Asli Demirgüç-Kunt and Edward J. Kane, 'Deposit Insurance around the Globe: Where Does It Works?' (2001) *National Bureau of Economic Research Working Paper* 8493.
29 John Raymond LaBrosse and David G. Mayes, 'Promoting Financial Stability through Effective Depositor Protection: The Case for Explicit Limited Deposit Insurance' (n13), 17.
30 Bernard Shull, 'How Should Bank Regulatory Agencies Be Organized?' (1993) 11 *Contemporary Economic Policy,* 99.
31 David S. Hoelscher, Michael W. Taylor and Ulrich H. Klueh, 'The Design and Implementation of Deposit Insurance Systems' (2006) International Monetary Fund, Occasional Paper No. 251, 9.
32 See Financial Stability Forum, 'Guidance for Developing Effective Deposit Insurance Systems' (n10).
33 Further discussion in Charles Goodhart and Dirk Schoenmaker, 'Should the Functions of Monetary Policy and Banking Supervision Be Separated?' (1995) 47 *Oxford Economic Papers*, 539, 560.
34 Financial Stability Board (FSB), 'Thematic Review on Deposit Insurance Systems Peer Review Report' (8 February 2012) < http://www.fsb.org/wp-content/uploads/r_120208.pdf?page_moved=1> accessed 11 January 2024.
35 Bert Ely, 'Regulatory Moral Hazard: The Real Moral Hazard in Federal Deposit Insurance' (1999) 4 *The Independent Review* 241,254.
36 See Financial Stability Forum 'Guidance for Developing Effective Deposit Insurance Systems' (n15).
37 *Ibid.*
38 David Folkerts-Landau and Lindgren Carl-Johan 'Word Economic and Financial Survey: Toward a Framework for Financial Stability' (International Monetary Fund, 1998) < http://www.imf.org/external/pubs/ft/wefs/toward/pdf/file03.pdf> accessed 7 November 2023.
39 George J. Benston and George G. Kaufman, 'Regulating Bank Safety and Performances' in James Rosenfeld (ed), *The Selected Works of George J Benston, Volume 1: Banking and Financial Services* (Oxford University Press 2010) 92.
40 George A. Akerlof and Paul M. Romer, 'Looting: The Economic Underworld of Bankruptcy for Profit' (1993) 2 *Brookings Paper on Economic Activity,* 70.
41 Wilson Ervin, 'Understanding "Ring-Fencing" and How It Could Make Banking Riskier' (Brookings Institute, February 2018) <https://www.brookings.edu/research/understanding-ring-fencing-and-how-it-could-make-banking-riskier/> accessed 2 January 2024.
42 Narayana Kocherlakota and Ilhyock Shim, 'Forbearance and Prompt Corrective Action' (2005) Bank for International Settlements (BIS) Working Paper No. 177.
43 Financial Stability Board (FSB), 'Thematic Review on Deposit Insurance Systems Peer Review Report' (n34). Reimbursement can also be called as 'payoff' or 'payout'.
44 *Ibid.*
45 Willian Su, 'General Guidance for the Resolution of Bank Failures' in Andrew Campbell (eds), *Deposit Insurance* (Palgrave Macmillan 2007) 250.
46 Nicholas J. Ketcha Jr, 'Deposit Insurance System Design and Considerations' (1999) Bank for International Settlements (BIS), Policy Paper No. 7, 221.
47 Claire L. McGuire, 'Simple Tools to Assist in the Resolution of Troubled Banks' (the World Bank, 2012) <http://siteresources.worldbank.org/EXTFINANCIALSECTOR/Resources/Bank_Resolution_Toolkit.pdf> accessed 20 December 2023.

48 Samuel H. Talley and Iqnacio Mas, 'Deposit Insurance in Developing Countries' (1990) World Bank, Policy, Research, and External Affairs Working Paper, No. WPS 548.
49 *Ibid* at 252.
50 'Too big to fail' banks usually have remarkable influence on financial stability and social stability. See generally Charles G. Leathers and J. Partick Raines, 'Some Historical Perspectives on 'Too Big to Fail' Policies' in Benton E. Gup (ed), *Too Big to Fail: Policies and Practices in Government Bailouts* (Praeger Publishers, 2004) 16.
51 See Financial Stability Forum, 'Guidance for Developing Effective Deposit Insurance Systems' (n15).
52 Andrew Campbell, 'Bank Insolvency and the Problem of Nonperforming Loans' (2007) 9 *Journal of Banking Regulation,* 25.
53 *Ibid.*
54 Ring-fencing also could refer to 'Ringfencing' or 'Ringfence'.
55 Steven L. Schwarcz, 'Ring-Fencing' (2014) 69 *Southern California Law Review,* 72.
56 William D. Jackson, 'Glass-Steagall Act: Commercial vs. Investment Banking' (Congressional Research Service, 1987) <https://www.everycrsreport.com/files/19870629_IB87061_7206629ee76f98f929ca4286dd5388a9feb12635.pdf> accessed 20 January 2024.
57 Steven L. Schwarcz, 'Ring-Fencing' (n55), 100.
58 Arthur E. Wilmarth, Jr, 'The Transformation of the U.S. Financial Services Industry, 1975–2000: Competition, Consolidation, and Increased Risks' (2002) *University of Illinois Law Review* 219.
59 Sam Fleming, Sharlene Goff and Martin Arnold, 'Bank Horse-trade on Ringfence Fine Print' *Financial Times* (London, 14 August 2014) < https://www.ft.com/content/dfd4da64-23b2-11e4-8e29-00144feabdc0> accessed 10 March 2024.
60 Andrew Campbell and Paula Moffatt, 'Bank Insolvency: How Can Ring-Fencing Ensure the Continuity of Banking Services in an Insolvent Banking Group' (The INSOL Europe Academic Forum Annual Conference, Berlin, October 2015), and see Andrew Campbell and Paula Moffatt, 'Bank Insolvency: The Introduction of Ring-Fencing in the UK: An Example to be Followed?' (2019) 4 *Journal of Business Law,* 241, 261.
61 Paul Volcker is the former chairman of the Federal Reserve; see Paul Volcker, 'How to Reform Our Financial System' *N.Y. Times* (New York, 30 January 2010) < http://www.nytimes.com/2010/01/31/opinion/31volcker.html> accessed 11 February 2024.
62 Steven L. Schwarcz, 'Ring-Fencing' (n55), 73. Also see the Dodd-Frank Wall Street Reform and Consumer Protection Act.
63 Arthur E. Wilmarth, Jr, 'The Dodd-Frank Act: A Flawed and Inadequate Response to the Too-Big-to-Fail Problem' (2011) 89 *Oregon Law Review* 1044.
64 Arthur E. Wilmarth, Jr, 'Narrow Banking as a Structural Remedy for the Problem of Systemic Risk: A Comment on Professor Schwarcz's Ring-Fencing' (2014) 88 *Southern California Law Review Postscript,* 6.
65 Kimberly D. Krawiec, 'Don't "Screw Joe the Plumber"': The Sausage-Making of Financial Reform' (2013) 53 *Arizona Law Review,* 68–70. Major exceptions to the Volcker Rule include the ability of banks to engage in 'market making' and 'risk-mitigating hedging', and major exceptions to the Lincoln Amendment are similar to the Volcker Rule, allowing banks to engage in 'hedging and other similar risk-mitigating activities' and to trade certain categories of swaps.
66 Arthur E. Wilmarth, Jr, 'Narrow Banking as a Structural Remedy for the Problem of Systemic Risk: A Comment on Professor Schwarcz's Ring-Fencing' (n63), 6.
67 Steven L. Schwarcz, 'Ring-Fencing' (n55), 73.
68 Eugene White, 'Deposit Insurance' (1995) The World Bank, Policy Research Working Paper WPS 1541.

69 Ronald MacDonald, 'Deposit Insurance' (n7).
70 Edward J. Kane, *The S & L Insurance Mess: How did it Happen?* (Urban Institute Press 1989) 61.
71 *Ibid.*
72 Andrew Campbell and Peter Cartwright, 'Co-insurance and Moral Hazard: Some Reflections on Deposit Protection in the UK and USA' (2003) 5 *Journal of International Banking Regulation,* 10.
73 George G. Kaufman, 'Too Big to Fail in Banking: What Does It Mean?' (2014) 13 *Journal of Financial Stability,* 214, 223.
74 Ricki T. Helfer was the former Chairman and Chief Executive Officer of the FDIC. See Ricki Tigert Helfer 'What Deposit Insurance Can and Cannot Do' (1999) 36 *Finance and Development IMF,* 24.
75 Ibid.
76 Maximilian J. B. Hall, 'The Deposit Protection Scheme: The Case for Reform' (1987) *National Westminster Bank Quarterly Review,* 45.
77 Asli Demirgüç-Kunt and Enrica Detragiache, 'Does Deposit Insurance Increase Banking System Stability? An Empirical Investigation' (2002) 49 *Journal of Monetary Economics,* 1380.
78 Willam A. Lovett, 'Moral Hazard, Bank Supervision and Risk-Based Capital Requirements' (1989) 49 *Ohio State Law Journal,* 1365.
79 Patricia A. McCoy, 'The Moral Hazard Implications of Deposit Insurance: Theory and Evidence' Seminar on Current Development in Monetary and Financial Law, October 23–27, 2006 (IMF, Washington, DC).
80 Ricki Tigert Helfer 'What Deposit Insurance Can and Cannot Do' (n74), 25.
81 Lawrence Kryzanowski, 'Organizational Design and Positioning of the Deposit Insurance Function in the Financial System Safety Net' in Andrew Campbell (eds), *Deposit Insurance* (Palgrave Macmillan 2007) 102.
82 IADI, 'Enhanced Guidance for Effective Deposit Insurance Systems' (International Association of Deposit Insurers, May 2013)<http://www.iadi.org/en/assets/File/Papers/Approved%20Guidance%20Papers/IADI_Mitigating_Moral_Hazard_Enhanced_Guidance_2013-05.pdf> accessed 18 December 2023.
83 Andrew Campbell and Peter Cartwright, 'Co-insurance and Moral Hazard: Some Reflections on Deposit Protection in the UK and USA' (n72), 16.
84 Ibid, 16.
85 Financial Stability Forum, 'Guidance for Developing Effective Deposit Insurance Systems' (n5).
86 Gillian G. H. Garcia 'Deposit Insurance Actual and Good Practices: Good Practice for Deposit Insurance' (n22), 4.
87 *Ibid*
88 Gila Mehrez and Daniel Kaufmann, 'Transparency, Liberalization, and Financial Crisis' (2000) World Bank Policy Research Working Paper No. 2286.
89 IADI, 'Core Principles for Effective Deposit Insurance Systems' (n5).
90 Andrew Campbell, John Raymond LaBrosse, David G., Mayes and Dalvinder Singh, 'A New Standard for Deposit Insurance and Government Guarantees after the Crisis' (2009) 17 *Journal of Financial Regulation and Compliance,* 224.
91 Gillian G. H. Garcia, 'Deposit Insurance and Crisis Management' (2000) International Monetary Fund Working Paper No. 57, 23.
92 Financial Stability Forum, 'Guidance for Developing Effective Deposit Insurance Systems' (n15).
93 IADI, Enhanced Guidance for Effective Deposit Insurance Systems: Deposit Insurance Coverage Guidance Paper (International Association of Deposit Insurers, March 2013) <http://www.iadi.org/en/assets/File/Papers/Approved%20Guidance%20Papers/IADI_Coverage_Enhanced_Guidance_Paper.pdf> accessed 20 November 2023.

94 Deniz Anginer and Asli Demirgüç-Kunt, 'Bank Runs and Moral Hazard: A Review of Deposit Insurance' (n6).
95 Andrew Campbell and Paula Moffatt, 'UK Depositor Protection in the Aftermath of the Banking Crisis' (2010) 25 *Journal of International Banking Law and Regulation,* 287.
96 IADI, Enhanced Guidance for Effective Deposit Insurance Systems: Deposit Insurance Coverage Guidance Paper (n93).
97 *Ibid.*
98 Gillian G. H. Garcia 'Deposit Insurance and Crisis Management' (n91), 23.
99 IADI, Enhanced Guidance for Effective Deposit Insurance Systems: Deposit Insurance Coverage Guidance Paper (n91).
100 From the IMF's working paper on deposit insurance and crisis management and the IADI's guidance on deposit insurance coverage.
101 Patricia A. McCoy, 'The Moral Hazard Implications of Deposit Insurance: Theory and Evidence' (n79).
102 Luc Laeven, 'Pricing of Deposit Insurance' (2002) World Bank Policy Research Paper No. 2781, 54.
103 A. J. O. Wilkinson and Dermot Turing, 'Regulation of insolvent banks' in Fidelis Oditah (ed), *Insolvency of Banks: Managing the Risks: A Specially Commissioned Report* (FT Law & Tax 1996) 15.
104 Mads Andenas, 'Deposit Guarantee Schemes and Home Country Control' in Ross Cranston (ed), *The Single Market and the Law of Banking* (Lloyds of London Press 1995) 107.
105 Dalvinder Singh and John Raymond LaBrosse, 'Northern Rock, Depositors and Deposit Insurance Coverage: Some Critical Reflections' (2010) 2 *Journal of Business Law,* 56.
106 In this case, the UK applied coinsurance and a netting arrangement at that time, so all depositors of Northern Rock suffered a loss in its failure, and the bank paid out deposits first. In such situation, most depositors did not know the level of coverage.
107 Andrew Campbell and Peter Cartwright, 'Co-insurance and Moral Hazard: Some Reflections on Deposit Protection in the UK and USA' (n72), 12.
108 IADI, Enhanced Guidance for Effective Deposit Insurance Systems: Deposit Insurance Coverage Guidance Paper (n93).
109 Alexander Kyei, 'Deposit Protection Arrangements: A Comparative Study' (1995), International Monetary Fund Working Paper No. 95, 134.
110 Andrew Campbell and Peter Cartwright, 'Co-insurance and Moral hazard: Some Reflections on Deposit Protection in the UK and USA' (n73), 16.
111 Karishna G. Mantripragada, 'Depositors as a Source of Market Discipline' [1992] 9 *Yale Journal on Regulation*, 548.
112 *Ibid.*
113 John O'Keefe, Virginia Olin and Christopher A. Richardson, 'Bank Loan-Underwriting Practices: Can Examiners' Risk Assessments Contribute to Early-Warning System?' (2003), Federal Deposit Insurance Corporation Working Paper No. 2003-06, 16.
114 IADI, 'General Guidance for Developing Differential Premium Systems' (IADI, 2011) <https://www.iadi.org/en/assets/File/Papers/Approved%20Guidance%20Papers/IADI_Diff_prem_paper_FINAL_updated_Oct_31_2011_clean_version.pdf> accessed 20 December 2023.
115 Gillian G. H. Garcia 'Deposit Insurance and Crisis Management' (n91) 33.
116 Nicholas J. Ketcha Jr, 'Deposit Insurance System Design and Considerations' (BIS, 2016) <https://www.bis.org/publ/plcy07o.pdf> accessed 28 December 2023.
117 IADI, 'Governance of Deposit Insurance Systems Guidance Paper' (International Association of Deposit Insurers, 6 May 2009)<http://www.iadi.org/en/assets/File/Papers/Approved%20Guidance%20Papers/Governance%20Final%20Guidance%20Paper%206_May_2009.pdf> accessed 16 December 2023.

118 *Ibid* at 34.
119 Financial supervisors in this sentence include directors, officers and employees, agents, and anyone else acting on its behalf.
120 Andrew Campbell, 'To Protect or Not to Protect, That is the Question: Statutory Protections for Financial supervisors – How to Promote Financial Stability by Enacting the Right Law' Seminar on Current Developments in Monetary and Financial Law, October 23–27, 2006 (IMF, Washington, DC).
121 *Ibid* at 4.
122 IADI, 'Governance of Deposit Insurance Systems Guidance Paper' (n117).
123 Andrew Campbell, 'To Protect or Not to Protect, That is the Question: Statutory Protections for Financial supervisors – How to Promote Financial Stability by Enacting the Right Law' (n120).
124 *Ibid.*
125 IADI, 'IADI Core Principles for Effective Deposit Insurance Systems' (n5).
126 Financial Stability Forum, 'Guidance for Developing Effective Deposit Insurance Systems' (n15).
127 IADI, 'IADI Core Principles for Effective Deposit Insurance Systems' (n5).
128 Christine E. Blair, Frederick Carns, and Rose M. Kushmeider, 'Instituting a Deposit Insurance System: Why? How?' in Andrew Campbell, John Raymond Labrosse, David G. Mayes and Dalvinder Singh (eds), *Deposit Insurance* (Palgrave Macmillan 2007) 77.
129 IADI, 'Enhanced Guidance for Effective Deposit Insurance Systems: Ex-Ante Funding Guidance Paper' (International Association of Deposit Insurers, June 2015) <http://www.iadi.org/en/assets/File/Papers/Approved%20Guidance%20Papers/IADI_Enhanced_Guidance_on_Ex-Ante_Funding_June_2015.pdf> accessed 29 December 2023.
130 Jan P. Nolte and Isfandyar Z. Khan, 'Deposit Insurance Systems: Addressing Emerging Challenges in Funding, Investment, Risk-Based Contributions and Street Testing' (World Bank, 2017) <http://documents.worldbank.org/curated/en/824821511878338917/pdf/121708-REVISED-PUBLIC-FinSAC-Deposit-Insurance-Systems-Guidance-Papers-Nov-2017.pdf> accessed 20 January 2024.
131 Jessica Carboni et al., 'Deposit Protection in the EU: State of Play and Future Prospects' (2008) 9 *Journal of Banking Regulation*, 92.
132 David S. Hoelscher, Michael W Taylor and Ulrich H Klueh, 'The Design and Implementation of Deposit Insurance' (2006) International Monetary Fund, Occasional Paper No. 251, 19.
133 Beat Bernet and Susanna Walter, 'Design, Structure and Implementation of a Modern Deposit Insurance Scheme' (The European Money and Finance Forum, Vienna, 2009).
134 Gillian G. H. Garcia 'Deposit Insurance Actual and Good Practices: Good Practice for Deposit Insurance' (n23), 11.
135 Andrew Campbell et al., 'A New Standard for Deposit Insurance and Government Guarantees after the Crisis' (n90), 215.
136 IADI, 'IADI Core Principles for Effective Deposit Insurance Systems' (n5).
137 IADI, 'Funding of Deposit Insurance Systems Guidance Paper' (IADI, May 2009) <http://www.iadi.org/en/assets/File/Papers/Approved%20Guidance%20Papers/Funding%20Final%20Guidance%20Paper%206_May_2009.pdf> accessed 30 December 2023.
138 *Ibid*
139 *Ibid* at 11.
140 IADI, 'Enhanced Guidance for Effective Deposit Insurance Systems: Ex-Ante Funding Guidance Paper' (International Association of Deposit Insurers, June 2015)<http://www.iadi.org/en/assets/File/Papers/Approved%20Guidance%20Papers/IADI_

Enhanced_Guidance_on_Ex-Ante_Funding_June_2015.pdf> accessed 29 December 2023.

141 *Ibid.*

142 Gillian G. H. Garcia 'Deposit Insurance and Crisis Management' (n91), 46.

143 Mervyn King, Banking from Bagehot to Basel and Back Again (The Second Bagehot Lecture, New York, October 2010).

144 Rosa María Lastra, 'Systemic Risk, SIFIs and Financial Stability' (2011) 6 *Capital Markets Law Journal*, 197, 213.

145 IADI, 'Transitioning from a Blanket Guarantee or Extended Coverage to a Limited Coverage System' (IADI March 2012) <http://www.iadi.org/en/assets/File/Papers/Approved%20Research%20-%20Discussion%20Papers/Transitioning_Paper_29March2012_Final_for_Publication_1.pdf> accessed 10 June 2024.

146 IADI, 'Handling of Systemic Crises' (IADI October 2012) <http://www.iadi.org/en/assets/File/Papers/Approved%20Research%20-%20Discussion%20Papers/IADI_Research_Paper-Handling_of_Systemic_Crises-Final_201210(2012-12_to_IADI).pdf> accessed 25 January 2024.

147 Willem H. Buiter, 'Lesson from the 2007 Financial Crisis' (2007) Centre for Economic Policy Research Discussion Paper No. 6596.

148 Rym Ayadi, 'Deposit Insurance Systems during and after a Systemic Crisis' (Conference of European Forum of Deposit Insurers and Federal Deposit Insurance Corporation, Paris, 2009)

149 Asli Demirgüç-Kunt, Edward Kane and Luc Laeven, 'Adoption and Design of Deposit Insurance' in Asli Demirgüç-Kunt, Edward Kane and Luc Laeven (eds), *Deposit Insurance around the World: Issues of Design and Implementation* (The MIT Press, 2008), 29.

3 Deposit Insurance in the US

Experience, Country Specifics, and Institutional Structure and Reform

3.1 Introduction

Deposit insurance, one critical component of the financial safety net, has been applied to protect depositors, in full or in part, from bank failures in pursuit of financial stability. The world's first deposit insurance system was established in New York State in 1829.

After that, several states in the US learnt from New York State's experience and set up their respective deposit insurance schemes. The Wall Street crash in 1929 and the subsequent financial crisis and economic recessions led to the overhaul of financial legislation in the US. The Banking Act of 1933 gave rise to the establishment of the FDIC, the nationwide deposit insurer in the US, with an objective of maintaining financial stability and public confidence.[1]

At present, the FDIC is in charge of multiple regulatory functions as it plays a vital and indispensable role in the US financial regulatory regime. The FDIC has long been regarded as a pioneer in the global banking industry and provides a good example for other countries' financial reforms. So far, 140 countries have launched their own deposit insurance systems, many of which were modelled on the FDIC.[2] Despite the FDIC's advanced institutional and functional designs, it still witnesses some problems and deficiencies, such as its overly complex operating mechanism and the agency's discretion in resolving troubled financial institutions.

Against this backdrop, this chapter attempts to revisit and analyse the working mechanism of the FDIC as a multi-functional regulatory agency from the law and finance perspective. The focus concentrates on the FDIC's shifting role from a deposit insurer to a comprehensive trouble shooter for failing banks. This article is in five parts. Part one provides a brief overview of the historical development of US deposit insurance. Part two demystifies US banking regulation. Part three elaborates on the rationales of the FDIC. Part four describes how the FDIC resolves troubled banks. Finally, a conclusion will be drawn.

3.2 A Brief History of Deposit Insurance in the US

Prior to the creation of the FDIC by the Banking Act of 1933 (the Glass-Steagall Act), the earliest known deposit insurance programme in the US can be traced back to the early 19th century. In 1829, Joshua Forman, a businessman in New York

DOI: 10.4324/9781003612759-3

State, conceived the initial framework of a modern deposit insurance programme with three innovative improvements: all banks have to contribute to the funding of setting up deposit insurance; the system should grant examination powers to a board of commissioners to supervise banks; and it calls for a detailed list of investment activities to be covered by deposit insurance.[3] After the first state-level deposit insurance system in New York State, another 13 US states launched their own deposit protection arrangements between 1829 and 1917.[4] The motivation behind the rapid rise of deposit insurance throughout the 19th and early 20th centuries was to safeguard depositors' savings and communities from economic crises triggered by bank collapses.[5]

From 1829 to 1866, New York State and another five states initiated the so-called bank obligation insurance programmes, which could be regarded as the embryo of deposit insurance.[6] However, these programmes eventually failed owing to two inducements. First of all, the 'free banking' movement in the US banking industry lowered entry requirements for setting up banks and allowed banks to issue bonds and mortgages in equal amounts of their outstanding banking notes with state officials.[7] Consequently, banks that joined the 'free banking' movement were excluded from state-level insurance programmes, resulting in a decline in the number of members of state deposit insurance programmes. The second inducement was directly related to the unification of the federal banking system in the US. Congress started levying a 10 percent tax on state-chartered banks in 1865, and as a result, many state-chartered banks decided to convert themselves into federally chartered banks in order to avoid the tax payment. Thus, state-level insurance programmes finally ceased their operations due to a sharp decrease in member numbers and funding amounts.[8]

After this temporary setback, between 1907 and 1917, eight states started running new deposit insurance programmes. Nonetheless, the 1920s saw frequent economic disruptions and banking crises in the US, and these state-run deposit insurance programmes were unable to pay off all deposit claims because of their inadequate funding amounts.[9] Finally, policymakers drew the conclusion that state-run deposit insurance plans were impractical, leading to the complete end of state-run arrangements in 1930.

From a federal perspective, the demand for a national deposit insurance system can be dated back to 1886. From 1886 to 1933, there were approximately 150 proposals to introduce federal deposit insurance submitted to Congress. Out of the total submissions, three proposals were shortlisted: the first one concerned building an insurance fund which would raise money from member banks to compensate depositors; the second proposal was to ask the government to provide guarantees for deposits; and the final one was that deposits would be safeguarded by way of enforcing banks to buy safety bonds.[10] As summarised by Flood, these selected proposals were made in response to a series of problems exposed in the previous state-run deposit insurance programmes.[11]

During the Great Depression, around 9,000 banks encountered liquidity shortages and failed, causing financial losses to American depositors of up to $1.3 billion.[12] In addition, the Federal Reserve failed to inject sufficient liquidity into the

US banking industry, resulting in the severe disruption of the real economy. The financial crisis eventually pressed Congress to consider proposals to enact deposit insurance in pursuit of financial stability. By this time, there were growing public voices for establishing a federal-level deposit insurance. After persistent striving by advocates of deposit insurance, the Banking Act of 1933 that incorporated establishing the FDIC was finally signed by President Roosevelt.[13]

The FDIC had been running smoothly for half a century until the 1980s when over 2,000 depository institutions failed. This was the worst banking crisis since the Great Depression.[14] Then, in 1991, Congress promulgated the Federal Deposit Insurance Corporation Improvement Act (FDICIA) in response to this crisis, and it introduced risk-based premiums, the least cost test, and prompt corrective action, introduced by the FDICIA, are professional words in deposit insurance.

After its establishment in 1933, the FDIC assisted the US banking industry in withstanding, on several occasions, volatile economic conditions and successfully maintained financial stability and public confidence. Having set up deposit insurance, panic withdrawals and bank runs have generally become a thing of the past, and liquidity crises are no longer a main threat to the stability of the US banking sector. Aside from its primary role as the deposit insurer, the FDIC has gradually become a federal regulator of insured state-chartered banks and a receiver, or conservator, of failing financial institutions. After the global financial crisis, the Dodd-Frank Wall Street Reform and Consumer Protection Act (the Dodd-Frank Act) granted more powers and mandates to the FDIC, including resolution planning responsibilities for large and complex financial institutions.[15]

3.3 US Banking Regulation

In the US, since the Glass-Steagall Act first introduced deposit insurance varying the incentives of banks and depositors, deposit insurance has played a significant role in US banking regulation.[16] It is noteworthy that banking regulation in the US has been formulated by four sectors, including three traditional sectors and one emerging sector written in the Dodd-Frank Act. The four sectors of US banking regulation are:

- Safety and sound regulation;
- Deposit insurance;
- Capital regulation;
- Systemic risk (added by Dodd-Frank).[17]

Despite having prosperous financial markets with a comprehensive and complicated banking system, US banking regulation has been unanimously perceived as one of the most labyrinthine systems all over the world.[18] In particular, multiple banking regulators, either on the federal level or on the state level, have evolved into a dual banking system with overlapping jurisdictions.[19]

In the meantime, the dual banking system in the US has embarked on chartering depository institutions either by state regulators or by federal regulators.[20] That is to say, US banks wishing to take deposits from the public only have two regular routes to get chartered – chartered by state regulators or otherwise chartered by the Office of the Comptroller of the Currency (OCC), a primary federal regulator. Accordingly, state bank regulators are responsible for regulating state-chartered banks in line with state laws, whilst federally chartered banks should be regulated by the OCC in light of the National Bank Act 1864.[21] Although the US's dual banking system seems like a stubborn and old-fashioned system, Singh argues that, to some extent, the conversion between state-chartered banks and federally chartered banks is supposed to inject limited flexibility into this dual banking system.[22] However, he adds that separate chartering systems and membership mechanisms perhaps complicate the whole banking system.[23]

Alternatively, apart from the dual banking system, the membership mechanisms of the Federal Reserve and the FDIC have been fulfilling significant functions as the FDIC and the Federal Reserve Board (FRB) have been prudential regulators monitoring banking services run by their members. In practice, the primary regulator of national banks is the OCC; nonetheless, all national banks are designated to become members of the Federal Reserve and the FDIC.[24] Interestingly, when a national bank becomes a member of the Federal Reserve, this bank automatically becomes a member of the FDIC with access to the Deposit Insurance Fund (DIF), which merged the Bank Insurance Fund (BIF) and the Savings Association Insurance Fund (SAIF).[25]

Regarding state-chartered banks, the FRB is the primary regulator regulating most of them, and the FDIC is the primary regulator monitoring the rest that are not members of the Federal Reserve.[26] It is noteworthy that membership, in the current US banking system, not only means that the banks are shielded by primary financial regulators but also refers to the supervision and enforcement applicable to relevant banks. For instance, assuming there is a national bank, the OCC will be responsible for granting a charter and performing prudential supervision; the FDIC will carry out supervisory and enforceable powers to perform its obligations associated with the DIF; and the Federal Reserve will be obliged to implement discount windows and reserve requirements.[27]

Throughout the history of US financial markets, the US has demonstrated a strong preference for retaining multiple primary financial regulators rather than having a single regulator in charge of all financial sectors. However, it is a double-edged that the financial markets are regulated by multiple financial regulators. Weinberg, an economist from the Federal Reserve, has argued that:

> On the one hand, one might conclude that the need to compete with other agencies would motivate a regulator to perform its tasks as effectively and efficiently as possible. On the other hand, one might argue that the desire to attract more clients could drive a regulatory agency to be loose.[28]

After the GFC, several significant alterations seeking to overhaul multiple US financial regulators were made by the US Treasury in pursuit of sustaining rational mechanisms of financial regulation. The Office of Thrift Supervision (OTS), the former primary regulator of federal and state savings associations coupled with their holding companies, has been merged into the OCC, which can be perceived as one of the most significant reforms among US banking regulation.[29] Furthermore, notably, another reform made by the US Treasury was the creation of the Financial Stability Oversight Council (FSOC) in pursuit of identifying potential systemic risks and facilitating coordination among multiple US financial regulators.[30] At the present stage, the Federal Reserve, the OCC, and the FDIC are acting as primary regulatory bodies exercising prudential regulation. Viewed domestically, compared with the Federal Reserve, the FDIC and the OCC are anticipated to play greater roles in implementing bank regulation, supervision, and examination.

3.3.1 Major Individual Primary Regulators in US Banking System

Owing to the abolition of the OTC, the OCC has become the primary regulator monitoring both national banks and federal saving associations.[31] It is noteworthy that the head of the OCC, the Comptroller of the Currency, is a member of the board of the FDIC, as well as a voting member in the FSOC.[32] Not surprisingly, like other primary financial regulators, the OCC not only has an obligation to appoint examiners scrutinising the safety and soundness of national banks and federal saving associations, but also has enforceable powers to cease the operation and revoke the charter from member institutions.[33] Barring supervision and enforcement, the OCC is responsible for releasing quarterly reports regarding derivative activities in line with documents and information filed by member institutions.[34]

The FDIC, created in 1933 in response to a large number of bank failures in 1920, purports to protect unsophisticated depositors and communities by guaranteeing their savings are deposited in failed insured depository institutions.[35] Over the years, the FDIC has evolved from a single-function deposit insurer to a multi-functional federal financial regulator, as it has been an indispensable federal primary financial regulator safeguarding insured deposits, supervising state-chartered banks which are not members of the Federal Reserve, and acting as a receiver or conservator of failed banks. More significantly, the FDIC runs the DIF, which is mainly based on risk-based premiums levied from insured institutions, aimed at resolving failed insured banks by providing a maximum protection of $250,000 to individual insured depositors.[36]

The Federal Reserve, established in 1913, is targeted at maintaining financial stability through implementing monetary policy and banking supervision.[37] One essential function performed by the Federal Reserve is that, from the past to the present, the Federal Reserve, as a US central bank, has long been responsible for conducting monetary policy, providing capital liquidity, and issuing bank notes.[38] In the meantime, since the Dodd-Frank Act came into effect after 2008, the Federal Reserve has become the primary regulator responsible for supervising all systemically important financial firms and systemically important financial-market utilities in accordance with recommendations made by the FSOC.[39]

The FSOC, a new super-interagency committee introduced by the Dodd-Frank Act, is committed to facilitating coordination among multiple financial regulators and making recommendations for optimising the regulatory framework against potential systemic risks. It is important to note that focusing on financial regulation, the FSOC, in contemporary regulatory architecture, has been acting as a troubleshooter to reshape the regulatory framework and eliminate bad practices. For instance, the FSOC aims to identify potential systemic risks, regulatory gaps, heighten standards, and provide regulatory recommendations for primary financial regulators to implement regulatory improvements.[40] Besides, the FSOC, regarded as a conduit for collecting information and facilitating information sharing among multiple regulators, has the authority to convene meetings involving major primary financial regulators among the members of the FSOC to discuss the resolution of jurisdictional disputes, conflicting policies, and regulatory overlaps.[41] Although the FSOC does not have any substantial powers granted by Dodd-Frank to take actions to constrain potential systemic threats and mitigate regulatory gaps, the FSOC has the authority to direct primary financial regulators to abide by its recommendations concerning stricter prudential rules and heightened standards that can facilitate financial stability in US financial markets.[42]

The Federal Financial Institutions Examination Council (FFIEC) was established as an official interagency department unifying supervisory principles and supervisory standards, and for reporting forms of supervisory examination applied to financial institutions.[43] In the context of the current US regulatory architecture, due to the complexity of financial regulation, primary regulators sometimes have overlapping responsibilities and conflicting policies for supervising the same financial activities. Thus, the FFIEC, whose principal purpose is to strengthen consistency and uniformity, aims to harmonise auditing standards and supervisory practices. Furthermore, the FFIEC updates handbooks covering each area and specific prudential regulation concerns for examiners.

3.3.2 The Dilemma of US Banking Regulation

Undoubtedly, the multiple regulators mechanism has increased the demands for interagency coordination, collaboration, and communication, resulting in the increasing complexity of US banking regulation. Timothy Geithner, the former Treasury Secretary, has said:

> Our financial system operated with large gaps in meaningful oversight, and without sufficient constraints to limit risk. Even institutions that were overseen by our complicated, overlapping system of multiple regulators put themselves in a position of extreme vulnerability. These failures helped lay the foundation for the worst economic crisis in generations.[44]

Although the US banking system has successfully resisted various financial crises over the years, several deficiencies of the current banking system still exist. At present, the existence of overlap and duplication in the current US banking system has been a predominant hurdle, raising inefficiency and costs. For example, there is overlapping supervision between the OCC and the Federal Reserve, as the OCC is responsible for monitoring transactions between banking groups and their non-bank affiliates, and the Federal Reserve may carry out the same monitoring again when it probes into suspected affiliate transactions between banking groups and their nonbank affiliates. According to the data collected by Sczudlo, more than 70 percent of US commercial banks are supervised and regulated by at least two banking regulators and almost 50 percent of banking groups that have ownerships for those commercial banks are being supervised or regulated by three or more financial regulators.[45] Hence, the existence of overlap and duplication that leads to inefficiency and the delay of resolution has significantly imposed pressure on financial institutions and financial regulators, resulting in increasing costs for rescuing troubled banks and compliance work.

Furthermore, under the multiple regulators mechanism, different regulators who may have conflicts of interest with each other could trigger competition in laxity to a certain extent, as regulators may attempt to lure new members by lowering regulatory standards or offering beneficial advantages for their own member institutions.[46] Despite motivating regulators to compete with each other, the multiple regulators mechanism, however, due to mutual surveillance, forces them to maintain the status quo under the current US banking system.[47] Besides, conflicting responsibilities and powers among primary regulators have resulted in the absence of accountability, as it is time-consuming to identify which regulator is accountable for a particular action amid regulators passing the buck.[48]

Sczudlo advocates some suggestions for consolidating the current regulatory framework as the present complicated system engenders higher expenses accompanied by lower efficiency.[49] As a result, he adds that the US should consider reducing the number of banking regulators and examinations since the US banking industry is already one of the most heavily regulated banking industries in the world.[50]

However, arguments involving opponents in relation to consolidating the banking system are obviously cogent, mainly focused on two aspects: first, the current system so far has operated fairly well; and second, a single regulator is incapable of performing all responsibilities. It must be admitted that these arguments are difficult to be denied. Although current US banking regulation has imposed pressure on financial institutions, the US banking industry has long been profitable and a leading pioneer in global financial markets, so there is no urgent need to call for substantial changes to the current financial regulatory framework, in terms of evolving into a single financial regulator for US banking regulation.

Over the past decades, Congress has made great efforts to fortify uniformity and facilitate coordination. For example, the FFIEC and the FSOC, two super interagency committees designed to strengthen consistency and coordination, have been established in line with the Financial Institutions Regulatory and Interest Rate Control Act and the Dodd-Frank Act, respectively. Thus, employing a single regulator to break the equilibrium, in effect, is unrealistic and unable to resolve the dilemma of the US banking system. Simultaneously, as noted by the Federal Reserve, dramatic changes could engender uncertainty and instability in the banking market.[51] Thus, compared with maintaining the status quo, consolidating banking regulation may encounter strong opposition arising from financial regulators and legislation.

The US Treasury has unveiled a blueprint seeking to optimise regulatory structure in the US.[52] Focussing on this blueprint, it demonstrates that objectives-based regulation stands out in comparison with structural regulation and functional regulation, which is also named a three-regulator structure that consists of three regulators – a market stability regulator, a prudential regulator, and a business conduct regulator.[53] In light of this blueprint released by the US Treasury, the market stability regulator is mainly responsible for monitoring the whole financial markets and economy; the prudential financial regulator is responsible for regulating individual financial institutions and risk management; and the business conduct regulator is responsible for releasing conduct handbooks and setting good business practices across all financial sectors.

Nonetheless, the US Treasury admits that some hurdles have to be overcome and resolved to build an optimal structure. First, coordination is still an overarching issue eliminating the effectiveness of the current regulatory structure, as the multi-regulator approach that naturally introduces competition among financial regulators involves difficulties in coordination.[54] After realising the importance of coordination since the GFC, the Dodd-Frank Act has established and expected the FSOC to deepen coordination and collaboration among multiple regulators. Prior to 2008, the US General Accounting Office (GAO) had already suggested that information-sharing is essential for enhancing effective banking regulation, whereas regulators that attempted to cover up their members in the recent global financial crisis have proved that establishing effective coordination still has a long way to go.[55] Second, regulators in the optimal structure should ensure discipline by strictly abiding by the directive principles of regulation, for example, guidelines of regulatory procedures and compliance.[56] Therefore, the principles need to be written in a more sophisticated and innovative way rather than just using a one-size-fits-all approach to the whole system.

3.4 The Deposit Insurer: Revisiting the FDIC and the Operating Mechanism of Deposit Insurance in the US

Operating the federal deposit insurance scheme for US depositors has remained the fundamental responsibility of the FDIC. It is an essential tool of financial regulation to maintain financial stability and public confidence. At present, the FDIC is one of the most trustworthy deposit insurers around the world, due to its constant efforts to promote public awareness of deposit insurance and compensate savers in the event of banking failures. For example, when insured depository institutions fail, the FDIC gives their depositors prompt access to their savings and other related financial services. The FDIC has been praised by the International Monetary Fund for its advanced risk-based premiums assessment method.[57] Over the past 85 years, the FDIC has been constantly adapting its operating strategies and methods of addressing bank failures to the ever-changing banking industry. This section pays attention to the four most important areas of the FDIC's operating mechanism regarding the operation of deposit insurance: its institutional structure, the funding mechanism, the risk-based premiums assessment, and the coverage.

3.4.1 Institutional Structure of the FDIC

The FDIC is administered by a board of directors which consists of five members. The board is responsible for day-to-day management and decision-making. Three members of the board, the chair, vice chair, and one director, are appointed by the US President with the advice and consent of the Senate, the upper chamber of the US Congress. Each nominee serves a six-year term except for the chairman who has a five-year term.[58] The other two members of the board are ex-officio directors, which are served by the Comptroller of the Office of the Comptroller of the Currency (OCC) and the Director of the Consumer Financial Protection Bureau (CFPB).[59] It should be noted that, since 1993, no more than three members of the board should come from the same political party.[60]

Currently, the FDIC is administering three funds: the Orderly Liquidation Fund (OLF), the Federal Savings and Loan Insurance Corporation (FSLIC) Resolution Fund, and the Deposit Insurance Fund (DIF). By 2006, the FDIC was responsible for managing the Bank Insurance Fund (BIF) and the Savings Association Insurance Fund (SAIF). After the Federal Deposit Insurance Reform Act of 2005 (FDIRA) came into effect in 2006, the assets and liabilities of the BIF and SAIF were merged and then transferred to the newly established DIF.[61]

Pursuant to the Dodd-Frank Act, the OLF, a specialised fund for resolving failing financial institutions, has come under the management of the FDIC. However, the OLF will only be available when the FDIC is appointed as a receiver. In addition, the DIF, which is pre-funded by risk-based premiums charged to participating banks, aims to insure depositors of member depository institutions and to cope with failing financial institutions through resolutions that pass the least cost test.[62] Moreover, the FSLIC Resolution Fund is responsible for selling remaining assets and liabilities related to the former FSLIC, which was abolished by the Financial Institutions Reform, Recovery, and Enforcement Act of 1989.[63]

Congress requires the FDIC to submit an annual report regarding its operations, activities, budget, receipts, and expenditures, including:

- The current financial condition of the DIF and FSLIC Resolution Fund;
- The purpose, effect, and estimated cost of each resolution action taken for an insured depository institution;
- The actual costs of assistance provided for an insured depository institution;
- The exposure of the DIF to changes in those economic factors most likely to affect the condition of the fund:
- A current estimate of the resources needed for the DIF and the FSLIC Resolution Fund;
- Any evaluations considered appropriate to future resolution.[64]

3.4.2 Funding Mechanism

Over the past 85 years, the funding mechanism of the FDIC has evolved from a simple standard to a more complicated approach which charges premiums to insured institutions on a risk-based basis. The FDIC has embarked on a risk-based system since it was formally introduced by the FDICIA in 1993. Before that, all member institutions paid their premium contributions using the same ratio.[65]

The FDIC has always employed an ex-ante funding mechanism to ensure the sufficiency of its funds. Diane Ellis, Director of Insurance and Research at the FDIC, underlines that sufficient funds have long played an essential role in fulfilling well-functioning deposit insurance, and the US experience demonstrates that a good deposit insurance agency with adequate funds has effectively eliminated delays in the closing of failed banks, thus lowering the ultimate costs of a failure.[66] Clearly, the ex-ante funding mechanism is able to cover most future losses, which is necessary to maintain confidence and fortify financial stability. It is noteworthy that, apart from the FDIC's own resources, it can borrow up to $100 billion in supplementary funds from the Treasury and Federal Financing Bank in the event of emergency situations, which consolidates the compensating capability of the DIF.[67]

However, determining an optimal fund size has been a headache for every deposit insurer around the world. By the end of the Great Depression, owing to fewer bank failures and a better economic situation, the target fund size was not an imminent concern.[68] However, from 1980 to 1994, more than 2,900 banks and insured thrift institutions failed, causing approximately $200 billion in losses and market recession that significantly harmed the US economy.[69] As a result, due to having failed to set a target level, the DIF did not have adequate resources to compensate depositors' claims, and US taxpayers had to pay an extra $125 billion to recover failed thrift institutions.[70] Congress, in 1989, introduced the Designated Reserve Ratio (DRR) designed to calibrate the optimal fund size. Initially, the DRR was set at 1.25 percent of the estimated aggregated insured deposits, which then became a strict statutory benchmark in 1996.[71] However, in theory, the FDIC shall not take any action against well-capitalised and well-managed insured institutions when the funds reach the target size.[72]

Unfortunately, the rigid mechanism of the DRR resulted in a situation where almost 90 percent of the member institutions made little contributions, leading to a substantial deficit for the DIF.[73] Before the recent GFC, in order to correct this problem, Congress, in 2006, abandoned the 1.25 percent benchmark and gave certain autonomy to the FDIC, which can calibrate the DRR between 1.15 and 1.50 percent.[74] Unfortunately, during the GFC, the DIF was still considered insufficient. Therefore, Dodd-Frank, *de facto*, raised the minimum DRR to 1.35 percent, and Congress removed the upper limit cap for the DRR.[75]

Premium collection has been a key pillar supporting the DIF. Since the approval of Congress in 1993, risk-based premiums assessment, an advanced but highly technical system to calibrate accurate premium rates, has been employed by the FDIC. Before 2006, this system was simply based on capital ratios and supervisory ratings, but after the reform in 2006, the FDIC began to apply innovative and substantial changes to optimise the risk-based premiums assessment that will be discussed below.

Under the risk-based premiums assessment, with respect to small insured financial institutions, an approach that uses eight financial ratios coupled with supervisory ratings has been installed. As for large and highly complex insured financial institutions, a brand-new scoreboard measure, such as a straightforward indicator identifying risk and evaluating premiums, has been used to differentiate premiums.

3.4.3 Risk-Based Premiums Assessment

The assessment of risk-based premiums, a complex system based on insured banks' risk levels to differentiate premiums between each insured bank, has significantly shifted since 2006, as objects of risk-based premiums assessment were divided into three sections: highly complex, large, and small insured institutions.[76]

With respect to established insured small institutions, they have been placed into four risk classifications – Risk Category I, II, III, and IV – based on capital levels and supervisory ratings.[77] Meanwhile, insured small institutions have been categorised into three capital groups – well capitalised, adequately capitalised, and undercapitalised – according to the leverage ratio and three risk-based capital ratios used for regulatory goals.[78]

The supervisory groups, termed as Group A, Group B, and Group C, have been determined by primary regulators who utilise CAMELS Composite Ratings listed in Table 3.1 to evaluate insured small institutions.[79] Group A refers to financially sound small institutions coupled with CAMELS Composite Rating 1 or 2; Group B is formed by insured small institutions that slide to CAMELS Composite Rating 3 and pose severe threats to the DIF; and Group C encompasses insured small institutions combined with CAMELS Composite Ratings 4 or 5, which might expose substantial losses to the DIF. Furthermore, the final results of risk classifications evaluated by the capital groups and the supervisory groups are set out in Table 3.2.

Table 3.1 CAMELS Composite Ratings[80]

Composite Ratings	*Standards*
Rating 1	Insured financial institutions are sound in every respect. A few weaknesses appearing in the institutions can be resolved through regular action by the board of directors and management.
Rating 2	Insured financial institutions are fundamentally sound. A few moderate weaknesses appearing in the institutions can be corrected within the board of directors' and management's capabilities and willingness.
Rating 3	Insured financial institutions present some degree of supervisory concern. Weaknesses could range from moderate to severe, and management may lack the capability or willingness to handle them.
Rating 4	Insured financial institutions are unsafe and unsound. Serious managerial deficiencies result in unsatisfactory performance. The weaknesses are rated from severe to critically deficient and could not be resolved by the board of directors and management.
Rating 5	Insured financial institutions are extremely unsafe and unsound. The institutions present a critically deficient performance with the greatest supervisory concern. Those problems exceed management's capability or willingness to control them.

Data Source: Federal Deposit Insurance Corporation.

Table 3.2 Classification of Risk Category[81]

Capital Group	*Supervisory Group*		
	Group A CAMELS Composite Rating 1 or 2	*Group B CAMELS Composite Rating 3*	*Group C CAMELS Composite Rating 4 or 5*
Well Capitalised	Risk Category I	Risk Category II	Risk Category III
Adequately Capitalised	Risk Category II	Risk Category II	Risk Category III
Undercapitalised	Risk Category III	Risk Category III	Risk Category IV

Data Source: Government Publishing Office.

Table 3.3 The Current Total Base Assessment Rates for Established Insured Institutions (in basis points per annum)[82]

	Risk Category I	*Risk Category II*	*Risk Category III*	*Risk Category IV*
Initial Base Assessment Rate	3–7	12	19	30
Unsecured Debt Adjustment[83]	-5–0	-5–0	-5–0	-5–0
Total Base Assessment Rate	1.5–7[84]	7–12	14–19	25–30

Data Source: Federal Deposit Insurance Office.

Interestingly, as shown in Table 3.3, insured small institutions within Risk Category I have had differential assessment rates. The assessment rates of all institutions incorporated in Risk Category I vary from the minimum assessment rate to the maximum assessment rate, indicating a four-basis-points gap between each other.

Once a Risk Category I institution's assessment rate is below the minimum assessment rate, the institution is supposed to pay the minimum premiums to the DIF. When the assessment rate exceeds the maximum rate, the institution simply pays the maximum rate.

The financial ratios illustrated in Table 3.4 are specifically applied to differentiate insured small institutions' assessment rates with the combination of the weighted CAMELS Component Ratings.[85] Simultaneously, the financial ratios in Table 3.4 that are applied in Risk Category I intend to forecast the possibility of an insured institution being downgraded from Group A to Group B or worse.

The financial ratios and the fluctuating rates used in Risk Category I are not applicable for newly insured small institutions and insured branches of foreign institutions because they have specified assessment rates shown in Table 3.5. Contrary to Risk Category I, institutions falling into Risk Category II face fixed and higher assessment rates, and so on, for Risk Categories III and IV.

Unlike the insured small institutions that are positioned by the combination of financial ratios and supervisory ratings, the FDIC has now launched two similar scorecards assessing large institutions and highly complex institutions respectively.

Table 3.4 Financial Ratios for Assessing Established Small Institutions[86]

Financial Ratios in the Current Assessing System
Weighted Average CAMELS Component Rating
Leverage Ratio
Net Income before Taxes/Total Assets
Nonperforming Loans and Leases/Gross Assets
Brokered Deposit Ratio
One Year Asset Growth
Loan Mix Index

Data Source: Government Publishing Office.

Table 3.5 The Current Total Base Assessment Rates for Newly Insured Small Institutions (in basis points per annum)[87]

	Risk Category I	*Risk Category II*	*Risk Category III*	*Risk Category IV*
Initial Base Assessment Rate	7	12	19	30
Brokered Deposit Adjustment	N/A	0-10	0-10	0-10
Total Base Assessment Rate	7	12-22	19-29	30-40

Data Source: Federal Deposit Insurance Corporation.

Two scores, the performance score and the loss severity score, are deployed to pinpoint large or complex institutions. A higher score means a higher risk level, and the score of zero refers to the lowest risk level as scorecard measures directly reveal scores from a minimum of 0 to a maximum of 100, subsequently, the score is eventually converted to the initial assessment rate for a large or complex institution.

The performance score, a weighted average score that represents the final assessment result, has been formed by three parts: weighted average CAMEL rating score; ability to withstand asset-related stress score; and ability to withstand funding-related.[88] Table 3.6 elaborates on how to allocate weight and calculate the score for each components.

The loss severity score, a reflection of the loss severity measure, is intended to estimate potential losses to the FDIC in the event of encountering a large bank failure. This measure is composed of two standardised types of assumptions. One is the run-off assumption based on the empirical study of eleven large institutions' failures from 2007 to 2009, and the other is asset loss rate assumptions that estimate the recovery values of insured depository institutions.

With regard to highly complex institutions, the FDIC has made several changes compared to the performance score used in large institutions shown in Table 3.7. It can be seen that, for instance, the FDIC has adopted a completely different concentration measure and added a market risk measure evaluating the asset-related stress score for highly complex institutions. Additionally, the FDIC has added the 'average short-term funding to average total assets ratio' to assess the funding-related stress score.[90]

Table 3.6 Calculation of Performance Score[89]

Performance Score Components	*Weight (percent)*
Weighted Average CAMEL Rating	30
Ability to Withstand Asset-Related Stress	50
Ability to Withstand Funding-Related Stress	20

Data Source: Government Publishing Office.

Table 3.7 Comparisons of Performance Score between Large Institutions and Highly Complex Institutions

For Large Institutions	*For Highly Complex Institutions*
Weighted Average CAMEL Rating Ability to Withstand Asset-Related Stress • Tier 1 Leverage Ratio • Concentration Measure • Core Earnings/Average Quarter-End Total Assets • Credit Quality Measure Ability to Withstand Funding-Related Stress • Core Deposits/Total Liabilities • Balance Sheet Liquidity Ratio	Weighted Average CAMEL Rating Ability to Withstand Asset-Related Stress • Tier 1 Leverage Ratio • Concentration Measure • Core Earnings/Average Quarter-End Total Assets • Credit Quality Measure and Market Risk Measure Ability to Withstand Funding-Related Stress • Core Deposits/Total Liabilities • Balance Sheet Liquidity Ratio • Average Short-Term Funding/Average Total Assets

Data Source: Government Publishing Office.

Proponents of risk-based premiums assessment highlight that the most important aspect of this system is to counter moral hazard as bankers in pursuit of high-risk but high-return portfolios are no longer invisible, and they have to pay the costs for their risky business practices.[91] The second improvement has been actuarial fairness, which eliminates pricing inequality.[92] This is to say, instead of low-risk institutions paying comparatively higher premiums under the flat-rate premiums assessment, a sound insured bank under a well-functioning risk-based premiums assessment probably pays less in premiums than a riskier bank, as a direct reward for remaining sound and safe.[93]

However, one serious problem pointed out by Fissel is that charging riskier institutions high premiums probably impairs the DIF and the FDIC, because it is understandable that a riskier institution might indulge in forging an inaccurate balance sheet or other inaccurate financial statements to distract supervisory attention and escape from high premiums, thereby undermining the reliability of deposit insurance.[94]

Furthermore, riskier institutions have to bear higher premiums, but, in reality, it must be questioned whether they have the financial capability to pay such high premiums. However, in this situation, the lower premiums that financially sound institutions have to contribute put the adequacy of the DIF in doubt.

It is noteworthy that the assessment of current risk-based premiums based on book-value capital standards might trigger a dilemma where problematic banks escape from high premiums by making book-value look sound. It is to be anticipated that book-value would overvalue assets and underestimate the value of liabilities.

However, market-value-based standards are not panaceas for risk-based premium assessments. There are two main drawbacks restraining market-value-based standards. First, the adoption of market-value standards requires regulators to collect the most reliable and accurate information to help them make correct judgements. Second, the capital market, a constantly volatile market, is full of misleading information that attracts public attention. Therefore, in order to make timely correct decisions, regulators have to carefully and rapidly analyse information, thereby increasing burden and workloads, despite the fact that regulators already have intensive and pressing workloads.

Although the US has advanced databases and considerable experience in operating risk-based premiums assessments, a problematic logic behind the system is still living in the current stage. This system simply considers diminishing banks' incentives to take excessive risks by posting higher premiums for those banks that are going to take more risks, rather than encouraging depositors to pay attention to the risk level of banks with legislation enacting the responsibility.[95] However, it must be admitted that, in reality, most depositors are placed at a disadvantaged position due to information asymmetry, which creates a disequilibrium between consumers and banks. Even if depositors have had full information related to the host banks, without professional knowledge, it is virtually impossible for them to select information applicable to making the right decision.

Besides, the current risk-based premiums assessment that incurs disequilibrium between small and large institutions is noted by Thomas, who underlines that a comprehensive risk-based premiums assessment should be consistent for all institutions.[96] At present, assessments for large institutions and complex institutions are higher and stricter than assessments for small institutions, but in fact, according to the study of recent cases, large and complex institutions have made little contribution to recent losses of the DIF.[97]

By contrast, from the FDIC's point of view, when an insured institution fails, its liabilities, including insured deposits and secured liabilities, are eventually transferred to the FDIC, and, generally speaking, once large and complex institutions collapse, the losses they bring to the FDIC and the DIF would be significant figures. Thus, a higher standard risk-based premiums assessment for large and complex institutions is necessary to urge them to remain soundly managed and to keep pace with the objectives of the FDIC.[98] Moreover, as noted by Hawke, a former Comptroller of the Currency, the reality has been that most member institutions pay lower premiums to the DIF as they have sound management or the DIF reaches the target level. The OCC thus suggested that the FDIC should have more autonomy to implement a risk-based premiums assessment.[99]

Another criticism of introducing scorecard measures to large and complex institutions is complexity, which makes banks uncertain about what the FDIC wants to reward and penalise.[100] Nonetheless, many insured institutions have already adopted scorecard measures to evaluate counterparties' risk. More significantly, the FDIC understands that complicated scorecard measures could further differentiate risk among large and complex institutions, because the assessment for large institutions is entirely different from the standards used for small institutions as the FDIC has a very comprehensive database for putting forward standardised assessments related to small institutions.[101]

3.4.4 Coverage

Since 1933, the level of US deposit insurance has been raised from the original \$2,500 to the current \$250,000.[102] At present, after the passage of the Dodd-Frank Act in response to the recent GFC, the coverage of deposit insurance has been raised to \$250,000 per depositor, per bank, for eight specific categories of accounts.[103]

Moreover, qualified deposits in different branches of a single insured institution are protected up to a total amount of \$250,000, whereas other savings deposited in another insured bank are separately protected by another \$250,000 coverage. Exceptionally, a depositor might receive more than \$250,000 protection when deposits are held in different types of ownership.[104] Deposits denominated in a foreign currency are simultaneously covered by deposit insurance, but once a host bank becomes insolvent, the reimbursements of those deposits are paid through the equivalent value in US dollars based on the exchange rates on the date of default.[105]

Through a retrospective look at the development of US deposit insurance, there are three straightforward functions brought by increasing deposit insurance coverage. By studying the coverage increase cases that happened in 1966, 1974, and 1980 respectively, it was common that commercial banks and the securities industry offered higher interest rates to absorb deposits in the wake of the government unleashing the regulation of interest rate liberalisation. By contrast, the savings and loan associations, primary sources of mortgage loans, had then experienced dramatic withdrawals that engendered a large volume of deposit outflows, triggering a substantial decline in mortgage loans.[106]

To solve this problem, Congress encouraged the public to deposit their dollars in savings and loan associations by increasing deposit coverage directly, thereby converting spare dollars to deposits.[107] Gerald Ford, a former president who upheld the deposit coverage increase by signing the bill, asserted that raising the deposit insurance limit helps thrift institutions attract large depositors who would deposit their money in insured institutions they trust over many years to enhance savings based on various purposes amid higher coverage.[108]

Strengthening public confidence is the second benefit of the increase in coverage. During financial crises or recessions, lifting the deposit insurance limit is always an effective solution against the setback of confidence in the US financial markets, as the increase in coverage is regarded as a pledge issued by the government. This stimulates the public to put their money in financial institutions in response to an increasing probability of bank failures during a volatile period.

The third benefit of expanding coverage is to stimulate competition within the financial market. The FDIC has seen coverage increase as an opportunity for small banks to compete with large banks on the same starting line.[109] Shy *et al.,* in their research, found that lower deposit insurance coverage constrains interest rate competition between institutions. They examined that, with a lower coverage, the first thing large depositors consider is placing their uninsured money in rival banks beneath the insured amount so that they can get protection by deposit insurance.[110] Apparently, lower coverage reduces the effectiveness of interest rates and promotes the market power of banks in providing lower interest rates to customers.[111]

Trade-offs of coverage in conjunction with bank runs and depositor discipline have long troubled the FDIC since the introduction of deposit insurance, and depositors have always been standing at a crossroads. Without rational deposit protection, bank runs triggered by depositors' mounting withdrawals might occur, and the costs of stopping bank runs are immeasurable. However, in effect, by introducing generous coverage, depositor discipline might be distorted, and deposits will simply flow to high-yield banks that might pose potential threats to financial stability.

Therefore, there are different views surrounding coverage. Kaufman underscores that blocking depositor discipline has made federal deposit insurance more costly, and it is vital to enable depositor discipline to fulfil its functions because supervision cannot succeed without help from depositor discipline.[112] Nevertheless, Diamond and Dybvig hold an opposite opinion; compared with the tremendous costs of bank runs, 100 percent coverage is a comparatively economical weapon against costly bailout.[113] It is clear that the FDIC has adopted the latter suggestion, which seems like the most realistic option.

3.5 How the FDIC Resolves Failing Financial Institutions?

Owing to the special characteristics of the banking sector, banking resolution implemented by financial authorities is needed to resolve a failing bank by various resolution proceedings in pursuit of public interests and financial stability. Maintaining public confidence and financial stability, the ultimate goals of the FDIC, drives the FDIC to carry out effective resolutions needed to minimise the adverse impact of bank failures that exacerbate the local economy. During the resolution process, the FDIC basically implements two functions – a deposit insurer for insured deposits and a receiver of failed financial institutions.

Since the FDICIA took effect in 1991, two of the FDICIA's significant amendments – prompt corrective action (PCA) and the least cost test – have been introduced to cut down the costs to the DIF.[114] As a result, according to the FDICIA, when drawing up a bank resolution, the FDIC has been legislatively required to tackle the failing bank in the least costly way.

The FDIC has now embarked on developing two fundamental resolutions – Purchase and Assumption transactions (P&A) and deposit payoffs. A deposit payoff could perhaps be applied unless the FDIC has not received any bids or a least-cost bid.[115] Other resolutions used by the FDIC in the past, like Open Bank Assistance, which is substantially scrapped by the Dodd-Frank Act, are no longer able to shed global economic risks.

The final step of the resolution process is that the chartering authority closes a failing bank and appoints the FDIC as a receiver, thereby commencing the receivership process. Usually, the FDIC first closes a failing bank on a Friday, and the acquirer then continues to offer financial services to the failing bank's customers with unimpeded access to insured funds by the next business day. Having carried out all resolution procedures except loss-sharing P&As, the FDIC, as a receiver appointed by the chartering authority, shoulders the responsibility of conducting the receivership.

3.5.1 Resolution Process under the Dodd-Frank Act

Before stepping into resolution transactions and receivership procedures, the FDIC has to advance an orderly resolution process step by step. As long as the chartering authority has intervened in a failing bank that is determined to be critically undercapitalised through prompt corrective action, the FDIC formally proceeds with an orderly resolution process that basically takes 90 days under Title II of the Dodd-Frank Act.[116]

To strive for a credible and actionable resolution, the FDIC would have engaged in back-and-forth communication with senior management of a failing bank and executed in-depth on-site due diligence devoted to impartially marketing the institution. This includes offering potential bidders comprehensively detailed information related to the franchise value. A virtual Data Room, where potential acquirers can search for any documents of interest, is established by the FDIC to get more potential acquirers involved, facilitating a successful bid even if those potential acquirers are unfamiliar with the failing institution. Finally, a bid that contains two basic pricing targets – the franchise value and the assets – has to pass the least-cost test, after which the FDIC ceases the operation of the failing institution.

It is noteworthy that, by learning lessons from the recent global crisis, the federal financial regulators have deliberately adopted a negative attitude towards rescuing 'too big to fail' institutions with bailouts.[117] In the past, the US government placed financial stability first and believed only itself had the capability to conquer financial troubles; thereby, bailouts were believed to inhibit financial instability triggered by large, complex, and interconnected financial institutions.[118] However, since the GFC, 'too big to fail' institutions are allowed to go bankrupt under the Bankruptcy Code.

At the same time, banking and finance, two essential components of the US economy, are prone to producing financial instability and public panics. So, only having the Bankruptcy Code is obviously unable to handle the failures of big financial institutions. For instance, looking at the Lehman Brothers Holdings (Lehman) case, which was a landmark case of the GFC, it illustrated that more than $75 billion was unable to be recovered under the Bankruptcy Code. Until 2011, over $1.2

billion on legal services and other professional fees had been spent on Lehman's collapse.[119]

After exposing loopholes in this case, a new resolution, the Orderly Liquidation Authority, was created by Title II of the Dodd-Frank Act in response to 'too big to fail' instead of the Bankruptcy Code and bailouts, in which creditors and shareholders would 'bear the losses of financial companies', and the FDIC has been empowered against Systemically Important Financial Institutions (SIFIs) in terms of pricing the assets, minimising losses and risk, and spinning off moral hazard.[120]

From the FDIC's perspective, under Title II, several provisions enacted in this section have empowered the FDIC to confront large and complex financial institutions outside the Bankruptcy Code.

First, unlike specific rules within the Bankruptcy Code, the Dodd-Frank Act authorised the FDIC, which simultaneously acts as a receiver and a deposit insurer, to set up one or more bridge financial companies to maintain the going-concern value, key operations, services, and transactions in order to dodge market disorders.[121] The FDIC therefore not only looks after insured depositors by providing consecutive access to their deposits but also settles claims filed by shareholders, debt holders, and other creditors in receivership processes based on the orders in 210 (b) of the Dodd-Frank Act.[122] Meanwhile, Section 204 of the Dodd-Frank Act enables the FDIC to remove the board of directors and senior management of failed covered institutions whose misconduct is responsible for the failure, continue normal operations with remaining employees, and hire contractors who have specific knowledge to monitor operations.[123]

The second, which might be labelled continuity of qualified financial contracts, attempts to ensure that qualified financial contracts are inherited by the following acquirer or a bridge institution. Under the Bankruptcy Code, in the case of a debtor company becoming insolvent, the qualified financial contracts would not continue to work unless approved by counterparties. However, a SIFI usually possesses a vast number of qualified financial contracts in conjunction with services and transactions. In case of a failure, by getting through the Bankruptcy Code, counterparties that have contractual relationships with the SIFI might rush to negotiate the dissolution of contracts and recover remaining portions as much as possible, thus causing adverse effects to all related parties and US financial stability.[124]

Nevertheless, under the Orderly Resolution Authority of the Dodd-Frank Act, though a SIFI is in the receivership process, the Dodd-Frank Act legislatively enables the FDIC to continue those qualified financial contracts by transferring them to either a solvent financial institution or a bridge financial institution.

However, the resolution authority to resolve failing institutions is controversial. Both Scott and Kroener III sharply criticise that under the Dodd-Frank Act, the FDIC unduly depends on its discretion to deal with covered financial institutions.[125] It can be noted that, for instance, the FDIC sets up a bridge financial institution that is completely protected to transfer those assets and liabilities the FDIC considers fitting to the bridge institution. As described by Kroener III, it seems like 'picking winners and losers among the creditors', leaving a blank space for political interference.[126]

While Garcia underlines that, throughout the history of US financial regulation, although broad discretion has long been given to US financial regulators, they have failed to carry out enforcement actions before the financial institutions reach the verge of collapse. [127] It can be noticed that financial regulators are very tolerant and happy to give an opportunity to financial institutions. Therefore, she emphasises that when a country relies on supervisory discretion, strengthened supervisory accountability is necessary.[128]

Nonetheless, the FDIC insists that, pursuant to Title I of the Dodd-Frank Act, the proceedings to resolve problematic financial institutions have been more efficient than under the Bankruptcy Code. Under Dodd-Frank, the FDIC could schedule resolution in advance based on comprehensive on-site access to SIFIs, as well as by obtaining key information on day-to-day operations from resolution plans submitted by covered financial institutions. Therefore, the FDIC's capability to address imminent failures and coordinate with the Federal Reserve and other regulators has been consolidated.

Scott firmly opposes the excessive reliance on a powerful discretion that incurs low transparency and abuses of authority, neglecting 'meaningful judicial review and legal accountability'. He believes the resolution process should revert to the Bankruptcy Code.[129] By contrast with the Orderly Resolution Authority under the Dodd-Frank Act, once the FDIC proceeds with the resolution process in light of Chapter 14 of the Bankruptcy Code, the FDIC could attempt reorganisation, not liquidation, to maximise the value of a failed financial institution. Furthermore, the fair treatment creditors receive with respect to losses and claims in light of Chapter 14 has been an advantage over decisions made by the agency's discretion because the Bankruptcy Code provides strict rules on claim priorities, preferences, and authority, asserting certainty in the resolution process.

But, admittedly, in terms of addressing SIFIs, time is the enemy. Kroener III acknowledges that the advantage of bank resolution over the Bankruptcy Code is that the FDIC can make prompt decisions that accelerate the speed of bank resolution, with fewer administrative costs.[130] Objectively speaking, financial regulators stand in a much higher position to oversee risks, operations, transactions, and conditions of financial institutions, and resolution process via financial regulators is relatively time-saving compared with getting court orders. Barring time, financial regulators naturally have an advantage over the bankruptcy court due to their specific knowledge and on-site access. However, compared with the Bankruptcy Code, the presence of low transparency and uncertainty in agency discretion are, admittedly, indisputable facts.

3.5.2 Purchase and Assumption Transactions

The FDIC, since FDICIA, does not hide its preference for using P&As to resolve failing institutions. A P&A transaction, considered to be a least interruptive but flexible measure to the local economy, encourages sound institutions to purchase all or some assets of failing institutions and assume all or some liabilities.[131] Through many years of practice, P&As have evolved into diverse variations to satisfy the different interests of potential acquirers and a constantly changing market.

Basic P&A transactions, which impose restrictions on the level of cash and marketable securities, as well as offer flexible options of tangible assets to potential acquirers, are reciprocal for all participants in terms of providing full protection to customers' insured deposits without any disruptions and losses. As a result, basic P&As not only help the FDIC cut down workloads and costs but also help acquirers obtain new customers by offering consecutive access.[132] However, not surprisingly, the shortcomings of basic P&As unexceptionally exist as the clarity related to who would assume uninsured deposits and how many assets the potential acquirers are supposed to purchase is unclear.

Three stretched ramifications, namely whole bank P&A transactions, P&A transactions with optional shared losses, and bridge bank P&A transactions, have been developed from Basic P&A transactions along with all benefits discussed above.

Whole bank P&A transactions, as the name implies, attempt to persuade potential acquirers to bid for all the assets of failing banks based on a *tale quale* value basis. Three reasons appear to suggest that the FDIC could benefit from this type of transaction. The first, which underscores continuity, ensures that loan customers are served coherently by acquirers in the same way as at previous failed institutions. Second, by way of having bidders that acquire all the assets of failed institutions, whole bank P&As, which waive further financial obligation associated with the FDIC, help the FDIC reduce cash outlay. The third, which could be marked as a relief of burden, means that the FDIC no longer needs to be responsible for liquidating assets as acquirers merge a vast majority of assets of failed institutions. A serious concern to most acquirers is that a bidder makes a negative acquisition that would have a long-term adverse effect on profit, clouding the prospect of the bidder.

P&A transactions with optional shared losses have been viewed as one type of transaction to tackle distressed assets that are not attractive to potential acquirers. Under this approach, the FDIC could partially share losses with bidders on certain assets. According to the practice used during the global financial crisis, the FDIC generally shared 20 percent of losses with acquirers, and further shared losses depended on the exact circumstances of bids.[133] This option, which is easier to negotiate with bidders, reduces the immediate cash needs of the FDIC and pushes forward P&A proceedings progressively in terms of maximising franchise value and bidding. In addition, the FDIC and acquirers usually start negotiating with different purposes. For instance, the FDIC prefers to deal with distressed assets as fast as possible, but acquirers are subject to business considerations. It should be noted that, throughout the global financial crisis, the FDIC has expressed its preference to sell distressed assets at a discount, which implicitly subsidises the acquirers by playing down the value of those assets. Nonetheless, dealing with distressed assets is projected to be sustained work; that is to say, it would be time-consuming for both the FDIC and bidders.

The last ramification of P&As is bridge bank P&As, in which the FDIC as an acquirer temporarily assumes the responsibility of operating a bridge bank chartered by the OCC. Normally, in order to pinpoint the most suitable acquirers, two years with maximum three-year extensions are given to the bridge bank before it has been sold or otherwise resolved by a P&A transaction, an acquisition, a stock sale, or a payoff.[134] Nevertheless, compared to other P&As, these P&As have produced an enormous number of difficulties for the FDIC. Duplication of these P&As has been troublesome for the FDIC because it would be simultaneously dealing with three proceedings: closing the failing bank, operating the bridge bank, and ceasing the bridge bank. Notably, in the event high-quality customers and employees quit the bridge bank, the franchise value the bridge bank owns would be substantially reduced, resulting in another difficulty in attracting potential bidders after the transition period.

Undoubtedly, the pressure of dealing with failing institutions has been successfully relieved by P&A transactions, which have been a predominant resolution since 1933, accounting for over 60 percent of all transactions.[135] Viewed objectively, maintaining continuity is the biggest advantage over other resolutions. From the perspective of customers, despite the closing down of an original bank, they would be consistently served by the assuming bank. Additionally, from the FDIC's standpoint, P&A transactions ensure that assets and liabilities have been maximally circulated in the private sector, thereby reducing cash outlays.

3.5.3 Deposit Payoffs

A deposit payoff is the subordinated option behind P&A transactions in light of the least-cost test. Theoretically, unlike P&As, in a deposit payoff, no liabilities and no assets have to be assumed by another institution. The FDIC therefore undertakes responsibility for paying depositors the equal amount of their insured deposits. Nowadays, three forms of deposit payoffs – straight deposit payoffs, Insured Deposit Transfer (IDT), and Deposit Insurance National Bank (DINB) – have been generally adopted by the FDIC.

A straight deposit payoff, a resolution that is only applied when liquidation, closure, or winding up could be the least costly resolution, requires the FDIC to confirm the accounts of insured deposits and pay directly to each depositor by mailing a cheque. Meanwhile, the FDIC, as a receiver, bears the responsibility of receivership and the costs of liquidation.

The IDT, an alternative to a straight deposit payoff, is one type of deposit payoff where the FDIC hands insured deposits to an agent bank, allowing customers of the failed bank to withdraw their deposits from the agent bank by having created new accounts pursuant to 12 C.F.R. Part 330.[136]

Unlike the two types of deposit payoffs stated above, creating a DINB looks more complex. The chartering authority is supposed to first nominate the FDIC as the receiver of a failing bank, then the FDIC creates a DINB to operate as a transition bank that starts up with no capitalisation and confined functions. If there is no acquirer assuming the insured deposits, a DINB is created to protect depositors, especially those who live in underserved areas, by offering them consecutive access to insured deposits and leaving time to open new accounts in other insured banks as well. Generally speaking, a DINB enables customers to have sufficient time to start new banking relationships without any barriers, as it provides convenience through direct deposit transfer and automated payments from original accounts to receiving banks. Although a DINB can last for a maximum period of two years, the majority of recent cases demonstrate a tendency that a DINB can work within 30 days.[137]

3.6 Conclusion

Having experienced several financial crises, the FDIC has evolved from a deposit insurer to a multifunctional authority that plays an important and indispensable role in the US banking regulatory system. This article provides a comprehensive study of how the FDIC works in relation to its functions regarding deposit insurance and banking resolution.

As a deposit insurer, the FDIC has proved to be a good example around the world, since it has successfully overcome multiple difficulties during enormous crises. This has been achieved mainly through using risk-based premiums and increasing coverage. However, the FDIC simultaneously faces some challenges, such as the risk-based premiums assessment. Although this is one of the most advanced techniques, it is often said to be complicated and needs extra support from a very comprehensive database. When implementing this, the FDIC has to ensure that it can continue to optimise a strong database and justify correct information.

As a receiver of failed banks, the FDIC is responsible for dealing with failing financial institutions that pose significant threats to financial stability. After the GFC, the Dodd-Frank Act extended the FDIC's jurisdiction to systemically important complex and large financial institutions. However, some scholars question whether resolving failing banks based on an agency's discretion incurs opacity and abuse of power, arguing that Chapter 14 of the Bankruptcy Code via court orders is the preferable choice. But in reality, the FDIC has advantages over Chapter 14, such as professional staff and on-site due diligence. Therefore, accountability and transparency should be strengthened within the FDIC.

Meanwhile, it is noteworthy that the Trump administration has placed deregulation on the agenda and President Trump has signed the bank bill rolling back some regulations, including Dodd-Frank.[138] Thus, the prospect of an Orderly Liquidation Authority that enables the FDIC to counter systemically important complex and large financial institutions is uncertain.

Overall, although there is some uncertainty relating to the future of the FDIC, it is undoubtedly still playing a vital role in deposit insurance and banking resolution. Meanwhile, many countries could learn lessons from the FDIC. The FDIC still provides a good template for emerging economies that wish to establish or reform their respective banking regulatory regimes.

Notes

1 Federal Deposit Insurance Corporation (FDIC), 'A Brief History of Deposit Insurance' (FDIC, Washington DC, 1998) < https://www.fdic.gov/bank/historical/brief/brhist.pdf> accessed 16 September 2023.

2 International Association of Deposit Insurers (IADI), 'Deposit Insurance System Worldwide' (IADI, Basel, 2018) < https://www.iadi.org/en/deposit-insurance-systems/dis-worldwide/> accessed 20 October 2023.
3 FDIC, 'The First Fifty Years – A history of the FDIC 1933–1983' (FDIC, Washington DC, 1984) < https://www.fdic.gov/bank/analytical/firstfifty/> accessed 17 September 2024.
4 The following states were Vermont, Indiana, Michigan, Ohio, Iowa, Texas, Oklahoma, Kansas, Nebraska, Mississippi, South Dakota, North Dakota, and Washington.
5 Cater H. Golembe, 'The Deposit Insurance Legislation of 1933: An Examination of Its Antecedents and Its Purposes' (1960) 25 *Political Science Quarterly,* 189.
6 These five states were Vermont, Indiana, Michigan, Ohio, and Iowa. In this situation, the first four programmes primarily covered circulating notes and deposits. New York State later set restrictions on circulating notes, but Ohio and Iowa only extended coverage to circulating notes. Only Ohio and Iowa offered immediate payment with adequate funds for insured obligations. In New York, Vermont, and Michigan, creditors were paid only after the liquidation of a failed bank. Creditors in Indiana depended on liquidation proceeds and stockholder contributions.
7 FDIC, 'The First Fifty Years – A history of the FDIC 1933–1983' (n3). In this situation, the 'free banking' movement introduced banks to an alternative to deposit insurance. With the increasing number of 'free banks', members of state insurance programmes decreased.
8 FDIC, 'The First Fifty Years – A history of the FDIC 1933–1983' (n3).
9 Deposit insurance in eight states only covered deposits, and Kansas temporarily imposed a limit on coverage. Depositors in Kansas and Mississippi received dividends by having interest-bearing certificates paid from liquidation proceeds; the balance due was paid by insurance funds. In the remaining six states, depositors could be reimbursed immediately by insurance funds.
10 FDIC, 'The First Fifty Years – A history of the FDIC 1933–1983' (n3).
11 Mark D. Flood, 'The Great Deposit Insurance Debate' (1992) 74 *Federal Reserve Bank of St. Louis Review*, 51, 77.
12 Nicholas Crafts and Peter Fearon, 'Lessons from the 1930s Great Depression' (2010) 26 *Oxford Review of Economic Policy*, 304, 305.
13 FDIC, 'The First Fifty Years – A history of the FDIC 1933–1983' (n3).
14 George J. Benston and George G. Kaufman, 'Deposit Insurance Reform in the FDIC Improvement Act: the Experience to Date' (1998) 22 *Economic Perspectives*, 2.
15 Usually, the FDIC works jointly with the Federal Reserve Board. See FDIC, 'FDIC Strategic Plan 2015–2019' (FDIC, Washington DC, 2015) <https://www.fdic.gov/about/strategic/strategic/strategic_plan_2015_2019.pdf> accessed 9 October 2023.
16 Mark R. Williamson, 'Regulatory Theory and Deposit Insurance Reform' (1994) 42 *Cleveland State Law Review,* 105.
17 Mark Jickling and Edward V. Murphy, 'Who Regulates Whom? An Overview of US Financial Supervision' (Congressional Research Service, Washington DC, 2010) <https://fas.org/sgp/crs/misc/R40249.pdf> accessed 10 September 2024. Safety and soundness regulation under the context of banking regulation refers to the examination and regulation pertaining to the possibility of a bank's default, and the losses towards depositors and creditors. Deposit insurance is supposed to stabilise the liquidity of banks and to provide guarantees for the savings of American citizens. Capital regulation in this context means the availability of a bank's total assets against losses. Systemic risk as an emerging part of banking regulation in the US basically refers to risks sprawl in the whole financial system that could not be solved by examining individual institutions or markets.
18 Mark R. Williamson, 'Regulatory Theory and Deposit Insurance Reform' (n16).
19 Mark Jickling and Edward V. Murphy, 'Who Regulates Whom? An Overview of US Financial Supervision' (n17).

20 Nilufer Ozdemir, 'Implications of the Dual Banking System in the US' (2016) 44 *Atlantic Economic Journal*, 92.
21 12 USC, § 1.
22 Dalvinder Singh, *Banking Regulation of UK and US Financial Markets* (Ashgate Publishing 2007) 32.
23 Ibid.
24 12 USC, § 282.
25 12 USC, § 1814 (b). After the implementation of the Federal Deposit Insurance Reform Act of 2005, the assets and liabilities of the BIF and the SAIF have been merged and transferred into the new DIF.
26 12 USC, § 321 and § 282.
27 To solve temporary shortages of liquidity, the discount window is a monetary instrument utilised by the Federal Reserve, allowing qualified banks to borrow money from the Federal Reserve on a short-term basis.
28 John A. Weinberg, 'Competition among Bank regulators', (2002) 88 *Economic Quarterly*, 19.
29 See https://www.occ.treas.gov/about/who-we-are/occ-for-you/bankers/ots-integration.html.
30 See https://www.treasury.gov/initiatives/fsoc/about/Pages/default.aspx.
31 See https://www.occ.treas.gov/about/what-we-do/mission/index-about.html.
32 Edward V. Murphy, 'Who Regulates Whom and How? An Overview of US Financial Regulatory Policy for Banking and Securities Markets' (Congressional Research Service, Washington DC, 2015) < https://fas.org/sgp/crs/misc/R43087.pdf> accessed 20 October 2023.
33 12 USC, § 5414.
34 See https://www.occ.gov/topics/capital-markets/financial-markets/derivatives/derivatives-quarterly-report.html.
35 The Banking Act of 1933.
36 See https://www.fdic.gov/deposit/insurance/.
37 Federal Reserve Act of 1913.
38 12 USC, § 411 and § 441.
39 12 USC, §321, § 1841, and § 3101.
40 12 USC, § 5322.
41 *Ibid.*
42 12 USC, § 5330 and § 5331.
43 12 USC, § 3301 and §3302.
44 Timothy Geithner, 'Secretary Geithner Introduces Financial Stability Plan' (US Department of the Treasury Press Center, 2009) <https://www.treasury.gov/press-center/press-releases/Pages/tg18.aspx> accessed 11 November 2023.
45 Raymond S. Sczudlo, 'Consolidation of US banking Regulation Proposed' (1994) 13 *International Financial Law Review*, 20.
46 Rose M. Kushmeider, 'The US Federal Financial Regulatory System: Restructuring Federal Bank Regulation' (2005) 17 *FDIC Banking Review*, 8.
47 John A. Weinberg, 'Competition among Bank Regulators' (n28).
48 Rose M. Kushmeider, 'The US Federal Financial Regulatory System: Restructuring Federal Bank Regulation' (n38).
49 Raymond S. Sczudlo, 'Consolidation of US banking Regulation Proposed' (n45) 20.
50 *Ibid.*
51 Sabrina R. Pellerin, John R. Walter and Patricia E. Wescot, 'The Consolidation of Financial Market Regulation: Pros, Cons, and Implications for the United States' (Federal Reserve Bank of Richmond, May 2009) <https://www.richmondfed.org/~/media/richmondfedorg/publications/research/working_papers/2009/pdf/wp09-8.pdf> accessed 15 November 2023.

52 The US Department of the Treasury, 'Blueprint for a Modern Financial Regulatory Structure' (The US Department of the Treasury, March 2008) <https://www.treasury.gov/press-center/press-releases/Documents/Blueprint.pdf> accessed 20 November 2023.
53 *Ibid.*
54 Xavier Vives, 'Competition Policy in Banking' (2011) 27 *Oxford Review of Economic Policy*, 479, 297.
55 The United States General Accounting Office, 'Financial Services Regulators: Better Information Sharing Could Reduce Fraud' (GAO, March 2001) <http://www.gao.gov/new.items/d01478t.pdf> accessed 20 November 2023.
56 The US Department of the Treasury, 'Financial Regulatory Reform: A New Foundation: Rebuilding Financial Supervision and Regulation' (The US Department of Treasury, October 2009) <https://www.treasury.gov/initiatives/Documents/FinalReport_web.pdf> accessed 25 November 2019.
57 David S. Hoelscher, Michael W. Taylor and Ulrich H. Klueh, 'The Design and Implementation of Deposit Insurance' (IMF, Washington DC, December 2006) <https://www.imf.org/en/Publications/Occasional-Papers/Issues/2016/12/31/The-Design-and-Implementation-of-Deposit-Insurance-Systems-18683> accessed 12 October 2023.
58 12 USC, § 1812.
59 *Ibid.*
60 *Ibid.*
61 Pub. L. 109-171, § 2102.
62 FDIC, '2016 Annual Report' (FDIC, Washington DC, February 2017) <https://www.fdic.gov/about/strategic/report/2016annualreport/2016ar_final.pdf> accessed 20 November 2023.
63 *Ibid.*
64 12 USC, § 1827.
65 12 USC, § 1817.
66 Diane Ellis, 'Deposit Insurance Funding: Assuring Confidence', (FDIC, Washington DC, November 2013) < https://www.fdic.gov/deposit/insurance/assuringconfidence.pdf> accessed 22 November 2023.
67 FDIC, '2016 Annual Report' (n62).
68 FDIC, 'Options Paper' (FDIC, Washington DC, August 2000) <https://www.fdic.gov/deposit/insurance/initiative/options_080700m.pdf> accessed 25 November 2023.
69 FDIC, 'Managing the Crisis: The FDIC and RTC Experience: 1980–1994', (FDIC, Washington DC, 1998) <https://www.fdic.gov/bank/historical/managing/> accessed 25 November 2023.
70 *Ibid.* Also see FDIC, 'Historical Statistics on Banking' at https://www5.fdic.gov/hsob/SelectRpt.asp?EntryTyp=20&Header=1 accessed 26 November 2023.
71 Pub. L. 101-73, § 208 (4) (1) (B).
72 12 USC, § 1825.
73 Diane Ellis, 'Deposit Insurance Funding: Assuring Confidence' (n66).
74 P. L. 109-171, § 2105 (B).
75 12 USC, § 1817.
76 12 USC, § 1817. In general, a small bank refers to a bank with total assets of less than $10 billion.
77 Ibid.
78 12 CFR, § 327. A supplementary leverage ratio used for determining capital groups commences from 1 January 2020. The leverage ratio is supposed to affect the capital group assignment of few, if any, small banks.
79 Primary regulators refer to small banks' primary federal regulators and state regulators. The CAMELS rating system is a supervisory rating developed in the US to reflect the banks' condition. This system is based on a ratio analysis of the financial state-

ments combined with on-site examinations executed by a designated primary regulator. Constituents of CAMELS rating system include: capital adequacy, asset quality, management, earnings, liquidity, and sensitivity.

80 Source: FDIC Law, Regulations, Related Acts available at https://www.fdic.gov/regulations/laws/rules/5000-900.html. CAMELS composite ratings are based on a careful assessment related to an institution's managerial, operational, financial, and compliance performance. The six key constituents of CAMELS rating system are regularly used for assessing insured institutions.

81 Government Publishing Office (GAO), 'Part III: Federal Deposit Insurance Corporation' (2016) 81 *Federal Register*, 321080. <https://www.gpo.gov/fdsys/pkg/FR-2016-05-20/pdf/2016-11181.pdf> accessed 10 July 2024.

82 The date collected from the FDIC: Current Assessment Calculators, which was updated since 30 September 2017. Available at https://www.fdic.gov/deposit/insurance/calculator.html.

83 The unsecured debt adjustment cannot exceed the lesser of 5 basis points or 50 percent of an insured depository institution's initial base assessment rate, and it is not applicable for new banks or insured branches of foreign banks.

84 The total base assessment rate should be at least 1.5 basis points.

85 The weighted CAMELS Component Ratings are applied in following rules: 25 percent each for capital adequacy and management; 20 percent for asset quality; 10 percent each for earnings, liquidity, and sensitivity. The Component Ratings system is used for deposit insurance assessment purposes.

86 Government Publishing Office (GAO), 'Part III: Federal Deposit Insurance Corporation' (2016) 81 *Federal Register*, 32183, and the FDIC official website about calculating assessment rates, available at https://www.gpo.gov/fdsys/pkg/FR-2016-05-20/pdf/2016-11181.pdf and https://www.fdic.gov/deposit/insurance/calculator.html respectively.

87 The date collected from the FDIC: Current Assessment Calculators, which was updated since 30 September 2017. Available at https://www.fdic.gov/deposit/insurance/calculator.html.

88 GAO, 'Part II: Federal Deposit Insurance Corporation' (2011) 76 *Federal Register*, 10690. <https://www.fdic.gov/deposit/insurance/11rulead35.pdf> accessed 20 July 2024.

89 GAO, 'Part II: Federal Deposit Insurance Corporation' (2011) 76 *Federal Register*, 10690. <https://www.fdic.gov/deposit/insurance/11rulead35.pdf> accessed 20 July 2024.

90 Unlike the concentration measure used in large institutions, which considers the higher-risk assets to Tier 1 capital and reserve score or the growth-adjusted portfolio concentrations score, the concentration measure for complex institutions depends on the top 20 counterparty exposures to Tier 1 capital and reserves ratio and the largest counterparty exposure to Tier 1 and reserve ratio.

91 Mark D. Flood, 'Deposit Insurance: Problems and Solutions' (1993) 75 *Economic Review*, 29.

92 Gary S. Fissel, 'Risk Measurement, Actuarially-Fair Deposit Insurance Premiums and the FDIC's Risk-Related Premium System' (1994) 7 *FDIC Banking Review*, 18.

93 Marcia M. Cornett, Hamid Mehran and Hassan Tehranian, 'The Impact of Risk-Based Premiums on FDIC-Insured Institutions' (1998) 13 *Journal of Financial Services Research*, 164.

94 Gary S. Fissel, 'Risk Measurement, Actuarially-Fair Deposit Insurance Premiums and the FDIC's Risk-Related Premium System' (n92).

95 Andrew Campbell and Peter Cartwright, 'Co-insurance and Moral Hazard: Some Reflections on Deposit Protection in the UK and USA' (2003) 5 *Journal of International Banking Regulation*, 16.

96 Kenneth H. Thomas, 'FDIC Premium Plan is Too Little, Too Late' *American Banker* (New York, 23 June 2015) <https://www.americanbanker.com/opinion/fdic-premium-plan-is-too-little-too-late> accessed 17 December 2023.
97 Larry D. Wall, 'The Change in the FDIC Assessment Base' (2015) Centre for Financial Innovation and Stability of Federal Reserve Bank of Atlanta' <https://www.frbatlanta.org/cenfis/publications/notesfromthevault/1503.aspx> assessed 10 June 2024.
98 Andrew Kuritzkes, Til Schuermann, and Scott Weiner, 'Deposit Insurance and Risk Management of the US Banking System: How Much? How Safe? Who Pays?' The Wharton Financial Institutions Centre of University of Pennsylvania <http://citeseerx.ist.psu.edu/viewdoc/download?doi=10.1.1.129.5678&rep=rep1&type=pdf> accessed 15 July 2024.
99 The OCC, 'Eliminating Constraints on Risk-based Pricing' Statement of John D. Hawke, Jr., Comptroller of the Currency before the Committee on Banking, Housing, and Urban Affairs (the OCC, February 2003) <https://www.occ.gov/static/news-issuances/congressional-testimony/2003/pub-test-2003-12-oral.pdf> accessed 13 June 2024.
100 Karey Wutkowski and Tim Dobbyn, 'Update 2-US FDIC Proposes large banks pay for their risk' *Reuters* (London, 13 April 2010) <https://www.reuters.com/article/banks-fdic/update-2-us-fdic-proposes-large-banks-pay-for-their-risk-idUSN1321819820100413> accessed 15 July 2024.
101 Diane Ellis, 'Deposit Insurance Funding: Assuring Confidence' (n67).
102 Christine M. Bradley, 'A Historical Perspective on Deposit Insurance Coverage' (2000) 13 *FDIC Banking Review*, 14, 18.
103 Eight specific accounts include: single accounts, qualifying retirement accounts, joint accounts, revocable trust accounts, irrevocable trust accounts, accounts of a corporation or partnership, government accounts, and employee-benefit plan accounts.
104 12 CFR, § 330.4.
105 12 CFR, §330.3(e). If there is a specified agreement about a particular exchange rate, according to the agreement.
106 James R. Barth, *The Great Savings and Loan Debacle* (American Enterprise Institute Press Feb 1991) 40, 110.
107 Christine M. Bradley, 'A Historical Perspective on Deposit Insurance Coverage' (n102).
108 Gerald R. Ford, Public Papers of the Presidents of the United States (General Services Administration, 1974) available at https://quod.lib.umich.edu/p/ppotpus/4732025.1974.001?view=toc accessed 16 December 2023.
109 Christine M. Bradley, 'A Historical Perspective on Deposit Insurance Coverage' (n102).
110 Oz Shy, Rune Stenbacka and Vladimir Yankov, 'Limited Deposit Insurance Coverage and Bank Competition' (2016) 71 *Journal of Banking & Finance*, 103, 104.
111 *Ibid.*
112 George G. Kaufman, 'Bank Runs: Causes, Benefits, and Costs' (1988) 7 *Cato Journal*, 571.
113 Douglas W. Diamond and Philip H. Dybvig, 'Banking Runs: Causes, Benefits, and Costs' (1988) 7 *Cato Journal*, 559, 598.
114 Robert A. Eisenbeis and Larry D. Wall, 'Reforming Deposit Insurance and FDICIA' (2002) 87 *Economic Review*, 6, 7.
115 John F. Bovenzi and Arthur J. Murton, 'Resolution Costs of Bank Failures' (1988) 1 *FDIC Banking Review*, 2.
116 12 USC, § 1831.
117 Jerome H. Powell, 'Ending "Too Big to Fail"' (Institute of International Bankers 2013 Washington Conference, Washington DC, March 2013).

118 Sheila C. Bair, 'We Must Resolve to End Too Big To Fail' (2011) 5 *FDIC Quarterly*, 25.
119 Jacqueline Palank, 'Law Firm's Lehman Tab May Reach $ 430 Million' *Wall Street Journal* (New York, 5 July 2012) <https://www.wsj.com/articles/SB10001424052702304550004577509002044284314> accessed 15 January 2024.
120 12 USC, § 5384 and 5390.
121 12 USC, § 1821.
122 12 USC, § 5390.
123 12 USC, § 5384.
124 FDIC, 'The Orderly Liquidation of Lehman Brothers Holding Inc. under the Dodd-Frank Act' (2011) 5 *FDIC Quarterly*, 38.
125 Kenneth E. Scott, 'A Guide to The Resolution of Failed Financial Institutions' in Kenneth E. Scott and John B. Taylor (eds), *Bankruptcy Not Bailout: A Special Chapter 14* (Hoover Institution Press, 2012) and William F. Kroener III, 'Comment on Orderly Liquidation under Title II of Dodd-Frank and Chapter 14' in Kenneth E. Scott and John B. Taylor (eds), *Bankruptcy Not Bailout: A Special Chapter 14* (Hoover Institution Press, 2012).
126 *Ibid.*
127 Gillian G. Garcia, 'Failing Prompt Corrective Action' (2010) 11 *Journal of Banking Regulation*, 183.
128 *Ibid* at 188.
129 Kenneth E. Scott, 'A Guide to The Resolution of Failed Financial Institutions' (n125).
130 William F. Kroener III, 'Expanding FDIC-Style Resolution Authority' in Kenneth E. Scott (ed.), *Ending Government Bailouts as We Know Them* (Hoover Institution Press, 2010).
131 Rosalind L. Bennett, 'Failure Resolution and Asset Liquidation: Results of an International Survey of Deposit Insurers' (2001) 14 *FDIC Banking Review*, 13.
132 IADI, 'General Guidance for the Resolution of Bank Failures' (IADI, Basel, Dec 2005) <http://www.iadi.org/en/assets/File/Papers/Approved%20Guidance%20Papers/Guidance_Bank_Resol.pdf> accessed 10 January 2024.
133 William R. Baxter, Ryan D. Sheller, and Robert F. Storch, 'FDIC Loss-Sharing Agreement: A Primer' (2010) 7 *Supervisory Insights*, 3.
134 FDIC, 'Resolutions Handbook' (FDIC, Washington DC, Dec 2014) <https://www.fdic.gov/about/freedom/drr_handbook.pdf> accessed 15 February 2024.
135 FDIC, 'Federal Deposit Insurance Corporation Failures and Assistance Transactions 1934-2007 Table BF02' available at https://www5.fdic.gov/hsob/HSOBSummaryRpt.asp?BegYear=1934&EndYear=2017&State=2&Header=0 accessed 2 January 2020. These are official historical statistics showing details and data about failed banks.
136 12 CFR, § 330.7.
137 12 U.S.C. § 1821.
138 Elizabeth Dexheimer, 'Trump Signs Biggest Rollback of Bank Rules Since Dodd-Frank Act' *Bloomberg* (London, 25 May 2018) <https://www.bloomberg.com/news/articles/2018-05-24/trump-signs-biggest-rollback-of-bank-rules-since-dodd-frank-act> accessed 16 January 2024.

4 Deposit Insurance in the UK

Experience, Country Specifics, and Institutional Structure and Reform

4.1 Introduction

The Deposit Protection Scheme, echoing the banking crisis between 1973 and 1975 and the call for the harmonisation of banking regulation in the European Union (EU), became the first formal deposit insurance scheme in the UK after the Banking Act 1979.[1]

However, the failure of the Bank of Credit and Commerce International in the 1990s, which consumed massive scheme funding, led to a large discussion regarding reforms in UK banking regulation. Later on, the UK enacted the Financial Services and Markets Act 2000 (FSMA) to completely revamp its banking regulatory architecture and launch a new deposit protection scheme called the FSCS, which continues to operate the UK deposit insurance scheme today.

At present, the FSCS, operating a pay box model, is only responsible for discharging the basic functions of deposit insurance in terms of deposit payouts and compensation claims. During the GFC, the Northern Rock run dealt a blow to the low-profile FSCS as it revealed many deficiencies in the UK's deposit insurance scheme but helped the UK strengthen the FSCS. As a result, the FSCS has undergone a series of significant developments in pursuit of facilitating a well-functioning deposit insurance scheme. It is said that the FSCS has now evolved into a pay box plus model with strengthened powers amid the implementation of the Single Customer View.[2] Despite strengthened functions and powers, the FSCS, so far, has no regulatory power to deal with troubled financial institutions.

Against this backdrop, this chapter seeks to reconsider and analyse the operating mechanism of the FSCS as a classical pay box model in line with the IADI's classification. The focal point of this chapter concentrates on the FSCS's significant reforms since the Northern Rock run during the GFC and suggestions for future reforms of the FSCS. This chapter is in four parts. Part one provides a historical overview of the deposit protection scheme in the UK. Part two examines the designs of the FSCS. Part three discusses the lessons learned from the Northern Rock crisis. Part four provides a discussion on prospective reforms of the FSCS. Finally, a conclusion will be drawn.

DOI: 10.4324/9781003612759-4

4.2 The Development of the UK Deposit Insurance Scheme

4.2.1 The Deposit Protection Scheme

The Banking Act 1979 was the first formal banking regulatory legislation in UK history, as a result of the secondary banking crisis between 1973 and 1975, and the appeal to harmonise banking regulation amid the adoption of the first European Economic Community (EEC) Banking Directive of 1977 in coordination with laws, regulations, and administrative provisions associated with credit institutions. It was clear that the Act made progress in explicitly clarifying the Bank of England's regulatory powers and initiating the Deposit Protection Scheme.[3]

The Deposit Protection Scheme, the UK's first formal deposit protection scheme, took effect on 19 February 1982, following the second part of the Banking Act 1979, as a result of the popularity of safeguarding vulnerable depositors from bank failures.[4] Nevertheless, large and safe banks had hostile attitudes towards the scheme, partly because flat rate contributions that required all depository institutions to pay the same rate possibly subsidised risky banks.[5]

However, before the commencement of the Deposit Protection Scheme, only implicit deposit protection was in effect, as stated by Campbell and Cartwright, 'whenever a bank experienced serious financial difficulties, the government and Bank of England were deciding on appropriate action on an *ad hoc* basis'.[6] In the meantime, without a specific Banking Act, the Bank of England was responsible for implementing banking supervision in line with a number of sections enacted in different acts.

Under the scheme, the Deposit Protection Board was mainly set up with the power to manage the Deposit Protection Fund and levy contributions from authorised depository banks and other authorised depository institutions.[7] Contributions from a minimum of £2,500 to a maximum of £300,000 were levied by the Board. Notably, once a single institution paid contributions of more than 0.3 percent of its total deposits, no further contributions were required.[8] In addition, the scheme adopted co-insurance, insuring 75 percent of the maximum £10,000 of any single depositor's total deposits in insured deposit-taking institutions, with 25 percent co-insurance of £10,000.[9]

By 1987, the scheme had witnessed two significant changes to its rationales. First, building societies, concentrating on receiving deposits from individuals and lending to individuals in the UK mortgage market were incorporated into the scheme.[10] The second, which could be perceived as the increase of deposit insurance coverage amid the promulgation of the Banking Act 1987, raised the maximum protection from £10,000 to £20,000 with the same level of co-insurance.[11] By the end of 1996, the Scheme had paid out a total of £144 million, with £78.4 million of this relating to the collapse of Bank of Credit and Commerce International, the largest bank failure in that period.[12] Ultimately, this collapse led to reflections on UK banking supervision and depositor protection, resulting in a series of reforms for UK financial markets.

4.2.2 The Financial Services Compensation Scheme

The Bank of England Act 1998 established the Financial Services Authority (FSA), taking charge of banking regulation from the Bank of England.[13] When the Labour Government came into power, it established the FSA as a sole powerful financial regulator supervising all financial services and service providers. Then, when the FSMA 2000 came into effect, the powerful FSA formally took control, and the FSCS commenced its operation on 1 December 2001.

The FSCS, concentrating on protecting consumers involving the full range of financial services, was established by the FSA with the granting of an independent legal personality. Nevertheless, the powers of making rules and implementing banking resolution were not given to the FSCS. In accordance with Section 212 of the FSMA 2000, the FSCS, a non-profit independent deposit insurer responsible for compensating consumers who suffer losses from the failures of authorised financial service providers, formally assumed responsibilities for maintaining public confidence and facilitating consumer protection.[14] Moreover, Section 213 of the FSMA 2000 detailed three preconditions regarding the circumstances depositors would be eligible to receive compensation, how much compensation would be paid out, and how to fund the scheme.[15]

Before the GFC, the FSA had significantly improved the coverage limit. Focussing on the FSA's overhaul, the first £2,000 was given 100 percent protection. The next £33,000 only received 90 percent protection, thereby retaining co-insurance of 10 percent. This is to say, the maximum compensation limit was enhanced to £31,700.[16] Since 2007, the UK deposit insurance coverage limit has undergone four stages: first, for compensation claims from 1 October 2007 to 6 October 2008, the coverage limit had been enhanced to 100 percent of the first £35,000; from 7 October 2008 to 29 June 2009, the coverage limit had been raised to £50,000; from 30 June 2009 to 30 December 2010, the limit of 100 percent protection had been raised to £50,000 per person; and, since 31 December 2010, the coverage limit has been increased to 100 percent coverage of the first £85,000.

Simultaneously, the EU Directive on Deposit Guarantee Schemes was another factor in the increase of the UK deposit insurance coverage limit. The directive, as amended at the end of 2008, required members to raise their coverage limits to €50,000.[17] The FSCS provided depositors with 100 percent protection of £50,000, which exceeded the minimum required by the directive. When the directive increased coverage to €100,000 in December 2010, the UK increased its deposit insurance coverage to £85,000 rather than €100,000. This means that the current deposit insurance coverage is actually lower than the minimum amount required by the directive because of the continuous devaluation of British pounds.[18]

The shortcomings of the FSCS mirrored the weaknesses the UK had in place. When the GFC erupted, the FSCS acknowledged that very few consumers considered seeking assistance from the low-key depositor protection scheme provided by the FSCS.[19] Between 2008 and 2009, depositors from five banks – Bradford & Bingley, Icesave, Kaupthing Singer and Friedlander, Heritable Bank, and London Scottish Bank – received payouts from the FSCS, which was worth approximately

£20 billion in compensation, putting financial pressure on the FSCS, as most of the money was borrowed from the UK Treasury and then repaid by deposit insurance contributions and substantial recoveries.[20] Besides, the long queues outside each branch of Northern Rock revealed that public awareness of the FSCS was not only much lower than the accepted level but also incapable of blocking bank runs. Apart from public awareness, at the beginning of the GFC, the UK deposit insurance scheme that adopted co-insurance with a very low level of full protection failed to restore public confidence, as depositors who had more than £2,000 in savings became concerned over the losses of their savings arising from bank failures due to the existence of co-insurance. Therefore, after the GFC, the FSCS commenced its overhaul.

Lord Turner in his review underlines the reflection on deposit insurance and bank resolution, calling for the overhaul of depositor protection and consumer protection in the UK.[21] Since 1 April 2013, two powerful successor regulators, the Prudential Regulation Authority (PRA) and the Financial Conduct Authority (FCA), have been established to continue performing the major functions of the FSA.[22] Under the new 'twin peaks' regulatory framework, the PRA, a new prudential regulator under the Bank of England, has been responsible for regulating and supervising over 1,500 systemically important banks, building societies, and large financial investment firms.[23] In the meantime, the FCA, an independent conduct regulator that has inherited the majority of functions from the FSA, has been responsible for monitoring more than 56,000 financial firms.[24] Unlike the PRA, the FCA is more focused on enhancing market integrity, promoting competition, and protecting consumers, so as to create a fair and effective market for consumers.[25] In addition, the Financial Policy Committee (FPC), a consultant committee with powers of discretion for identifying potential systemic risks and making recommendations, was simultaneously set up to urge regulators to implement specific policy tools and deliver recommendations to direct financial regulators in maintaining financial stability.[26]

It is noteworthy that, after the cessation of the FSA, the powers of the FSA have been transferred to the PRA and the FCA respectively. Therefore, both the PRA and the FCA jointly have powers over the governance of the FSCS, and the FSCS, in turn, is ultimately accountable to them. Pursuant to the amended FSMA 2000, the FSCS, the PRA, and the FCA have a compulsory obligation to collaborate together.[27]

4.3 Revisiting the FSCS and the Operating Mechanisms of the FSCS

4.3.1 Institutional Reforms after the GFC

Since the GFC, the UK has witnessed significant financial regulatory reform that converted the single regulator mechanism into the twin peaks model. Three emerging regulatory bodies – the FPC, the PRA, and the FCA – have been established and replaced the single regulator mechanism since the promulgation of the Financial Services Act 2012.

Alongside the reform, the PRA and the FCA, two new regulatory bodies under the new twin peaks model, have been responsible for taking charge of prudential regulation and conduct supervision in the UK's financial markets. The PRA, as the UK prudential regulator created within the Bank of England, is mainly responsible for conducting micro prudential regulation and overseeing systemically important financial institutions. Simultaneously, the FCA, an independent regulatory body separate from the Bank of England, has inherited all other functions and responsibilities from the FSA monitoring the business and conduct carried out by all UK-authorised financial institutions. In addition, the FPC has been responsible for macroeconomic issues, such as capital and leverage ratio requirements and housing market controls, in pursuit of financial stability.[28]

The FSCS, a non-profit body created under the FSMA 2000, accountable to the FCA, the PRA, and HM Treasury, has been acting as a designated scheme manager for paying out consumers who have suffered losses arising from the failures of authorised financial firms. After the implementation of the new twin peaks model, the appointment of directors of the FSCS has been determined by the PRA and the FCA, whilst the chairman and chief executive of the FSCS simultaneously have to be approved by HM Treasury.[29] However, the terms of appointment of the board, in which members are limited to 'public interest representatives', should ensure that the FSCS operates independently without any intervention by the PRA and the FCA, even though the PRA and the FCA have jointly written scheme rules pertaining to assessments and compensation for relevant claims.[30]

At the present stage, in order to pay out promptly, the FSCS is working closely with the FCA and the PRA, which are primary UK financial regulators supervising all financial institutions that sell financial services and products. In turn, the FCA and the PRA have an obligation to ensure that the FSCS is capable of performing functions on time. Notably, Section 217A of the FSMA 2000 has put forward a responsibility of collaboration by requiring all of them to prepare and maintain a memorandum in compliance with the functions under Part 15 and Part 15A of the FSMA 2000.

4.3.2 The Funding Mechanism of the FSCS

By way of continuous optimisations involving the FSMA 2000, the FSCS currently has adopted a hybrid funding mechanism that consists of ex-ante deposit insurance levies and supplementary levies.[31] In the meantime, the Banking Act 2009 swept away barriers for the FSCS to raise supplementary funds against contingent failures that might take place at any time.[32] The new hybrid funding mechanism enables the FSCS to levy financial institutions based on actual costs and flexible adjustments.

Normally, the FSCS's target funding pool is made up of management expense levies, specific cost levies, and compensation cost levies: first, management expense levies utilised to run the FSCS arise from the regulatory costs that all authorised financial firms have to pay, with an annual limit capped by the FCA and the PRA; second, the PRA and the FCA collect levies from each sub-class and promulgate maximum limits of specific cost levies covering claims and proceed payments, and compensation cost levies.[33]

It is noteworthy, since July 2017, that the UK has adopted risk-based levies for compensation cost levies.[34] The PRA is responsible for calculating final weighted scores based on eight risk indicators demonstrated in Table 4.2 and the FSCS then calculates the risk-based levies in light of the aggregate risk scores and the adjustment factor suggested by the PRA. After the levy calculation, the FCA starts charging levies with offering levies invoice.[35]

In light of the current funding mechanism in the UK, in order to fulfil compensation claims, the FSCS has set out eight broad classes and nine sub-schemes in line with the relevant compensation limits determined by the PRA and FCA, as shown in Table 4.1. It is important to note that these limits represent the maximum amounts the FSCS can levy from each sub-scheme for compensation payments.

The first three classes and sub-schemes are perceived as the PRA classes, and the remainder are counted in the FCA classes. Except for deposits, all other classes are simultaneously split into eight categories. What kind of categories a financial

Table 4.1 Classification of Compensation for Each Sub-Scheme

Class	*Sub-Scheme*	*Limits of Compensation Payments for each Sub-Scheme*
Deposits	Deposits	£1,500 million
Life and Pensions	Life and Pensions Provision	£690 million
General Insurance	General Insurance Provision	£600 million
General Insurance Intermediation	Investment Provision	£200 million
Life and Pensions Intermediation	General Insurance Intermediation	£300 million
Investment Intermediation	Life and Pensions Intermediation	£100 million
Investment	Investment Intermediation	£150 million
Home Finance	Home Finance Intermediation	£40 million
	Debt Management	£20 million

Data Source: the FSCS.

Table 4.2 The UK Measure to Calculate the Aggregate Risk Score

Risk Indicator	*Weight*
Leverage Ratio	12%
Common Equity Tier Ratio	12%
Liquidity Coverage Ratio	24%
Non-performing Loans Ratio	18%
Risk-Weighted Asset/Total Assets	8.5%
Return on Assets	8.5%
Unencumbered Assets/Covered Deposits	17%
Total	100%

Data Source: PRA.

firm should be in is determined by the activities the firm is permitted to conduct and a firm could be placed into one or multiple categories. Unlike the PRA sub-schemes without mutual subsidies, the FCA sub-schemes may subsidise each other through the retail pool once the ultimate compensation costs of a class surpass the levy cap. Under the current funding mechanism, two retail pool models have been employed for the FCA classes, one for intermediary failures and the other for investment provider failures. The only difference between the two models is that the FCA provider contribution classes are not required to pay an additional £260 million to the retail pool used for intermediary failures.[36]

However, critics are concerned that the enforcement of a cross-subsidy might trigger unfairness among member institutions, especially in the case of the failure of Keydata Investment Services Ltd (Keydata).[37] Keydata had been a financial service provider selling financial products provided by Luxembourg-based companies SLS and Lifemark, and these products, which attempted to qualify as tax-free Individual Savings Accounts, were designed to return interest on capital invested based on portfolios of life insurance policies sold to American elderly people.[38] Nonetheless, these products failed to be recognised by the FSA with tax-free status, and the bonds were found to be worthless, resulting in Keydata going into administration. In this case, the FSCS had contributed a total of £247 million interim levies to cover losses arising from the failure of Keydata, leading to 217 contributing firms requesting a judicial review action against the FSCS's decision to cover the losses of Keydata.[39]

Although the FSCS's decision on Keydata has been successfully upheld against the judicial review request of its procedures, there are still some doubts relating to the FSCS's procedural unfairness. The selection of contributing members and the decision-making process of spreading financial losses to member financial institutions, which are mainly based on the FSCS's discretion, have been two prominent issues leading to industry concerns.[40] Therefore, an open, clear, and transparent procedure in making decisions regarding member selection and cross-subsidy is needed to dodge adverse impacts on UK financial industries.

Notably, unlike previous compensation cost levies merely based on the total volume of covered deposits in an insured financial institution, the UK, to date, has eventually progressed to a risk-based levies system for its compensation cost levies. The new risk-based levies mechanism is similar to the US's scoreboard measure for large and complex financial institutions, which weighs each risk indicator into a total score. Before calculating the aggregate risk score, each risk indicator outputs an individual score demonstrating deposit takers' risk levels, which then would be weighted into a total score.[41] The weight of each risk indicator in the UK calculating measure can be seen in Table 4.2, and the specialised weight of each risk indicator in the calculating measure for credit unions is shown in Table 4.3.

After working out the aggregate risk scores, the PRA would convert them into final weighted scores, delivering the final scores to the FSCS.[42] Subsequently, the FSCS would figure out the risk adjustment factor based on the aggregate risk weight and tariff database. As a result, the FSCS will determine each deposit taker's risk-based levies in accordance with the risk adjustment factor.[43] Compared

Table 4.3 Measure to Calculate the Aggregate Risk Score for Credit Unions

Risk Indicator	*Weight*
Leverage Ratio	25%
Liquidity Ratio	25%
Non-Performing Loans Ratio	25%
Return on Assets	25%
Total	100%

Data Sources: PRA.

with the US scoreboard measure, this approach seems simpler, partly because it is a newly launched assessment which needs to be tested and to accumulate experience over the years.

At the same time, the members of the FSCS would be refunded by the FSCS once the surplus funding is over £20 million, whilst the decision on refunding might be taken into consideration in case of the surplus funding exceeding £10 million.[44] In contrast to refunding, merely under the reasonable and precise expectation and forecast, the FSCS is capable of charging supplementary levies against funding shortfalls. It can be seen that, for example, the actual costs for life and pensions intermediation in 2017 and 2018 climbed to approximately £146 million due to the growing number of pension transfers, but the maximum levy limit for life and pensions intermediation maintained at £100 million.[45] In response to the shortfall, the FSCS determined to raise an additional £24 million from the life and pensions intermediation class, coupled with the retail pool, against extra costs. Nonetheless, with regard of extra remaining funds, unlike extra levies imposed on the life and pensions intermediation class, the FSCS has returned £20 million, regarded as surplus funds, to the firms falling in general insurance provision class.[46]

Although the UK has transitioned from a pure ex-post funding with flat rates scheme or pay-as-you-go model to a hybrid funding approach, given the ascending costs of running a bank, it is noteworthy that the financial services providers in the UK have fiercely resisted ex-ante funding proposals.[47] The British Bankers' Association echoed that the ex-post funding scheme is completely achievable for the demands of the UK financial markets in terms of the UK banking market's concentrated nature, and the ex-ante funding scheme could tighten capital availability, which, however, eliminates the effectiveness of capital utilisation, resulting in a meaningless drought of banks' liquidity.[48] However, a small-sized deposit insurance fund is financially incapable of tackling 'too big to fail' bank failures due to the massive demands of compensation, sufficient capital resources, and diversified risks, thereby bolstering public confidence to a limited extent.

Besides, the Treasury Committee disagrees with the British Bankers' Association's notion and argues that two fundamental disadvantages of the previous funding scheme were obvious.[49] First, the pay-as-you-go model or the ex-post levies mechanism failed to restore depositors' confidence in financial stability because of the absence of prompt funding resources.[50] Second, the pay-as-you-go approach or the ex-post levies mechanism may exacerbate banks' fiscal circumstances as this approach levies banks during financial turmoil, whereas the ex-ante funding scheme enables the FSCS to levy banks during stable periods with sufficient capital.[51] By and large, the Treasury Committee is apt to install an ex-ante funding scheme despite the expensive costs.

Besides, the IADI illustrates the same preference and makes recommendations for installing an ex-ante funding mechanism. One important lesson learnt from the GFC is that the lack of public confidence might trigger market panics and the escalation of panic withdrawals, leading to a systemic crisis. Thus, the IADI suggests that adopting an ex-ante funding approach in the face of bank failures not only increases certainty and public confidence but also equally spreads losses among financial institutions. In addition, compared with an ex-post funding scheme that spreads losses to surviving financial institutions, an ex-ante funding scheme is equitable, although it is very costly due to the intrinsic feature of moral hazard.[52]

At the present stage, after optimising the funding scheme over the years, the UK deposit insurance scheme, the FSCS, has adopted a hybrid approach that consists of ex-ante levies and supplementary levies. The majority of funds arise from annual levies via charging sub-schemes with maximum limits, while a minority of funds are raised for supplementary costs. In the meantime, the FCA and the PRA have framed a tariff base for sub-schemes in order to pinpoint financial service providers more accurately and reasonably. However, this enhances complexity, causing a mounting amount of management costs.

4.3.3 Coverage and Compensation Limit

Prior to 1 October 2007, the UK deposit insurance scheme had long involved co-insurance that attempted to compel depositors to afford fractional losses of bank failures, simply because the UK government, before the Northern Rock run, believed that the rationale behind co-insurance was to minimise moral hazard by encouraging depositors to pay attention to monitoring host banks' conditions carefully.[53] However, although the FSA and Hall underline that depositors should retain an incentive to remain vigilant towards risks involved in receiving banks, co-insurance was broadly criticised by scholars.[54] In practice, consumers of financial institutions usually have very limited access to the latest information and financial statements, making it is very difficult for them to make an accurate judgement on the risk level concerning host banks. It can be noted that, for instance, Campbell and Cartwright argue that the lack of 'user-friendly' information has hindered most depositors from assessing the riskiness involved in host banks.[55] At the same time, MacDonald also underlines that, unlike purchasing fashion brands, it is hard for depositors to subscribe to the most recent information of banks.[56] Therefore, expecting depositors to remain vigilant and afford losses is unfair, leading to setbacks in public confidence and financial stability. Especially compared with financial regulators, depositors are always at a disadvantage due to their lack of specific and professional experience and knowledge.

Having realised the significant importance of public confidence since the Northern Rock run, the UK has eventually given up co-insurance and established 100 percent protection with a high but limited coverage. As of the end of September 2007, 100 percent of £35,000 came into effect. Subsequently, in order to abide by two modifications of the coverage limit of the Deposit Guarantee Schemes Directive (DGSD), the UK compensation limit has been boosted from £50,000 to £85,000.

At present, unlike the US deposit insurance scheme covering foreign banks and various types of deposits, the FSCS only protects customers arising from financial services providers authorised by either the FCA or the PRA or each EU state regulator. Nonetheless, simultaneously, the UK has extended deposit insurance coverage to a larger range including deposits, investments, home finance, insurance business, and general insurance advice and arranging.[57] Furthermore, there are different compensation limits targeting different types of financial services, which are shown in Table 4.4.

It is noteworthy that, under the current UK banking market, consumers could hold multiple accounts in various banks, building societies, or credit unions that are subsidiaries of a big banking group. For example, Lloyds Bank, the Bank of Scotland and Halifax are all owned by the Lloyds Banking Group but operate business independently, with the Bank of Scotland and Halifax sharing the same single banking license. In response to such a situation, if a bank or a building society is separately authorised by the PRA, like Lloyds Bank and the Bank of Scotland, the FSCS would separately pay out a maximum of £85,000 per person per account. However, when the FSCS faces different banking brands that run business based on the same banking license, like what the Bank of Scotland and Halifax have done in the UK banking sector, customers holding multiple accounts in those different brands would receive compensation up to £85,000 in total, no matter how many accounts they have.[58]

Notably, the intention behind the current coverage limit is to meet the de facto coverage limit of the DGSD that requires each member state to comply with minimum protection at €100,000. Additionally, the FSCS increased its coverage limit

Table 4.4 Compensation Limits for Each Type of Financial Services

Types of Financial Services	*Compensation Limits*
Deposits	100% protection of £85,000
Investments	100% protection of £50,000
Home Finance	100% protection of £50,000
Insurance and General Insurance Advice and Arranging	1. No upper limit and 100% protection of claims that arise from compulsory insurance, professional indemnity insurance, and the death or incapacity of the policyholder due to injury, sickness, or infirmity. 2. 90% protection of other types of policy with no upper limit, excluding Goods in Transit, Marine, Aviation, Credit Insurance, and Contracts of reinsurance.

Data Source: the FSCS' official website.

by £10,000, from £75,000 to £85,000, on 30 January 2017, due to the continuous devaluation of the British pound after Brexit.[59] However, 'Does the UK need such a high coverage limit?' is in doubt, as this limit intends to primarily comply with the DGSD, neglecting the domestic situation.

According to Figure 4.1, until July 2018, amid weak wage growth and falling real incomes, the growth rates for personal savings have slowed to a record low level at 1.2 percent since the banking data started working in progress.[60] Despite the continuous decline of personal deposits in the wake of other weak economic data since 2016, the coverage limit has been boosted. Additionally, in light of the data disclosed by the UK Finance and Office for National Statistics, the total amount of personal deposits held in personal current and savings accounts have been approximately £841.9 billion, and the latest population estimate, including residents who have resided in the UK for more than 12 months, is around 66 million.[61] Thus, in light of an '80/20' rule proposed by the IADI that covers 80y percent of depositors but 20 to 30 percent of the value of total deposits,[62] the coverage limit of the FSCS should be from £31,890 to £47,835, which is far below the current £85,000.[63]

As elaborated in Figure 4.2, these statistics published by the Office for National Statistics in March 2018 reveal that the majority of people's total financial assets are far below £85,000, and the current UK coverage limit seems extremely high, protecting at least 88 percent of residences in the UK. Therefore, the majority of UK depositors, obviously, just need to care about interest returns with no incentive to oversee banks' performance before saving hard-earned deposits in host banks.

In other words, this coverage limit seems like an umbrella for wealthy communities. Individuals with more than £85,000 in savings can still get full protection by tactfully putting their excess money in different banks that have been separately authorised by either the PRA or the FCA. This indicates that wealthy individuals are going to get more advantages over ordinary depositors, and people with more than £85,000 in savings are the real beneficiaries of this high coverage limit.

Under this situation, UK financial regulators might pay equal attention to deposit insurance in comparison to prudential regulation, the principal participant of the financial safety net bolstering deposit protection, due to the absence of sufficient

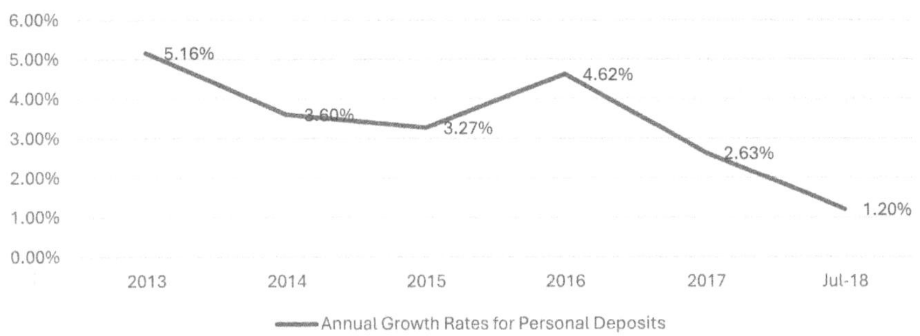

Figure 4.1 Annual Growth Rates for Personal Deposits
(Data Source: UK Finance)

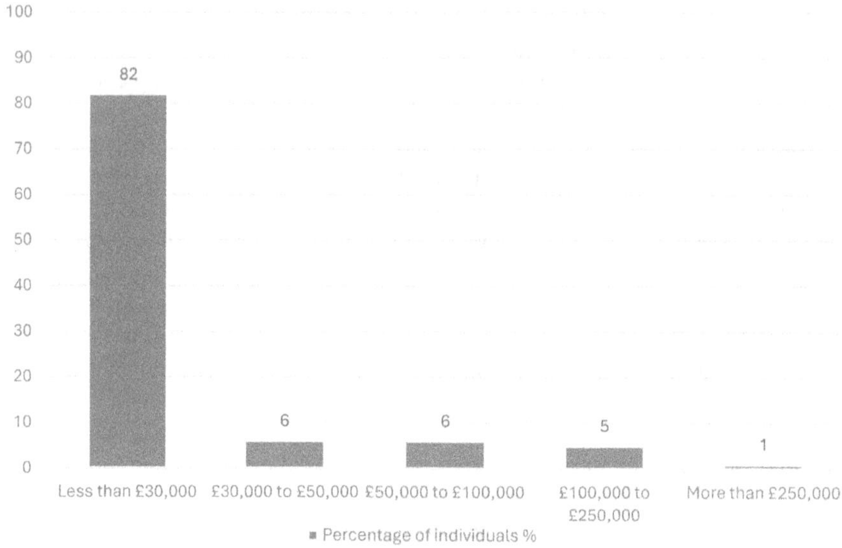

Figure 4.2 Total Value of All Formal Financial Assets Banded for All Individuals 16 Years and Over, UK July 2014 to June 2016

(Data Source: Office of National Statistics)

incentives for exerting market discipline from the majority of depositors. With a high coverage limit, it is unrealistic to incentivise depositors to monitor their bank accounts and banks' performance, which, however, may increase workloads for the regulators but give bankers relief.

The UK attempted to discipline both depositors and bankers by the introduction of co-insurance, but ultimately it proved unsuccessful during the Northern Rock run. Mervyn King, former Governor of the Bank of England, objects to co-insurance and says:

> If you have deposit insurance, there is no point having 90%, because that will not stop the bank run, as we saw, it has to be 100% but only up to some limit. In order to prevent banks taking excessive risks on the back of that deposit insurance – the moral hazard risk – it is much more important to have in place the special resolution regime whereby the authorities can get control of a bank that has been taking too many risks, particularly on the liquidity front.[64]

Besides, Blair *et al.* stress that co-insurance is a double-edged sword, as it not only offers an incentive for depositors to police banks but also increases the possibility of bank runs, simply because depositors are exposed to proportional losses.[65]

Therefore, setting a reasonable compensation limit that strikes a balance between public confidence and moral hazard is necessary for the UK deposit insurance scheme, as the current coverage limit of £85,000 might be too high and generous to protect a vast majority of depositors. A reasonable and fair coverage limit is not just revealed by a cold number, as it should consider various economic indexes including inflation and savings. After Brexit, without minimum requirements imposed by EU directives, the UK may have the autonomy to decide its own compensation limit in terms of reducing the current limit and setting its coverage limit based on the IADI's 80/20 rule.

4.3.4 Compensation

In terms of compensation, the FSCS has been responsible for paying out covered depositors in pursuit of reasonably possible and cost-effective results.[66] Under the current scheme, the FSCS, instead of depositors, undertakes outright legal rights to claim covered deposits back. Regarding covered deposits, the FSCS has super-preferred priority in the insolvency proceedings, indicating that covered deposits would be paid first. In addition, uncovered deposits of individuals and small and medium-sized enterprises (SMEs) still have a priority over unsecured creditors but behind covered deposits. This is to say, in most cases, the FSCS acts as a creditor with priority.

Simultaneously, to achieve reasonably possible and cost-effective results, the Banking Act 2009 provides natural advantages for the FSCS to claim insured deposits back. In Section 99 of the Banking Act 2009:

(1) A bank liquidator has two objectives;
(2) Objective 1 is to work with the FSCS so as to ensure that, as soon as is reasonably practicable, each eligible depositor;
    (a) has the relevant account transferred to another financial institution, or;
    (b) receives payment from (or on behalf of) the FSCS;
(3) Objective 2 is to wind up the affairs of the bank so as to achieve the best result for the bank's creditors as a whole;
(4) Objective 1 takes precedence over Objective 2.[67]

In light of this section, the FSCS, aimed at paying out depositors within seven days after a failure, is capable of performing functions in bank insolvency by working closely with bank liquidators and handing over prompt payouts to depositors by requesting information from a banking liquidator.[68]

Meanwhile, the Single Customer View (SCV), an approach to seize the vast majority of individuals' deposit accounts, is being applied by the FSCS, enabling each deposit taker to file precise information in relation to individuals' deposit accounts.[69] Along with the SCV, the FSCS is capable of requiring a banking liquidator to provide further information it needs to accomplish a faster payout.[70] As a result, the FDIC has adopted the SCV to carry out faster payouts, indicating that accurate account data and the latest information submitted by banking liquidators and deposit takers play an essential role in the pursuit of reimbursing depositors within seven days after a failure. When a payout is completed, the FSCS automatically replaces covered depositors and becomes a creditor of failing banks, and a member of the Liquidation Committee collaborates with bank liquidators to reach the maximum value of a banks' assets.

However, although the procedures for payouts in the UK have been accelerated, some challenges faced by the FSCS still exist and need to be addressed. First, the SCV mainly relies on accurate data and the latest information in relation to depositors' accounts. So, one big challenge is that the FSCS has very weak agency discretion to ensure that all deposit takers can submit and update information required on time. Given the current UK regulatory architecture, enacting hard rules within relevant laws for the FSCS to require deposit takers to notify any substantial change is necessary. Second, conducting a faster payout can be regarded as a team effort with various parties involved in this process. This is to say, cohesive and consistent regulatory collaboration and regulatory arrangements should be well-designed.

4.4 Lessons Learned from the Run on the Rock

4.4.1 Lessons on UK Institutional Structure

In the wake of the GFC following the US sub-prime mortgage crisis, Northern Rock, the UK's fifth-largest mortgage lender headquartered in the North East of England, became the first UK bank to fail due to a bank run since 1878.[71] Owing to aggressive expansion in international lending markets and a global liquidity squeeze, Northern Rock eventually encountered a liquidity shortage and called for liquidity support from the Bank of England, which was responsible for acting as a lender of last resort in the UK.[72] Later, the Tripartite Authorities (including HM Treasury, the Bank of England and the Financial Services Authority) unanimously reached an agreement to provide liquidity support. However, in the meantime, market rumours of Northern Rock's liquidity crisis spread to the public domain, resulting in thousands of depositors queuing outside branches of Northern Rock to withdraw their savings.[73] Eventually, despite the Bank of England providing liquidity support, it failed to relieve public concerns, and Northern Rock became insolvent.

The 'Run on the Rock' has led to the overhaul of the previous regulatory framework in the UK. Before the current 'twin peaks' regulatory structure, the UK had adopted the Tripartite Authorities since the election of the Labour Government in 1997. Under the former Tripartite regulatory architecture, both the Bank of England and the FSA received critical criticism for their failures in monitoring Northern Rock.[74] In this case, the FSA was responsible for taking charge of prudential regulation and supervision, and the Bank of England was responsible for maintaining financial stability and implementing the functions of lender of last resort. However, the FSA failed to issue a warning on the aggressive strategy of Northern Rock, and the Bank of England rejected Northern Rock's first request for liquidity support. Alongside the Northern Rock run, the Bank of England, regarded as the guardian of financial stability, lacked efficient access to individual institutions, which, in contrast, was the responsibility of the FSA. As noted by Campbell, the Bank of England seemed unconscious of the looming loopholes of Northern Rock for some time, implying poor communication and coordination between the two major UK financial authorities despite the existence of a Memorandum of Understanding.[75]

Having realised this problem, a comprehensive overhaul of the UK financial regulatory institutional structure was put in place. The most essential reform was the introduction of the twin peaks regulatory model, in which the function of prudential regulation was transferred to the PRA, a new prudential regulator created under the Bank of England, and conduct supervision was distributed to the FCA, an independent regulator inheriting most functions from the FSA apart from prudential regulation. These institutional changes reflected the UK's solution to addressing poor coordination. However, MacNeil points out that flaws still exist in the new regulatory framework, such as the ambiguity of responsibility between prudential regulation and conduct supervision, and the expansion of mandates of the Bank of England.[76]

4.4.2 Lessons on the UK Deposit Insurance Scheme

The Northern Rock run has simultaneously compelled the UK government to reconsider deposit protection. Deposit insurance, as a significant participant of the financial safety net, has also been a suggested integration into the regulatory framework since the Northern Rock crisis.[77] The Northern Rock crisis demonstrated a complete failure of the UK deposit protection scheme, as it can be proved that, after the Northern Rock run, the government blanket guarantee eventually stepped in to restore public confidence and maintain financial stability. Alistair Darling, the former Chancellor, made an announcement:

> Should it be necessary, we, with the Bank of England, would put in place arrangements that would guarantee all the existing deposits in Northern Rock during the current instability in the financial markets. This means that people can continue to take their money out of Northern Rock. But if they choose to leave their money in Northern Rock, it will be guaranteed safe and secure.[78]

Failure to prevent the collapse of Northern Rock implies a total failure of the FSCS, the UK's deposit insurance scheme.

During the Northern Rock run, the UK adopted co-insurance that provided depositors with 100 percent protection of the first £2,000 but 90 percent protection of the next £33,000, indicating maximum losses of £3,300.[79] It was not surprising that depositors of Northern Rock queued in a long line to withdraw their savings, because the coverage limit, at that time, was considered to be inadequate and depositors could only receive full protection of the first £2,000.

Besides, co-insurance means that depositors' compensation claims could not be fulfilled in full, so that they might become creditors of failed banks, in a disadvantaged position.[80] Even though the motivation of co-insurance is to encourage depositors to monitor host banks by allowing depositors to suffer losses, most depositors, at the beginning stage of the Northern Rock run, seemed unaware of the FSCS and how they were protected by the UK deposit insurance scheme. However, in practice, it is unfair to allow most depositors who are in a disadvantaged place to afford losses, as information asymmetry is the principal hurdle impeding depositors from understanding what dangers they have to encounter with host banks. In addition, deposit insurance is totally different from commercial insurance, as in normal commercial insurance, the insured people have control over their behaviours. For example, drivers could drive cars carefully in order to mitigate car accidents, thereby receiving lower premiums on their next car insurance contract as a reward.

However, depositors could not carry out any real action to stop a bank failure. Unlike public goods, the banking sector is too skilled and specific, so it is unrealistic to have high expectations of encouraging depositors, especially most ordinary depositors, to exert market discipline. Therefore, what financial regulators should do is carefully oversee banks' activities in lieu of depositors, because they have powers and mandates granted by legislation and have annual budgets arising from taxpayers. The FSA, the Bank of England, and HM Treasury published a consultation paper to acknowledge that although co-insurance produces incentives for depositors to monitor banks, it drives depositors to withdraw their savings when a bank appears to have financial difficulties.[81] The Northern Rock run was a landmark case demonstrating that co-insurance did not work well and that 100 percent protection with a high but limited coverage could be more appropriate. Ultimately, 100 percent coverage with a high but limited coverage limit has been applied to UK deposit insurance.

At the same time, the Northern Rock run reflected an inadequate coverage limit within the UK deposit insurance scheme. It is clear that a high coverage limit could bring confidence to depositors, but a rational limit is significantly needed. The previous £35,000 was obviously too low to meet depositors' expectations, and long queues outside each branch of Northern Rock were convincing evidence reflecting the reality of depositors' anxiety. Subsequently, the UK coverage limit was increased to £50,000, and, as of the end of 2010, the limit was boosted to the current limit of £85,000. Interestingly, the current limit of £85,000 has been determined by EU directives, not by the actual UK situation. Nevertheless, as discussed above, the current UK coverage limit is too generous, as it is far from the average level.[82] Of course, the EU directive is a key element, but political pressure, aimed at retaining a stable economy and social order, is also a prominent influence, especially when the Northern Rock run commenced, the UK government had considered raising the limit to £100,000.[83] As critically viewed by Campbell:

> A government which is perceived as having taken no action to prevent the failure of a bank may find that its popularity with voters has diminished and this could, of course, have an adverse effect on its chances of re-election.[84]

Ideally, the deposit insurance coverage limit should be dynamic to follow real economic conditions, including the growth of wages, the average saving amount, and fintech, so as to maintain financial stability and consistently protect the most ordinary depositors, not just a small proportion of wealthy depositors. The IADI also suggests that the deposit insurance coverage limit should be reviewed periodically, as the coverage limit may become impractical over time, for example, in the UK's co-insurance used during the Northern Rock run.[85] However, in reality, adjustments to a dynamic deposit insurance coverage limit might be expensive and frequent, requiring deposit insurers to keep depositors updated on any substantial changes, which could produce extra costs and confuse the public.

Public awareness that refers to depositors' perception of the risk of saving money in a bank and the characteristics of a deposit insurance system is another deficiency exposed during the Northern Rock run. Prior to the 'Run on the Rock', the FSCS and the FSA did not work well on promoting consumer understanding in relation to financial services and UK financial markets. Given the absence of publicising what deposit insurance is and what deposit insurance can protect, it was to be understood that public concerns and confusion regarding Northern Rock were reasonable. Singh and LaBrosse add that UK consumers underrate threats posed by banks and financial derivatives.[86] A parliamentary report with respect to the Northern Rock run again emphasises the importance of depositors' awareness, saying that not only is a well-advertised scheme a prerequisite for maintaining financial stability, but also depositors should understand the basic features of deposit insurance.[87]

Modern banks that play an irreplaceable role in people's daily lives are highly interconnected, so one bank run could trigger contagion across the entire banking industry, severely impacting countries' economic growth and people's lives. Therefore, time is the enemy, and it is not reasonable to apply liquidation proceedings or court orders. Financial regulators should carry out effective intervention and resolution as fast as possible. The FSCS has been the last resort for depositors who have deposited their money in the UK. However, until now, the FSCS still has no power in rule-making and dealing with failing banks, except banks in default. The Northern Rock run has been a great opportunity for FSCS to evolve from a pay box model to a risk-minimiser with government backing to collect ex-ante premiums.[88] As a deposit insurer, the FSCS has an advantage over other financial regulators in addressing failing banks, as it captures comprehensive information on individual saving accounts through the SCV. However, unfortunately, the only thing the FSCS can do in banking resolution at the present stage, is provide the required information. By and large, the most impressive lesson learnt from the Northern Rock run is that it is compulsory to have effective deposit protection.[89]

4.5 Prospective Reforms of the UK Deposit Insurance Scheme

Since the Northern Rock run, owing to a constantly changing economic climate, the UK deposit insurance scheme still needs to be improved. In the meantime, compared with the FDIC in the US, the FSCS is placed in a very weak position against bank collapses, for instance, the failure of Northern Rock. Although there has been no bank run since the Northern Rock run, the UK government should have a vision for optimising its deposit insurance scheme against future crises, as pro-cyclicality is the basic feature of the financial system.[90]

As a risk-based levies mechanism has been initiated in the UK, it is time to integrate the FSCS into the UK financial regulatory framework and expand the

FSCS's powers and mandates in banking resolution. At present, prudential regulation and supervision, deposit insurance, and lender of last resort, the three major pillars of the financial safety net, have fulfilled an important function in maintaining financial stability.[91] Under present UK financial regulation, the PRA and the FCA take charge of prudential regulation and supervision and conduct supervision; the FSCS is responsible for managing the UK deposit insurance scheme; and the Bank of England undertakes the function of lender of last resort. Although the deposit insurer is so important in financial regulation, since the launch of the FSCS in 2001, the FSCS has not been granted legislative discretion, powers, or mandates to carry out de facto regulatory action that protects depositors, barring the function of compensating depositors.

Simultaneously, the function of 'SCV' that helps the FSCS capture the latest information associated with individual depositors should be extended, as the FSCS is expected to engage in bank resolution by having access to implement on-site examinations and on-site due diligence when a bank encounters financial difficulties that might trigger a bank run. One important reason to carry out such developments is directly related to time saving, because preventing a bank run is a race against time, as proven by the cases of Northern Rock and Lehman Brothers. When the FSCS discovers urgent flaws in deposit takers, due to the absence of regulatory powers and mandates, the FSCS cannot cope with flaws in a timely manner and might request further information regarding individual saving accounts from bank liquidators in order to prompt payouts, thereby missing the golden opportunity to save a bank.

Along with broad mandates, the FSCS could accomplish its mission of maintaining public confidence and protecting consumers. In the Northern Rock run, it was clear that the FSCS did not actively engage in stopping the run, despite very few bank runs in the UK. The Northern Rock run has illustrated that the FSCS, with a pay box model could not achieve its major objective of maintaining public confidence and consumer protection. This implies that the UK should ponder a proactive overhaul to pinpoint the role of the FSCS because the current arrangement of the FSCS is neither well-designed nor fully functioning to achieve its purpose.

As a starting point, the UK should rearrange statutory objectives for each financial regulator within relevant laws, as well as balance different objectives among multiple financial regulators. Kryzanowski suggests that pay box model deposit insurance schemes incur higher losses arising from bank failures and delay the timing of closing a troubled bank that may try to recapitalise in pursuit of survival.[92] He simultaneously underlines that encouraging uninsured depositors and other interested parties to join the monitoring team has been proven unreliable by studying US bank and thrift failures, and that having a deposit insurer with broad mandates is achievable to diversify judgements on the same case, thereby averting the significant errors made by concentrated regulatory framework, as a deposit insurer with broad mandates could make decisions from different points of view.[93]

If the UK determines to shift the FSCS from a pay box model to a risk-minimiser model, the whole UK regulatory structure would have to be reshuffled. At the very beginning, the legislation should appropriately redefine and distinguish the mandates, responsibilities, and powers between the FSCS and other financial regulators, because under this assumption the FSCS will have substantial powers and mandates to address troubled banks via various measures such as closure or liquidation proceedings.[94] Subsequently, the FSCS should be enabled to implement prompt corrective action and engage in a special resolution regime when necessary for tackling a troubled bank. Compared with the US banking sector that currently has 4,805 banks, the UK banking sector, which currently has a total of 345 banks and building societies, is much smaller and more concentrated, implying that the implementation of prompt corrective action in the UK might be easier and faster to bring into effect.[95] The implementation of prompt corrective action based on capital categories in the US has been considered successful in maintaining financial stability. Hence, the easiest way for the UK is to follow the most successful pioneer, as the UK in 2017 followed the US to initiate a risk-based levies mechanism, despite the use of a simpler measure faced with US measures.[96]

In theory, prompt corrective action might be a good weapon for the FSCS when it becomes a risk-minimiser deposit insurer. This is to say, the FSCS is capable of determining which bank should be closed based on prompt corrective action, coupled with knowing the latest risk level of each bank through using risk-based levies. During the Northern Rock run, the FSCS seemed like a spectator that could not do anything, and the hesitation of the Tripartite Authorities led to the delay of closure that cost billions of taxpayers' money. This assumption empowers the FSCS to take prerequisite action devoted to stopping banks' deterioration, as well as to close troubled banks before they get worse. Simultaneously, as stated by Kaufman, a feasible closure of a bank must contain prompt corrective action because it not only offers sufficient time for financial regulators to act promptly but also pushes financial regulators to close financially troubled banks that breach the minimum capital requirement without surprise and delay.[97]

Besides, the FSCS could boldly go further by acting as a banking liquidator. Modern banks, after years of evolution, have become so special and influential in current society that people's day-to-day lives and business transactions cannot proceed without banks. In the meantime, the most visible characteristic modern banks have is that they are interconnected, meaning that one bank could trigger a 'domino effect' in financial markets, leading to outright financial markets so as to lead to systemic crisis. Therefore, a specific financial authority is needed to promptly resolve bank collapses in pursuit of financial stability.

In the current UK situation, the FSCS can be regarded as a good option to take over the function of being a banking liquidator. First, the FSCS taking charge of all legal rights of depositors to claim deposits back is a natural advantage over other UK financial regulators, indicating that the FSCS can be deemed a creditor with priority in claiming covered deposits, which provides the FSCS with convenience in bank liquidation proceedings. This is to say, the FSCS has already been placed in an ideal position before it actually becomes a banking liquidator. Thus, it is expected that the FSCS could be given a strengthened role in banking liquidation proceedings in relation to depositor protection and banking resolution. Additionally, although the SCV has obtained the majority of individual saving accounts, under the current legal framework it still sometimes needs additional help from banking liquidators. Apart from mandates, time is the biggest enemy against bank runs, which has been proved by many bank failures, particularly the Northern Rock crisis. Therefore, enabling the FSCS to become a banking liquidator might make banking resolution time-saving and more efficient, as the FSCS can first pay out covered depositors and then respond to other creditors' claims in compliance with winding-up orders.

Moreover, this assumption of strengthening the functions of the FSCS in bank resolution and bank insolvency means that the UK's way to resolve troubled banks deviates from court orders and turns to the US's mechanism for dealing with troubled banks. However, even the US has massive debates about whether to tackle bank insolvency via court orders or agency discretion. Apparently, the most notable contribution brought by agency discretion is time-saving and efficiency, despite weaknesses including political interference and regulatory forbearance by way of agency discretion.[98]

The major advantage of consolidating the role of the FSCS in banking resolution is that a clear and consistent policy and objective would be in place to resolve troubled banks from the verge of collapse to insolvency proceedings. This hypothesis would maintain public confidence by eliminating uncertainty concerning how depositors will be repaid in case of banking liquidation, as uncertainty is a main driving force behind bank runs and most depositors would rush to withdraw their savings as soon as possible in order to get the full amounts of their savings back. Besides, policies and objectives should remain flexible and leave freedom for regulatory decisions made by the FSCS. The Treasury Committee of the House of Commons has recommended that the UK deposit insurer can learn lessons from the FDIC, which undertakes responsibilities to resolve troubled banks and manage deposit insurance.[99] Furthermore, given the prospect of the FSCS, various options and recommendations proposed by the IADI and other international financial organisations for being a risk-minimising deposit insurer can be taken into account.

Public awareness is the other essential foundation for the UK to build up an effective deposit insurance scheme. Northern Rock was a profound lesson that taught the UK how important public understanding of how deposit insurance runs in practice is. At the same time, the FSCS has been criticised for not providing necessary information related to deposit protection. At the present stage, depositor protection rules of the PRA Rulebook require all authorised banks, building societies, and credit unions to inform all their customers about the responsibility, mission, and existence of the FSCS.[100] Alongside depositor protection rules, all authorised deposit takers have to display the FSCS's posters in a prominent place in each branch.[101] Although the FSCS has made a great effort to enhance public education on deposit insurance since Northern Rock, it is not enough, and the FSCS still needs to strive for a credible image like the FDIC and the Canada Deposit Insurance Corporation (CDIC). As for public education, the FDIC runs a public education programme that uses various tools to promote the understanding of deposit insurance in the long term, for example, delivering seminars and training to employees or bankers of insured financial institutions and broadcasting a series of advertisements about deposit insurance via national and regional media.[102] Next to the US, the CDIC also has a sufficient budget for running a long-term education and training programme on the rationale and shortcomings of deposit insurance.

Therefore, for promoting public awareness of deposit insurance in the UK, some suggestions should be taken into account. First, the FSCS should be strengthened with broad mandates and powers to perform the functions of deposit insurance, so that the FSCS is capable of collecting information associated with deposit protection in a more efficient way that ensures the FSCS has sufficient preparation in response to bank runs.[103] And then, by learning lessons from Northern Rock, the FSCS should set up a specific budget to run various public education programmes including advertisements on deposit insurance, regular training sessions for bankers, employees, and depositors, and communication tools on a regular basis. Finally, with a strengthened role, the FSCS should closely coordinate with the Bank of England, the PRA, and the FCA in order to avoid information asymmetry, the main hurdle for making a correct determination.

4.6 Conclusion

After the Northern Rock run during the GFC, the FSCS underwent a series of significant alterations attempting to consolidate the FSCS's role in dealing with troubled financial institutions in the UK banking industry. This chapter has provided a comprehensive study of how the FSCS works, associated with its functions regarding deposit protection, and radical suggestions for the FSCS's further involvement in banking resolution.

The FSCS is a classical pay box model deposit insurer in accordance with the IADI's classification of worldwide deposit insurers. The collapse of Northern Rock during the GFC has completely demonstrated a total failure of the UK deposit insurance scheme, revealing various shortcomings of the FSCS. After the GFC, the FSCS has shifted from a basic pay box model to a pay-box-plus model, with a strengthened role in promoting the effectiveness of deposit insurance and resolving troubled banks. For example, it can be seen that co-insurance, which was proven useless and unrealistic by the Northern Rock Run, was repealed, a risk-based premiums assessment has been installed, and the new function of the SCV has been allocated to the FSCS for capturing individual saving accounts from deposit takers. However, these improvements are not enough to meet current demands.

It is suggested by the author that the FSCS should be granted the responsibility to carry out prompt action against troubled deposit takers that threaten financial stability. By comparing the FDIC, it is evident that a deposit insurer with broad mandates and sufficient information may take prompt and accurate action against troubled banks, as the SCV, a new measure for the FSCS to collect information, could assist the FSCS in capturing detailed and accurate account information, providing the FSCS with a natural advantage over other financial regulators in dealing with troubled financial institutions.

In addition, it is noteworthy that, after Brexit, the FSCS may not need to comply with minimum requirements set out by EU directives, which produces uncertainty for the future direction of the UK deposit insurance scheme. Therefore, the prospect of the FSCS that currently abides by EU directives is uncertain. By and large, although there is uncertainty associated with the future of the FSCS, it is clear that the FSCS will still play a consistent role in the UK deposit insurance scheme. Despite having been criticised during the GFC, the FSCS is still regarded as a good example for emerging countries that wish to build up a primary deposit insurance scheme.

Notes

1 Catherine R. Schenk, 'Summer in the City: Banking Failures of 1974 and the Development of International Banking Supervision' (2014) 129 *The English Historical Review*, 1129, 1156.
2 The Single Customer View will be explained and discussed in the Compensation section.
3 Edward P. M. Gardener, 'Supervision in the United Kingdom' in Edward P. M. Gardener (ed), *UK Banking Supervision: Evolution, Practice and Issues* (Allen & Unwin, 1986).
4 *Ibid.*
5 Andrew Campbell and Peter Cartwright, 'Co-insurance and Moral Hazard: Some Reflections on Deposit Protection in the UK and USA' (2003) 5 *Journal of International Banking Regulation*, 11.
6 Andrew Campbell and Peter Cartwright, *Banks in Crisis: The Legal Response* (Ashgate, 2002).
7 The Banking Act 1979, s 21.
8 The Banking Act 1979, s 27.
9 The Banking Act 1979, s 29.
10 Mike Buckle and John Thompson, *The UK Financial System: Theory and Practice* (Manchester University Press, 2004).
11 The Banking Act 1987, s 31.
12 Patricia Jackson, 'Deposit Protection and Bank Failures in the United Kingdom' (1996) 38 *Financial Stability Review*, 39.
13 Farah Halime et al., 'Financial Regulation: Who is Watching Whom' *Financial Times* (London, 30 July 2009) <http://ig-legacy.ft.com/content/313aeca4-7864-11de-bb06-00144feabdc0#axzz5HTlfzfNy> accessed 20 January 2024.
14 The Financial Services and Markets Act 2000, s 212.
15 The Financial Services and Markets Act 2000, s 213.
16 Andrew Campbell and Peter Cartwright, 'Co-insurance and Moral Hazard: Some Reflections on Deposit Protection in the UK and USA' (n5) 19.
17 Directive 2014/49/EU of the European Parliament and of the Council of 14 April 2014 on Deposit Guarantee Schemes.
18 Nikoletta Kleftouri, 'Rethink UK and EU Bank Deposit Insurance' (2013) 24 *European Business Law Review*, 105.
19 FSCS, 'Vision for a Confident Future' (FSCS, London, 2015) <https://www.fscs.org.uk/uploaded_files/Publications/201219_fscs_5-year_vision_2014_web.pdf> accessed 10 October 2023.
20 *Ibid.*
21 FSA, 'The Turner Review: A Regulatory Response to the Global Banking Crisis' (FSA, London, 2009) <http://www.fsa.gov.uk/pubs/other/turner_review.pdf> accessed 10 January 2024.
22 Brooke Masters, 'FSA to Give Away to "Twin Peaks' System"' *Financial Times* (London, 1 April 2013) <https://www.ft.com/content/32ebdd78-97bf-11e2-97e0-00144feabdc0> accessed 10 December 2023.

23 FSMA 2000, s 2 A.
24 FCA, 'FCA Mission: Our Approach to Authorisation' (FCA, December 2017) <https://www.fca.org.uk/publication/corporate/our-approach-authorisation.pdf> accessed 20 December 2023.
25 FSMA 2000, s 1 B
26 Bank of England Act, s 9 C.
27 FSMA 2000, s 217 A.
28 Timothy Edmonds, 'Banking Services: Reform and Issues' (House of Commons, London, December 2017) < https://researchbriefings.parliament.uk/ResearchBriefing/Summary/CBP-7234> accessed 20 December 2023.
29 FSCS, 'Annual Report and Account 2016/17' (FSCS, London, 2017) <https://secure.viewer.zmags.com/publication/381260a7#/381260a7/1> accessed 12 December 2019.
30 FSMA 2000, s 212 and s 213.
31 FSMA 2000, s 214 A.
32 Banking Act 2009, s 170 (1).
33 FCA, 'Financial Services Compensation Scheme Funding Review Instrument 2018' (FCA, London, 2018) <https://www.handbook.fca.org.uk/instrument/2018/FCA_2018_29.pdf> accessed 13 December 2019.
34 See Bank of England at https://www.bankofengland.co.uk/prudential-regulation/authorisations/financial-services-compensation-scheme.
35 Ibid.
36 See the FSCS 'Levy Information' https://www.fscs.org.uk/industry/funding/levy-information/.
37 Nick Kochan, 'The Fuss over FSCS' (2001) 12 *Operational Risk & Regulation*, 30.
38 Ian Pollock, 'Keydata: Where Did £450m of Investors' Money Go?' BBC (London, 16 June 2010) < https://www.bbc.co.uk/news/10273314> accessed 10 October 2023.
39 Joanna Gray, 'Judicial Review of Financial Services Compensation Scheme's Exercise of Power to Impose Compensation Costs Levy' (2011) 19 *Journal of Financial Regulation and Compliance*, 203.
40 Nick Kochan, 'The Fuss over FSCS' (n37).
41 PRA, 'Calculating risk-based levies for the Financial Services Compensation Scheme Deposit Class' (PRA, London, 2017) <https://www.bankofengland.co.uk/-/media/boe/files/prudential-regulation/statement-of-policy/2017/calculating-risk-based-levies-for-the-fscs-deposits-class-sop-update.pdf?la=en&hash=AAA45341CF34A1584C02C425F459CA20FF59BEBE> accessed 19 October 2023.
42 The aggregate risk weight ranges from 75 percent to 150 percent based on European Banking Authority Guidelines.
43 PRA, 'Calculating risk-based levies for the Financial Services Compensation Scheme Deposit Class' (n41).
44 FCA, 'Handbook Fee 6 Financial Services Compensation Scheme Funding' (FCA, London) < https://www.handbook.fca.org.uk/handbook/FEES/6/?view=chapter> accessed 10 September 2023.
45 See FSCS letter, available at https://www.fca.org.uk/publication/fees-information/fscs-supplementary-levies-march-2018.pdf.
46 FSCS, 'Class Statements 2017/18' (FSCS, June 2018) <https://www.fscs.org.uk/globalassets/annual-reports-and-class-statements/fscs-class-statements-2017-18.pdf> accessed 20 October 2023.
47 Treasury Committee, *The Run on the Rock (fifth report)* (HC 2007-08, 56-) 98-103.
48 Bank of England, HM Treasury and FSA, 'Financial Stability and Depositor Protection: Further Consultation' (Bank of England, HM Treasury, and FSA, July 2008) <https://assets.publishing.service.gov.uk/government/uploads/system/uploads/attachment_data/file/243379/7436.pdf> accessed 17 July 2023.
49 Treasury Committee, *The Run on the Rock* (n47).

50 Ibid.
51 Ibid.
52 IADI, 'Enhanced Guidance for Effective Deposit Insurance Systems: Ex-Ante Funding Guidance Paper' (International Association of Deposit Insurer, June 2015) <http://www.iadi.org/en/assets/File/Papers/Approved%20Guidance%20Papers/IADI_Enhanced_Guidance_on_Ex-Ante_Funding_June_2015.pdf> accessed 9 July 2024.
53 Following the meltdown of the Bank of Credit and Commerce International (BCCI), the deposit protection scheme guaranteed 75 percent of a maximum qualified £20,000. After that, prior to 1 October 2007, the FSCS provided 100 percent protection to the first £2,000 and 90 percent protection of next £33,000.
54 FSA, 'Consumer Compensation: A Further Consultation' (FSA, London, June 1999) <https://www.fscs.org.uk/uploaded_files/Publications/unknown/Consultation_24.pdf> accessed 20 July 2019, also see Maximilian J. B. Hall, 'The Reform of Federal Deposit Insurance: The Options' (1990) 43 *PSL Quarterly Review*, 445.
55 Andrew Campbell and Peter Cartwright, 'Co-insurance and Moral Hazard: Some Reflections on Deposit Protection in the UK and USA' (n5) 16.
56 Ronald MacDonald, 'Deposit Insurance' (1996) Bank of England, Handbooks in Central Banking No. 9.
57 See the FSCS official website at https://www.fscs.org.uk/what-we-cover/compensation-limits/).
58 See the FSCS official website at https://www.fscs.org.uk/what-we-cover/banks-building-societies/.
59 Directive 2014/49/EU of the European Parliament and of the Council of 16 April 2014 on Deposit Guarantee Schemes recasting Directives 94/19/EC [2014] OJ L173/149.
60 Fergal O'Brien, 'UK Squeeze Hits Workers as Savings Rate Falls to Record Low' *Bloomberg* (London, 24 August) available at <https://www.bloomberg.com/news/articles/2018-08-24/u-k-squeeze-hits-workers-as-savings-rate-falls-to-record-low> accessed 10 January 2024.
61 The data on savings was gathered from UK Finance, and the population numbers are from the Office for National Statistics.
62 IADI, 'Enhanced Guidance for Effective Deposit Insurance Systems: Deposit Insurance Coverage' (IADI, March 2013) <https://www.iadi.org/en/assets/File/Papers/Approved%20Guidance%20Papers/IADI_Coverage_Enhanced_Guidance_Paper.pdf> accessed 10 July 2024.
63 The statistics of total sterling deposits are made by UK Finance, available at https://www.ukfinance.org.uk/statistics/high-street-banking/, and the population estimate is cast by the Office for National Statistics, available at https://www.ons.gov.uk/peoplepopulationandcommunity/populationandmigration/populationestimates.
64 Treasury Committee, Examination of Witness on Mervyn King and Sir John Gieve (HC 2007-08) Questions 1740, 1749.
65 Christine E. Blair, Frederick Carns, and Rose M. Kushmeider, 'Instituting a Deposit Insurance System: Why? How?' In Andrew Campbell, John Raymond Labrosse, David G. Mayes, and Dalvinder Singh (eds), *Deposit Insurance* (Palgrave 2007).
66 See FSCS official website, available at https://www.fscs.org.uk/about-fscs/technical-information/sub-schemes/funding/recoveries/.
67 The Banking Act 2009, s 99.
68 FSMA, s 200 and 201A.
69 COMP 17.2.4R and COMP 17.2.3R(2).
70 FSMA, s 200 and 201A.
71 *The Economist*, 'Lessons of the Fall: Northern Rock' *The Economist* (London, 18 October 2007) available at https://www.economist.com/briefing/2007/10/18/lessons-of-the-fall accessed 17 November 2023.
72 Treasury Committee, *The Run on the Rock* (n47).

73 Dominic O'Connell, 'The Collapse of Northern Rock: Ten Years On' BBC (London, 12 September 2017) available at https://www.bbc.co.uk/news/business-41229513 accessed 17 November 2023.

74 Andrew Campbell, 'The Run on the Rock and Its Consequences' (2008) 9 *Journal of Banking Regulation*, 62.

75 *Ibid.*

76 Iain MacNeil, 'The Trajectory of Regulatory Reform in the UK in the Wake of the Financial Crisis' (2010) 11 *European Business Organization Law Review*, 492.

77 Andrew Campbell, 'The Run on the Rock and Its Consequences' (n74).

78 Richard Blackden and Katie Franklin, 'Government Guarantees Northern Rock Funds' *The Telegraph* (London, 17 September 2007) available at https://www.telegraph.co.uk/news/uknews/1563321/Government-guarantees-Northern-Rock-funds.html accessed 10 November 2023.

79 Andrew Campbell and Peter Cartwright, 'Co-insurance and Moral Hazard: Some Reflections on Deposit Protection in the UK and USA' (n5).

80 Dalvinder Singh and John R. LaBrosse, 'Northern Rock, Depositors and Deposit Insurance Coverage: Some Critical Reflections' (2010) 2 *Journal of Business Law*, 66.

81 HM Treasury, FSA, and Bank of England, 'Financial Stability and Depositor Protection: Strengthening the Framework' (London, January 2008) <https://assets.publishing.service.gov.uk/government/uploads/system/uploads/attachment_data/file/243413/7308.pdf> accessed 20 October 2023.

82 EU Directive of Deposit Guarantee Schemes requires each member state to increase coverage to €100,000.

83 David G. Mayes and Geoffrey Wood, 'Lessons from the Northern Rock Episode' in Robert R. Bliss and George G. Kaufman (eds) *Financial Institutions and Markets: 2007–2008 The Year of Crisis* (Springer 2009).

84 Andrew Campbell, 'Bank Insolvency and the Interests of Creditors' (2004) 7 *Journal of Banking Regulation*, 133.

85 IADI, 'Enhanced Guidance for Effective Deposit Insurance Systems: Deposit Insurance Coverage' (n62).

86 Dalvinder Singh and John R. LaBrosse, 'Northern Rock, Depositors and Deposit Insurance Coverage: Some Critical Reflections' (n80).

87 Treasury Committee, *The Run on the Rock* (n47).

88 John R. LaBrosse, 'Time to Fix the Plumbing: Improving the UK Framework Following the Collapse of Northern Rock' (2008) 9 *Journal of Banking Regulation*, 295.

89 Andrew Campbell and Paula Moffatt, 'UK Depositor Protection in the Aftermath of the Banking Crisis' (2010) 25 *Journal of International Banking Law and Regulation*, 487.

90 Xiaochuan Zhou, 'Changing Pro-Cyclicality for Financial and Economic Stability' (G20 Meeting of Financial Ministers and Central Bank Governors, São Paulo, 15 November 2008).

91 Financial Stability Forum, 'Guidance for Developing Effective Insurance Systems' (FSF, Basel, September 2001) <http://www.fsb.org/wp-content/uploads/r_0109b.pdf?page_moved=1> accessed 10 November 2023.

92 Lawrence Kryzanowski, 'Organizational Design and Positioning of the Deposit Insurance Function in the Financial System Safety Net' in Andrew Campbell, John Raymond LaBrosse, David G, Mayes and Dalvinder Singh (eds), *Deposit Insurance* (Palgrave 2007).

93 *Ibid.*

94 The IADI recommends that the mandate selected for a deposit insurer should be clearly and formally specified. A deposit insurer should have all powers necessary to fulfil its mandate, and all these mandates and powers should be clearly defined and formally specified via legislation or documents accompanying legislation. See IADI, 'Core Principles for Effective Deposit Insurance Systems: A Methodology for Compliance

Assessment' (Basel, December 2010) <https://www.bis.org/publ/bcbs192.pdf> accessed 16 November 2023.

95 The number of banks in the US can be found in the 'Conditions and Incomes for All Insured US Banks Report' by the Federal Financial Institutions Examination Council at https://ycharts.com/indicators/sources/ffiec, and the number of banks in the UK can be shown in the 'List of Banks' as Compiled by the Bank of England at https://www.bankofengland.co.uk/-/media/boe/files/prudential-regulation/authorisations/which-firms-does-the-pra-regulate/bankslist1801.pdf.

96 George G. Kaufman, *Prompt Corrective Action: 10 Years Later* (JAI/Elsevier Science, 2002).

97 George G. Kaufman, 'Using Efficient Bank Insolvency Resolution to Solve the Deposit Insurance Problem' in Andrew Campbell, John Raymond LaBrosse, David G. Mayes, and Dalvinder Singh (eds), *Deposit Insurance* (Palgrave 2007).

98 Kenneth E. Scott, 'A Guide to The Resolution of Failed Financial Institutions' in Kenneth E. Scott and John B. Taylor (eds), *Bankruptcy Not Bailout: A Special Chapter 14* (Hoover Institution Press, 2012) and William F. Kroener III, 'Comment on Orderly Liquidation under Title II of Dodd-Frank and Chapter 14' in Kenneth E. Scott and John B. Taylor (eds), *Bankruptcy Not Bailout: A Special Chapter 14* (Hoover Institution Press, 2012).

99 Treasury Committee, *The Run on the Rock* (n47).

100 PRA, 'Depositor and Dormant Account Protection' (PRA, London, 2015) available at: https://www.bankofengland.co.uk/-/media/boe/files/prudential-regulation/policy-statement/2015/ps615 accessed 10 May 2024.

101 *Ibid.*

102 See '2018 Annual Performance Plan' on the FDIC website, available at https://www.fdic.gov/about/strategic/performance/insurance.html.

103 John R. LaBrosse, 'Time to Fix the Plumbing: Improving the UK Framework Following the Collapse of Northern Rock' (n88).

5 Deposit Insurance in China

Experience, Country Specifics, and Institutional Structure and Reform

5.1 Introduction

Deposit insurance has made a great contribution to financial stability in the US and the UK, whereas it is a nascent system in China. During the GFC, although China claims that it successfully resisted the damage brought by the crisis and maintained its financial stability, hidden dangers emerged. Since a flurry of market-oriented reforms in 1979, state-owned commercial banks continue to play an irreplaceable role in China's financial system, with active government involvement still prevalent, which significantly jeopardises competition among China's financial markets and adversely impacts customers and private capital. In addition, bailouts or blanket guarantees backed by the government are believed to be provided to maintain financial and social stability during a financial crisis. In the past, without explicit deposit insurance, China provided bailouts and substantial financial support to save financially troubled state-owned commercial banks.

In 2015, China made two bold changes in its banking sector; one was to liberalise interest rates, and the other was to allow private capital to run entirely privately funded banks. To build a modern and market-based banking system, China introduced its first explicit deposit insurance scheme on 1 May 2015. However, this scheme is still in its early stages compared to advanced markets like the UK and US, which means there is considerable room for further optimisation.

In this context, this chapter attempts to provide a complete analysis of the working mechanisms of China's deposit insurance scheme. The main points will be more focused on the characteristics and overhaul of the Chinese deposit insurance scheme, as well as lessons on building a sound deposit insurance scheme drawn from international principles and advanced markets' experiences like the UK and the US. This chapter explores the reasons why China requires an effective deposit insurance scheme, outlines the key developments and characteristics of the Chinese deposit insurance scheme, and examines its shortcomings.

For this purpose, this chapter proceeds in seven parts. Part two provides a retrospective review of the history of banking regulation and deposit insurance in China. Then, part three discusses current banking regulatory structures in China. The fourth part examines the features of implicit deposit insurance in China, with three selected cases demonstrating how the central government resolves problematic banks. After that, parts five, six, and seven examine the operating mechanisms

DOI: 10.4324/9781003612759-5

of China's explicit deposit insurance scheme and give suggestions and reflections on prospective improvements. Finally, a conclusion will be drawn.

5.2 The Reforms of China's Banking System

5.2.1 Mono-Banking System between 1949 and 1978

Since the People's Republic of China (hereafter China) was founded in 1949, China's financial system has been divided into four stages: 1949–1978, 1979–1994, 1994–2008, and 2008–present. In the first stage between 1949 and 1979, China launched a unified financial system under the centrally planned economy policy, in which the central government had extremely strict control over all sectors of the financial system.[1] The People's Bank of China (PBOC), almost the only financial institution during this period, played a dual role as both a central bank and a commercial bank, and all its conduct was subject to the central government's commands.[2] As a result, under the influence of leftist ideology during this period, the PBOC, which performed all the functions of being a central bank and the only commercial bank, was responsible for all savings, credit, business transactions, foreign exchange, and national macro-economic control.[3]

5.2.2 The Exploration and Practice of China's Banking System from 1979 to 1994

The year 1978 was a turning point for China's financial system. Deng Xiaoping first introduced 'the reform and opening-up policy' at the 11th National Congress of the ruling Communist Party of China, paving the way to revamp China's financial system. Along with 'the reform and opening-up policy' and Deng's theory on China's financial system, in September 1983, the State Council promulgated the 'Decision on People's Bank of China Specifically Exercising the Function of the Central Bank' to designate the PBOC as the central bank of China. Simultaneously, between 1978 and 1986, the 'Big Four,' Agricultural Bank of China (ABC), Bank of China (BOC), China Construction Bank (CCB), and Industrial and Commercial Bank of China (ICBC), were created to take over all functions of being a commercial bank from the PBOC.[4] These four state-owned commercial banks were targeted at providing government-backed financing resources to state-owned enterprises (SOEs) and designated sectors of the economy with no competition. It was noteworthy that the Big Four were total financial intermediaries in China due to the lack of a stock exchange and a bond and insurance market.

After the 'Decision on Reform of the Economic Structure' at the Third Plenary Session of the 12th National Congress in 1984, the PBOC promulgated a policy that not only allowed the 'Big Four' to run any financial services permitted without any restrictions but also gave customers autonomy to choose between them, which first introduced competition within China's banking system.[5] Since then, a new form of commercial bank, joint-stock commercial banks with a shareholding ownership structure, was permitted to start up in China's banking market, which was a significant step forward in China's banking reform. Bank of Communications

(BCM), the fifth state-owned commercial bank, was the first joint-stock commercial bank with a shareholding ownership.

Along with BCM, another eight joint-stock commercial banks, with a shareholding ownership structure, were created to diversify China's financial markets and customer selection, though they are still controlled by the government or SOEs.[6] China, at the present stage, has made intensive progress in its financial system, and a two-tier banking system has basically been set up in the wake of the establishment of a central bank, the Big Four, and nine joint-stock commercial banks. However, the regret of China's banking reform in this period was that commercial banks were still policy-driven, not market-oriented, and their loans were mainly utilised for national or regional economic objectives without any consideration of profitability.[7]

In addition to commercial banks, in the 1980s, there was a growing number of rural credit cooperatives (RCCs) and urban credit cooperatives (UCCs) expanding China's banking industry. Later, some were converted to city commercial banks and rural commercial banks. The principal purpose was to provide financing channels to small and medium-sized enterprises (SMEs) and individuals. However, these RCCs and UCCs were led by local governments, not by the PBOC, resulting in the presence of chaotic lending policies in China's banking market.

Since Deng Xiaoping said 'banks should be evolved into real banks' at the end of 1986, the PBOC, in 1987, initiated a socialist-style financial system and became the only financial supervisor under the 'Provisional Regulations of the People's Republic of China on the Control of Banks', in which nine joint-stock commercial banks plus the 'Big Four' were the principal financial institutions supervised and led by the PBOC.[8] However, it was unfortunate that they had to comply with the central government's policy on the utilisation of funds credited by the PBOC. But then, this situation changed with the issuance of the 'Decision of the State Council on Reform of the Financial System' in 1993. Commercial banks in China no longer had to obey the central government's policy as three policy banks – China Development Bank (CDB), Export-Import Bank of China (CEXIM), and Agricultural Development Bank of China (ADBC) – were specifically set up to undertake the function of policy-driven loans, making China's commercial banks look more market-oriented.

Nevertheless, China encountered financial chaos during this period, as commercial banks were widely involved in non-banking financial services in terms of trusts, securities, and investment, and non-banking financial institutions ran deposit-taking businesses to attract deposits from the public. In response to such financial chaos, China launched a separate operation that kept commercial banks from being involved in non-banking financial services and commenced separate supervision in its financial system after the China Securities Regulatory Commission and China Insurance Regulatory Commission were stripped from the PBOC.[9] That is to say, the PBOC was no longer the only financial supervisor administering every financial sector in China.

5.2.3 Banking Modernisation and Commercialisation from 1995 to 2008

The year 1995 was another significant year for China's banking system, as two laws pertaining to China's banking system came into effect. First, the Law of the People's Republic of China on People's Bank of China (PBOC Law), the first banking-related law in China's history, was promulgated to recognise the PBOC's role as the central bank of China, as well as to provide a legal basis for the implementation of separate supervision. Furthermore, under this law, the right to appoint senior management for each branch of the PBOC was eventually converted from local governments to the PBOC in pursuit of maintaining operational independence whilst constraining intervention arising from local governments. Second, China enacted the Law of the People's Republic of China on Commercial Banks (Chinese Commercial Bank Law). This law provided the legal basis for separate operations, allowing commercial banks to independently run their business based on profitability, capital adequacy, and liquidity. Nonetheless, owing to China's unique political regime, so far the senior management of the PBOC and each commercial bank have still been embedded into China's political hierarchy, meaning that the government still has an invisible hand interfering in their operation.

By the end of the 1990s, accompanied by an overheating economy and bold reforms, China's banking system faced the most serious crisis of non-performing loans since 1949. Until the end of 1999, due to the lack of financial disclosure, the PBOC estimated that non-performing loans (NPLs) of commercial banks in China might be over RMB 3.2 trillion, accounting for more than 25 percent of total loans.[10] In reality, the Big Four were de facto technically insolvent, and the Asian financial crisis in 1997, which severely destroyed Asian countries' economies, was an existing lesson for China to understand how a financial crisis can damage years of economic achievements.[11] Consequently, the central government decided to inject RMB 270 billion into the Big Four in 1998 and launched massive bailouts in the following year by establishing four state-owned asset management companies (AMCs) to take over approximately RMB 1.4 trillion NPLs from the Big Four.[12] Zhou Xiaochuan, the former Governor of the PBOC, says the material causing such huge amounts of NPLs could be attributed to: (1) excessive government interventions; (2) lending to SOEs; (3) a weak domestic legal system; and (4) the lack of good corporate governance in banks.[13]

Besides, having realised the significance of prudential regulation, the PBOC started monitoring the capital adequacy of commercial banks in light of the Basel Capital Accord since 1998. However, the result of introducing international standards was unfavourable, because most loans still flowed to a vast number of unprofitable SOEs, which were financially unable to repay loans. Consequently, the Chinese government carried out consecutive bailouts to assist commercial banks in stripping off RMB 3.4 trillion non-performing loans until 2008.[14]

Since 2001, China's banking industry has encountered challenges from foreign banks, particularly when China officially became a member of the World Trade Organisation (WTO). Under the most-favoured-nation treatment of the WTO, foreign banks in China are to be treated the same as domestic banks without any limitations, which forces China to speed up its pace in shaping a modern banking system, despite having a five-year transition period. Compared with foreign contenders, China's banking industry during this period could be recognised as having the following disadvantages: (1) low competitiveness; (2) a high level of non-performing loans; and (3) a low capital adequacy ratio.[15] Therefore, there were massive worries concerning whether foreign banks with advanced corporate governance and sufficient capital would squeeze the room for domestic banks to dominate China's banking market.[16] However, in contrast, it is clear that the WTO accession has broken up the long-term monopoly of the Big Four, compelling them to optimise corporate governance, customer services, and capital adequacy to benefit Chinese customers.

After 2003, the central government initiated the boldest reform in the banking industry since the 'Decisions on Strengthening the Socialist Market Economy'. To start with, the ownership structure of the Big Four evolved into joint-stock commercial banks with shareholding ownership, and major foreign financial institutions were introduced as foreign strategic investors. It could be said that this move was aimed at substantially promoting the competitiveness of the Big Four by directly bringing in capital and advanced corporate governance. For example, the Royal Bank of Scotland (RBS), in 2005, not only jointly invested $3.1 billion with Merrill Lynch and Hong Kong-based tycoon Li Ka-Shing in acquiring 10 percent of the BOC shares but also helped the BOC tailor credit card services and corporate banking business.[17] It is clear that major foreign banks involved in modernising state-owned commercial banks have made a positive impact, although they purchased shares at a comparatively cheaper price.

Having seen the dividends from introducing foreign strategic investors and shareholding ownership, for the sake of good corporate governance, capital adequacy, and market discipline, the central government proposed a 'going public' policy that encouraged the Big Four to be listed on the Shanghai Stock Exchange (SHSE) and Hong Kong Stock Exchange (HKSE) through initial public offerings (IPOs). For example, between 2006 and 2010, the ABC and the ICBC were listed on the SHSE and the HKSE, publicly raising $22.1 billion and $21.9 billion, respectively, which have become two of the world's largest IPOs in history.[18] Going public has been perceived as a milestone in modernising state-owned commercial banks. Before the end of 2010, the Big Four and most commercial banks had gone public with shareholding ownerships, barring some city commercial banks, rural commercial banks, and rural credit cooperatives. (Table 5.1)

At the same time, in 2003, the China Banking Regulatory Commission (CBRC), as a banking regulator and a prudential supervisor in China, was set up to take over the function of prudential regulation previously performed by the PBOC.[19] And then, the PBOC was more focused on monetary policy and macroprudential regulation. After the CBRC stepped into China's banking regulation, China's financial regulatory framework progressed into a new era of 'one bank and three commissions', namely 'Yihang Sanhui' in Chinese.[20]

Table 5.1 Going Public Process and Foreign Strategic Investor of the Big Four Plus the BCM

Bank	*Date of IPO*	*Place of IPO*	*Capital Raised from Public Shares*	*Foreign Strategic Investor*
BOC	1 June 2006 15 July 2007	HKSE SHSE	$9.7 billion	RBS Merrill Lynch Li Ka-Shing Temasek
CCB	27 October 2005 25 September 2007	HKSE SHSE	$8 billion	Bank of America
ICBC	27 October 2006	HKSE SHSE	$21.9 billion	Goldman Sachs Allianz SE American Express
ABC	16 July 2010 15 July 2010	HKSE SHSE	$22.1 billion	No
BCM	23 June 2005 15 May	HKSE SHSE	$5.5 billion	HSBC

Data Source: Each Bank's Official Website.

5.2.4 Continuous Reform in the Post-Crisis Era (2008–Present)

China's financial system has suffered very limited losses from the GFC, given its lack of sophistication and isolation from the global market.[21] Despite having good fortune in the global financial crisis, China continues to consolidate its gradual and ongoing financial reform. Along with the overhaul of state-owned commercial banks, joint-stock commercial banks, RCCs, RCBs, and CCBs have also undergone significant changes, as the government encourages them to accept foreign investors and build professional senior management. To date, there are eight joint-stock commercial banks, three UCBs, and one RCB listing their shares on the SHSE or the HKSE. In 2011, China began to launch pilot programmes that allow some selected commercial banks to form financial holding companies that can run businesses in all financial sectors.

China's banking system witnessed a breakthrough in 2014 as the CBRC initiated a pilot project that granted entry permits to five fully privately owned banks. In December 2014, Shenzhen Qianhai WeBank, the first privately owned bank founded by Tencent Holding Limited, started offering financial services and financial inclusion to underbanked groups and SMEs via its online platform named WeBank APP.[22] Since March 2015, all five privately owned banks have begun to provide financial services, mainly targeting underbanked individuals and SMEs.[23] It is common that all privately owned banks offer financial services based on internet finance and new internet technology, thereby lowering operating costs. In the meantime, the emergence of private banks is anticipated to significantly promote financial inclusion in China, simply because individuals and SMEs can have convenient and fast financing channels via online platforms developed by privately owned banks.

By the end of 2017, 17 privately owned banks were running banking businesses with total assets of RMB 338.14 billion, total deposits of RMB 113.51 billion, and an average non-performing loan ratio of 0.53 percent.[24] In addition to privately owned banks, private capital simultaneously played a vital role in supporting CCBs, RCBs, and RCCs. By the end of 2016, the share of private capital in RCBs and RCCs reached 88.3 percent and 86.3 percent respectively, and private capital in CCBs was RMB 11 trillion.[25]

In the following year, the Chinese government embarked on building a more open, diversified, and competitive banking industry. First, the PBOC accomplished its mission of removing the upper limit for interest rates on deposits and the lower limit for interest rates on loans, which marks that China's banking industry has basically become market-based.[26] Second, in response to market-based interest rates and a progressively market-oriented banking market, the State Council eventually set up China's first deposit insurance scheme that encourages competition in the banking market.

As of the end of 2017, under China's two-tier banking system, as shown in Figure 5.1, a total of 4,532 banking institutions with 4.17 million employees, in different forms, provided financial services; the total assets of all banking institutions reached RMB 252.4 billion; and the total deposits climbed to RMB 169.3 trillion.[27] However, Figure 5.2 indicates that state-owned commercial banks still dominate the domestic banking market, in spite of the consecutive decline of their market share. Compared with the US and UK banking systems, China's banking system has to accelerate the pace of modernising its banking system.

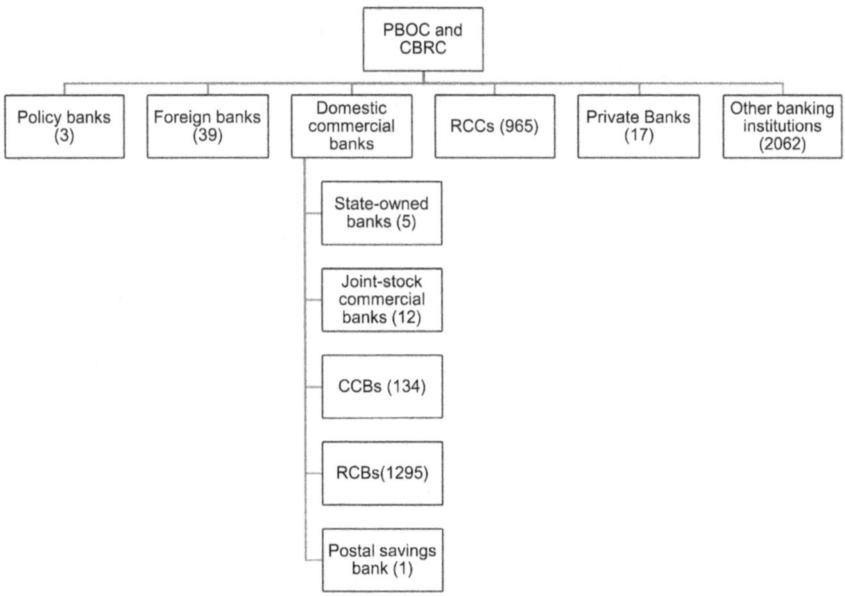

Figure 5.1 Chinas Two-Tier Banking System

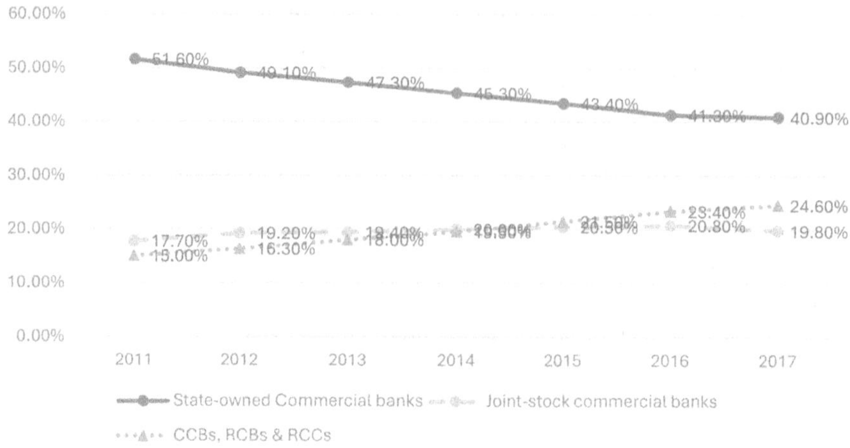

Figure 5.2 Market Share of Chinese Banks (by asset)
(Data Source: NFRA 2011–2017 Annual Reports)

5.3 The Current Architecture of China's Banking Regulation

5.3.1 The People's Bank of China

Before the establishment of the CBRC in 2003, the PBOC was the only regulatory agency overseeing China's banking system, implying that the PBOC was not only China's central bank but also China's banking regulator and supervisor. The PBOC Law was passed in 1995, giving the PBOC a certain degree of autonomy. The PBOC Law was amended in 2003 to fortify the PBOC's role in drawing up and implementing monetary policy, coupled with the power to supervise financial institutions from a macro-economic perspective. In addition, this law expounds that the PBOC has an obligation to safeguard China's banking market in terms of preventing systemic risks. Nevertheless, according to Article 5, the PBOC has to obtain approval from the State Council regarding money supply, interest rates and foreign exchange rates. As claimed by Zhou and Li, this law does not give the PBOC true autonomy to implement monetary policy.[28]

Along with the Bank of England and Federal Reserve, the PBOC, as a central bank, has been fulfilling the function of lender of last resort. However, unlike the Bank of England and Federal Reserve, decisions pertaining to liquidity assistance and bailouts made by the PBOC have to be approved by the State Council. For example, Article 32 of the PBOC Law underscores the leadership of the State Council in implementing financial assistance and bailouts, as any special-purpose loans via the PBOC must follow ex-ante decisions made by the State Council. Article 34 of the PBOC Law emphasises that when a bank has financial difficulty in honouring deposits that might lead to financial instability, the PBOC shall have the power to supervise and inspect the bank only after getting approval from the State Council in the interest of reaching financial stability. At the same time, the overlap of functioning LOLR between the PBOC and the CBRC confuses people. With respect to Article 29 of the Law of the People's Republic of China on Regulation and Supervision over the Banking Industry (Chinese Banking Regulation and Supervision Law), both the PBOC and CBRC, which are under the leadership of the State Council, collectively have the responsibility to tackle emergencies in China's banking market by drawing up a contingency plan together. This, however, indicates that the CBRC partially executes the function of LOLR, adding confusion to China's banking regulation.

In light of the PBOC Law, the PBOC has been redefined as a macro-prudential regulator for financial stability with no obligation to operate China's deposit insurance scheme. Indeed, the Deposit Insurance Regulations promulgated in May 2015 highlight that an independent deposit insurer under the leadership of the State Council is needed to be responsible for performing all functions of deposit insurance.[29] However, the State Council appointed the Financial Stability Bureau of the PBOC as a caretaker deposit insurer following the issuance of the Deposit Insurance Regulations. The State Council's response to this arrangement was that the central government thought it was unnecessary to have an independent deposit insurer running such an easy and rough deposit insurance scheme.[30] Nevertheless, in reality, the first reason is that China lacks a clear and structured legal framework for resolving bank failures, as the PBOC usually provides guarantees to depositors, especially when facing severe bank runs. Second, Articles 33 and 34 of the PBOC Law, which allow the PBOC to supervise and examine financial institutions if necessary and to request the CBRC to implement supervision and examine financial institutions suspected of posing threats to financial stability, can be regarded as preconditions to underpin the PBOC's leading status in safeguarding financial stability.[31]

However, though the PBOC is an interim deposit insurer managing China's deposit insurance scheme, in practice, because of the lack of a supportive and specific legal framework devoted to operating China's deposit insurance scheme, the PBOC cannot solely fulfil full functions of deposit insurance without external assistance from other relevant departments under the State Council. Furthermore, the absence of autonomy means the PBOC is only able to execute and update functions of deposit insurance only after obtaining approval from the State Council.

5.3.2 The National Financial Regulatory Administration

After the accession to the WTO, China accelerated its integration into global financial markets.[32] In 2003, given the competitive pressure and entrance of foreign banks, China took a significant step towards a more effective and modernised banking regulatory structure by creating the CBRC to take charge of banking regulatory and supervisory responsibilities instead of the PBOC, leaving the PBOC more focused on monetary policy. Since April 2018, amid a substantial overhaul of financial regulatory bodies led by the State Council, a new regulatory body, namely the China Banking and Insurance Regulatory Commission (CBIRC), has been created after the CIRC merged into the CBRC. The State Council promulgated the 2023 financial institutional reform on 7 March 2023, which repealed the CBIRC and established the new National Financial Regulatory Administration (NFRA) responsible for banking regulation and financial consumer protection.

The main purpose of separating banking supervision and monetary policy is to mitigate a conflict of interest that might strike a disequilibrium between monetary policy and banking supervision after injecting tremendous reserves into the banking sector.[33] This move attempts to show China's determination to develop effective and professional banking regulation under a sectoral regulation model by optimising existing separate regulation.

Since the end of 2003, the CBRC's position in supervising China's entire banking industry has been strengthened by enacting the Chinese Banking Regulation and Supervision Law, with detailed authorisations, provisions, and a code of conduct.[34] At the same time, the CBRC has been established to embark on four regulatory objectives based on prudential supervision: (1) safeguard the interests of depositors and consumers; (2) maintain public confidence; (3) promote public awareness, fairness, competition, and information disclosure; and (4) crack down on financial crimes. The CBRC's responsibilities are listed below:

- Compile rules and regulations monitoring the banking industry;
- Administer the establishment, changes, termination, and financial services provided by banking institutions;
- Execute on-site examinations and off-site surveillance of banking institutions with indispensable mandates against rule-breaking behaviours;
- Monitor senior management of banking institutions on the basis of fit-and-proper tests;
- Release statistics and reports associated with the banking industry periodically;
- Propose resolutions against troubled deposit takers in cooperation with related authorities;
- Take charge of the management of the supervisory boards of significantly important state-owned banking institutions and other affairs authorised by the State Council.[35]

It can be affirmed that, with these listed responsibilities, the CBRC, as a watchdog in China's banking industry, is very predominant in retaining China's banking market stability.

At present, regarding deposit insurance, it is perplexing to understand China's current institutional structure of deposit insurance. Although the NAFR should be responsible for protecting depositors in light of Article 1 of the Chinese Banking Regulation and Supervision Law, in reality, the PBOC is an interim deposit insurer with no legitimacy under the relevant legislation. Moreover, according to Article 35 of the Chinese Banking Regulation and Supervision Law, the powers to take over, close, and restructure banking institutions are granted to the NAFR, which makes the NAFR sound more like a deposit insurer than the PBOC. In addition, unlike the PBOC, the NAFR has the mandate to conduct on-site examinations for the sake of risk-based assessment so that it might have better insight into banks' risk levels, as well as to initiate risk-based premiums.

Like the PBOC, the NAFR is under the leadership of the State Council as well. In accordance with relevant law, all senior management of the NAFR have to be appointed by the State Council, observing the lack of regulatory independence that probably undermines its authority. China's political hierarchy is another long-standing issue affecting regulatory effectiveness. In practice, the chairmen and the CEOs of the Big Four, who have relevant administrative ranks, are also appointed by the China Communist Party and they might have the same administrative ranking as the chairman of the NAFR. This has undermined the authority of the NAFR, resulting in a severe 'too big to regulate' problem in China's banking market.[36]

5.3.3 Other Authorities

In addition to the NAFR and the PBOC, the Ministry of Finance (MOF) and State Taxation Administration, two departments under the leadership of the State Council, are related to deposit insurance. The MOF is responsible for formulating the corporate governance of state-owned financial companies and compiling tax policy for banking institutions in collaboration with the State Taxation Administration.[37] In October 2016, the MOF and State Taxation Administration collectively released the 'Notice of the MOF and State Taxation Administration on Charging Deposit Insurance Premium over Banking Institutions', which indicates that both the MOF and State Taxation Administration are authorised to set deposit insurance premium rates and charge premiums over deposit takers, complicating the current institutional structure of China's deposit insurance scheme.

5.3.4 Loopholes in China's Banking Regulation

China's banking market has been developing rapidly since the 'reform and opening up policy' issued at the end of 1970s, and the corresponding banking regulatory framework has witnessed significant changes in order to keep pace with banking reforms. Despite having made significant achievements, it cannot proclaim the perfection of China's banking regulation, especially when talking about the state grip on the banking system.

The lack of regulatory independence is an overarching weakness existing in contemporary China's banking regulation. At present, the PBOC and the NAFR, two irreplaceable financial regulators that play major functions in banking regulation, are still under the leadership of the State Council. Focusing on the regulatory independence of the PBOC, though there is a consensus that the central bank law legally confirms the PBOC's role as the central bank, two different attitudes towards this law among Chinese scholars have been clear. One view holds that this law is positive for modernising China's banking industry. As noted by Naughton, the central bank law strengthened the institutional integrity of the PBOC and was a milestone illustrating China's determination to build up a real central bank.[38] Yi Gang, the governor of the PBOC, agreed that given the transitional economy, the central bank law has guaranteed the implementation of a stable and consistent monetary policy, which contributes to the rapid development of China's banking market.[39] Chin further argues that since the global financial crisis, the US and many European countries also present political pressure to central banks with respect to monetary policy in pursuit of electoral advantages, as political interference in monetary policy is a concern in developed countries as well as in emerging countries.[40]

A contrary view holds that the PBOC falls short of the autonomy necessary to consolidate managing independent monetary policy, though the central bank law authorises the central bank status. Lardy argues that although Article 7 enables the PBOC to run monetary policy independently without any political interference from other ministries, provincial governments, social groups, and individuals, the State Council makes the ultimate decision on determining monetary policy, and the PBOC has to abide by the decision.[41] Additionally, Liew and Wu add that Article 5 requires the PBOC to obtain approval from the State Council before starting to work on monetary policy in relation to money supply, interest rates, and foreign exchange rates.[42] Shih, a long-standing observer of Chinese politics and economy, suggests that the PBOC usually relies on administrative decrees rather than monetary measures to achieve the goals of monetary policy, despite looking like a modern central bank.[43] Therefore, both Lardy and Shih argue that the independence of the PBOC is far below the proper level of independence, but they acknowledge the effective and efficient presence of the PBOC when it gets political backing.[44]

The other focal point refers to political intervention. The China Communist Party (CCP) is the only ruling party that directs and disciplines all governments and officials so that it has a tight grip on personnel management and decision-making.[45] Like other ministries and government organs, the personnel management of the PBOC and the NAFR is under the nomenklatura system managed by the Central Organization Department (COD) of the CCP, and their senior officials are placed into a bureaucratic hierarchy and the CCP system. For example, both the governors of the PBOC and the Chairman of the NAFR normally are members of the CCP Central Committee, which are positioned at the chief ministerial level.[46]

Surprisingly, the top executives of the Big Four and the other six state-owned financial groups are appointed by the COD following the nomenklatura system.[47] In practice, these top executives are quasi-government officials and cadres of the CCP, who might have the same ranking as the governor of the PBOC and the chairman of the NAFR under the CCP system.[48] Thus, in reality, these senior officers pursue a political career, not the bank's profitability, and the function of supervising senior officers of these ten banking institutions for misconduct is fulfilled by the Central Commission for Discipline Inspection of the CCP, not the PBOC or the NAFR.[49] From the CCP's point of view, a centralised banking market and regulatory bodies might be easier to manage and control. However, on the other hand, although China is striving to adopt international practices, Heilmann argues that political intervention over banking regulatory bodies and banking institutions by the CCP in light of the nomenklatura system is negative for building effective banking regulation in China when confronting political bias and potential manipulation.[50]

Undoubtedly, the ultimate destination for both the PBOC and the NAFR is to be truly independent financial regulatory bodies. Considering the social, political, and economic factors in China, although the IMF provides some suggestions of being an independent central bank or a financial regulator, there is no one-size-fits-all international norm in line with country specifics.[51] With the deepening of China's financial reform, it needs time for China to develop an approach step by step that can well address the current issues.

5.4 China's Resolution on Bank Troubles under Implicit Deposit Insurance

In past decades, China's banking system was strictly controlled by the government, which intervened in the operation of banks via administrative orders, the appointment of senior management, decision-making, and ownership control. Thus, many reckless decisions that incurred tremendous losses in China's banking industry were attributed to dictatorial political interferences.[52]

Implicit deposit insurance, primarily dependent on bailouts or blanket guarantees and taxpayers' contributions, was employed to reimburse depositors in the case of financial institution failures without any formal legislation.[53] Prior to 1 May 2015, China had followed this implicit deposit insurance scheme for many years, at the expense of trillions of RMB to rescue banks. Due to limited regulatory resources, the government frequently executed blanket guarantees to extend banks' lives, seen as political accomplishments that contributed to career advancement.

China normally had been through three ways to safeguard depositors. The first way was that the government and PBOC endorsed deposits after a closure. The second, which can be deemed as capital injection and non-performing loan disposal, was that the government and PBOC directly helped banks spin off non-performing loans and raise capital. Third, the government and the PBOC compelled healthy and sound banking institutions to merge with troubled institutions.

Notably, it can be seen that, under implicit deposit insurance, all measures have to be dependent on administrative orders. In other words, it can be said that the government and the PBOC were the saviours of Chinese depositors, which severely damaged market discipline. Up until now, though China still has not had a sound banking resolution regime, the launch of its deposit insurance scheme is a positive development and a step forward to inspire an integrated banking resolution mechanism.

5.4.1 Government Endorsement after a Closure

The PBOC used to close troubled deposit-taking institutions in order to stop bank runs that may trigger social instability and financial instability.[54] The principal legal basis is the Chinese Banking Regulation and Supervision Law, the PBOC Law, the Chinese Commercial Bank Law, and the Enterprise Bankruptcy Law of the People's Republic of China (Chinese Enterprise Bankruptcy Law). In practice, the PBOC often employs enforceable administrative measures to close failing banks and set up liquidation teams involved in winding up procedures. However, in accordance with China's administrative system, the provincial government has the same administrative powers as the PBOC, so some provincial governments might counter the PBOC's decisions on closing troubled banks if banks are influential in their regions. As a consequence, that is why there is only one bank closure case in China.

5.4.1.1 The Case of Hainan Development Bank

So far, Hainan Development Bank has been the first and the only commercial bank that was terminated by the PBOC. In the mid-1990s, Hainan province witnessed the burst of the real estate bubble, which gave a rise to an increasing number of troubled local trust and investment companies. In order to maintain financial stability, the Hainan provincial government decided to bail out five failing local trust and investment companies by establishing Hainan Development Bank to merge these five trust and investment companies.[55] However, only one of these five trust and investment companies was barely able to run a business, leaving an unfunded liability in excess of RMB 5 billion and posing a potential threat to the prospect of Hainan Development Bank.[56]

On 18 August 1995, Hainan Development Bank started running its banking business with a registered capital of RMB 1.677 billion and 43 shareholders, including the Hainan provincial government.[57] Nonetheless, only RMB 1.07 billion actually reached the account and RMB 0.92 billion was returned to the founding shareholders as loans.[58] Things appeared to change until the end of 1997. In the wake of the collapse of the real estate bubble, 28 UCCs were trapped in a liquidity shortage as their assets were concentrated in real estate. Along with the collapse, to make matters worse, these 28 UCCs offered extremely high interest rates to attract deposits. Consequently, the 28 UCCs failed to pay out deposits, and bank runs occurred.

To curb market panic and contagion, the Hainan provincial government and the PBOC made a reckless decision requiring Hainan Development Bank to acquire these 28 UCCs while undertaking all liabilities. However, compared to the 28 UCCs, the interest rate Hainan Development Bank offered was much lower, prompting depositors to transfer their money to other banks where higher interest rates were provided. Apart from interest rates, both Hainan Development Bank and these 28 UCCs suffered a significant hit in real estate market due to the overwhelming depreciation of real estate in Hainan province. As a result, a liquidity crisis and massive withdrawals occurred amid tremendous market panic.

After February 1998, as market panics peaked, there were long queues outside branches of Hainan Development Bank, though the PBOC announced a RMB 3.4 billion capital injection.[59] Against this backdrop, the PBOC promptly injected RMB 4 billion again; however, it seemed ineffective in stopping bank runs.[60] On 21 June 1998, the PBOC decided to close Hainan Development Bank and appointed the ICBC to assume all assets and liabilities. Subsequently, thanks to government backing and the good reputation of the ICBC, bank runs finally ceased and public confidence was restored.

This is to say, in the absence of an explicit deposit insurance scheme, no matter what risks Chinese depositors and banks take, the local governments and the

PBOC normally provide full guarantees to banks and depositors, if necessary. However, it is admitted that the failure of Hainan Development Bank was a sample case demonstrating how the local governments and the PBOC are accountable for the closure by wrong decision-making. Professional corporate governance and independence were absent in this case. Till the closure, vast amounts of taxpayers' money were spent on compensating depositors. Therefore, the lesson learnt is that an explicit deposit insurance scheme, not government guarantees, should be in place to resolve troubled banks; otherwise, depositors might believe that the government would provide a blanket guarantee, whilst not realising that they also have to make a contribution to the bill.

5.4.2 Capital Injection and Non-Performing Loan Disposal

Capital injection and non-performing loan disposal, a straightforward way to protect depositors' money by prolonging the life of a bank, have long been used by the central government, local governments, and the PBOC to maintain financial stability. Chinese commercial banks, especially state-owned commercial banks, have been vigorously lobbying to ask for liquidity support. In addition, in order to avoid social instability caused by bank runs and market panics, the Chinese government always maintains a moderate attitude towards banks' requests for capital.

5.4.2.1 The Large Scale Bailouts of the Big Four

Since the banking reform began in 1978, the Big Four have long played as shadows of the government, as they have to comply with government policy in terms of unconditionally financing government-favoured projects and undercapitalised state-owned enterprises that cannot repay loans.[61] Notwithstanding the high possibility of default, massive policy loans flowed to loss-suffering and struggling state-owned enterprises, resulting in giant numbers of NPLs in the Big Four.[62] Along with policy loans, the lack of good corporate governance and risk management also led to poor lending practices, resulting in massive amounts of NPLs.[63] As of the late 1990s, NPLs accumulated in the Big Four were around RMB 3.2 trillion, which accounted for over 25 percent of total outstanding loans and 40 percent of gross domestic product, leaving a time bomb in China's financial market and economy.[64] More seriously, by 1999, the Big Four took up 70 percent of market share by assets, raising concerns that the collapse of the Big Four could incur a catastrophic financial crisis that would wipe out years of efforts in China's economic growth.[65]

Potential social instability and financial instability arising from large-scale NPLs pressed the Chinese government to ponder comprehensive bailouts of the Big Four.[66] The first round of bailouts started between 1998 and 1999. In 1998, the Ministry of Finance directly provided a capital injection of RMB 270 billion to the Big Four by issuing specific treasury bonds.[67] However, this did not substantially tackle the fundamental issues associated with bad corporate governance and poor lending practices.[68] Since 1999, the Big Four again were trapped with tremendous non-performing loans. Subsequently, inspired by US's experience in resolving non-performing assets through the Resolution Trust Corporation, the Chinese government established four state-owned AMCs to implement unprecedented bail-outs assisting the Big Four to carve off RMB 1.4 trillion NPLS.[69] As a result, the capital adequacy ratio of the Big Four promptly plunged to well below 8 percent, the lower limit set by the Basel Accord.[70]

In the second round of massive capital injection from 2003 to 2005, a bold measure the Chinese government had worked out in response to a low capital adequacy ratio was to make use of foreign exchange reserves that had accumulated for years. In the meantime, the PBOC Law that prohibits the PBOC from owning shares of any commercial banks forced the State Council to establish a state-owned financial holding company, namely Central Huijin Investment Limited (Central Huijin), to receive foreign exchange reserves from the PBOC, as it utilised these foreign exchange reserves to acquire the shares of the Big Four. Since 2003, Central Huijin spent a total of RMB 486 billion, 15 percent of the whole foreign exchange reserves, on rescuing the Big Four, which made Central Huijin the biggest shareholder of the Big Four[71] (Table 5.2).

Between 2004 and 2005, the Chinese government's determination to overhaul the Big Four by getting rid of old-fashioned corporate governance via listing overseas resulted in massive spin-offs of NPLs, with more than RMB 780 billion of non-performing loans being transferred from the Big Four to four AMCs, lowering the average NPL ratio to 10.49 percent.[72] This was necessary because the Big Four, with negative balance sheets, were difficult to be listed on overseas stock exchanges without significant spin-offs of NPLs. By the end of 2008, while the average NPL ratio of the Big Four was reduced to 2.81 percent, this achievement resulted in the government spending over RMB 3.4 trillion from taxpayers' pockets.[73] Furthermore, in light of the most recent statistics promulgated by the CBRC in 2006, the overall recovery rate in cash was 20.84 percent, indicating a huge waste of public funding.[74]

Despite temporarily stabilising China's society and financial market, in the long run, direct capital injection and non-performing loan disposal have no longer been effective banking resolutions accommodating the modern banking system. In China, under the implicit deposit insurance scheme, depositors naturally prefer to save their money in the Big Four because both the government and depositors consider the Big Four as too big to fail financial institutions, and depositors have a fixed belief that the government would not allow them to go insolvent. This thought, however, clamps down on competition but inspires moral hazard.

Table 5.2 Shares Owned by Central Huijin Investment Limited for the Big Four (by Percentage)

Bank	*Shares Owned by Central Huijin*
ABC	40.42%
BOC	64.63%
CCB	57.31%
ICBC	34.99%

Source: Data collected from Central Huijin.

5.4.3 *Merger*

At an earlier stage, UCCs and RCCs that targeted particular groups including farmers and SMEs were playing a supplementary but essential role in integrating China's banking market. However, unlike the Big Four serving the macro economy, UCCs and RCCs that focused on regional economies became financing tools for local governments and local influential SOEs to conduct corrupt behaviours, such as money laundering and defalcation of state-owned assets.[75] The absence of an integrated legal framework motivated many RCCs and UCCs to reach the verge of crime, bypassing the law and policy to boldly make illegal money. For example, the most popular strategy of expanding deposit business among UCCs and RCCs in the past was to lure depositors by offering tempting interest rates that exceeded the maximum rates required by the PBOC, which meant that, when facing massive withdrawals, they could be hit by a liquidity crunch. During the late 1990s, the PBOC revoked licences of UCCs and more than 2,300 UCCs were merged into 90 CCBs when the PBOC vowed to end the chaos of UCCs. Nevertheless, many mergers had problems related to depositors' interests, whereas, by implicit deposit insurance schemes, local governments always took over responsibility for combating these problems instead of the PBOC and the CBRC.

5.4.3.1 *The Case of Zhengzhou Cooperative Bank*

Zhengzhou Cooperative Bank, which was made up of 48 UCCs, commenced business on 28 August 1996.[76] After the opening, like other UCCs' market strategy in attracting depositors, Zhengzhou Cooperative Bank lured depositors by providing alluring interest rates, revealing the fragility of the bank when liquidity became short. Faced with decreasing liquidity since August 1997, the PBOC lent RMB 4,290 million to Zhengzhou Cooperative Bank against the liquidity shortage.[77] Unfortunately, the suspension of providing tempting interest rates led to massive withdrawals, which triggered bank runs in 1998, estimating RMB 4,742 million needed to fill the funding gap.[78]

Since July 1998, the PBOC, involved in implementing on-site examination of Zhengzhou Cooperative Bank, found that moral hazard and corruption were severe amid extremely naive corporate governance. A total of 21 branches that operated as independent financial institutions conducted transactions off the balance sheet, resulting in losses worth up to RMB 30.8 million.[79] Simultaneously, NPLs had boomed due to large numbers of loans to unprofitable enterprises, with NPLs in 1998 valued at RMB 4,002 million, amounting to 78.81 percent of its total outstanding loans.[80] It is noteworthy that, as shown in Figure 5.3, a sharp growth of NPLs took place between 1997 and 1998. Combined with the volume of deposits, as illustrated by Figure 5.4, after ceasing high interest rates in 1998, a rapid slump in deposits can be found out between 1997 and 1998. Therefore, it can be assumed that increasing amounts of NPLs with declining volumes of deposits had an obvious impact on the liquidity crunch of Zhengzhou Cooperative Bank, which then triggered bank runs.

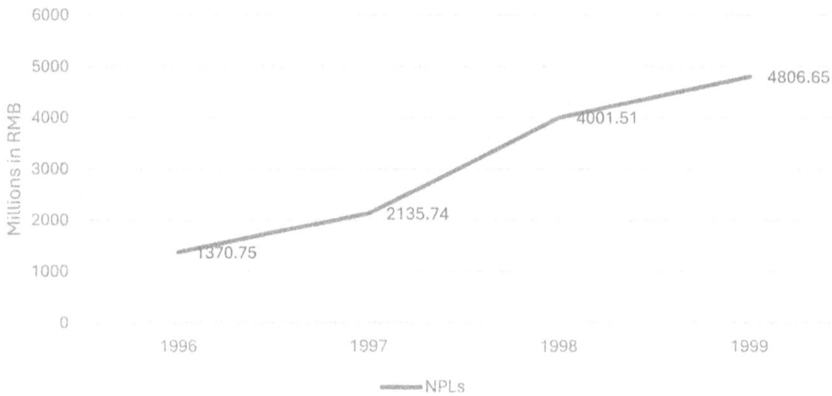

Figure 5.3 NPLs in Zhengzhou Cooperative Bank from 1996 to 1999
(Data Source: collected from the PBOC and Wind Information)

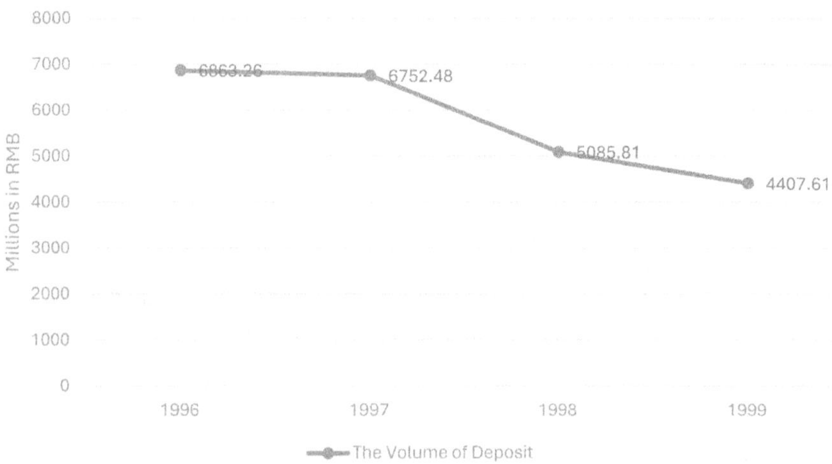

Figure 5.4 The Volume of Deposit from 1996 to 1999
(Data Source: collected from the PBOC and Wind Information)

After 1998, around 0.4 million depositors in Henan Province were unable to withdraw their money from Zhengzhou Cooperative Bank due to the liquidity shortage, which incurred tremendous panic and riots surrounding the branches. When the PBOC ceased capital support, the Henan provincial government and the Zhengzhou city government stepped in and rescued the bank in consideration of its influential status in maintaining financial and social stability within Henan Province. Interestingly, according to Article 64 of the Chinese Commercial Bank Law, the CBRC should take over management and carry out actions to protect depositors when confronting a banking crisis.[81] However, from 1999 to 2006, both the provincial and city governments replaced the PBOC and the CBRC to resolve the burdensome Zhengzhou Cooperative Bank by reshuffling senior management and paying for NPLs instead of auctioning NPLs to the market. Besides, the governments acted as guarantors to help Zhengzhou Cooperative gain sustained financial support from the PBOC. After receiving comprehensive bailouts from the government, Zhengzhou Cooperative Bank got back on track and renamed itself as Zhengzhou Bank, listing on the HKSE in 2015. However, so far both the Zhengzhou city government and the Henan provincial government still remain among the biggest shareholders in its ownership structure, accounting for 16 percent of the total shares.[82]

5.4.4 Problems under Implicit Deposit Insurance

The three cases discussed above illustrate that controversial government bailouts were the only resolution mechanism to rescue both large and small banking institutions under an implicit deposit insurance scheme in the past. Before 1979, given the utilisation of a planned economy and a monobanking system in which the central government directed the PBOC in every aspect of banking business, internal governance, and day-to-day operation, it was fair to say that government bailouts were adequate and effective in maintaining the stability of the financial system. The turning point of the banking system was in 1979, when China started steering its economy towards a socialist market economy following the reform and opening-up policy. Since then, almost all commercial banks sought to participate in the process of marketisation.

However, before 2015, implicit deposit insurance schemes had long been the mainstream resolution mechanism for troubled banking institutions in pursuit of financial and social stability. From depositors' perspectives, an implicit deposit insurance scheme with the government providing guarantees might be preferred, simply because the fears of social instability force the government to compensate depositors, and depositors would not bear any statutory responsibility for failing to monitor banks. Talley adds that the government is capable of not providing guarantees, but this rarely happens in practice.[83] As shown in the above three cases, it is clear that controversial government bailouts have eventually overcome difficulties, and Chinese depositors have got accustomed to being fully covered by the government as the central government, the PBOC, and local governments ultimately pay for the losses of depositors and banks in the event of bank failures.

Nevertheless, in contrast, LaBrosse and Mayes argue that although implicit deposit insurance demonstrates great potential to protect depositors, it exposes taxpayers, who contribute most to the state revenue, to enormous costs of rescuing troubled banks.[84] China is a vivid example illustrating how much taxpayers have to pay for the losses of troubled banks under implicit deposit insurance. By 2008, the GDP of China was RMB 30.067 trillion, but, in the meantime, China had spent approximately RMB 3.8 trillion of taxpayers' money rescuing troubled banks, accounting for more than 10 percent of GDP in China.[85]

Additionally, implicit deposit insurance, which does not clearly define the government's legal responsibility for deposit reimbursement or bank liabilities, creates uncertainty for depositors, creditors, and other involved parties. This is to say, government bailouts are discretionary and based on the preference of the government, leading to uncertainty and inequality between large and small banks. Focusing on the three cases stated above, it can be found that this phenomenon is pervasive, as, in comparison with small banks like Hainan Development Bank and Zhengzhou Cooperative Bank, large banks like the Big Four are comparatively more likely to receive unconditional and consistent financial support from the central government. This might introduce uncertainty for Chinese depositors about whether to put their deposits in large state-owned banks or small and medium banks, as large banks are preferred under the considerations of the government. By studying several landmark cases under China's implicit deposit insurance scheme, it is noteworthy that there was no specific authority for resolving troubled banks. The only way to resolve troubled banks was based on interim collaboration between the government, the court, and financial regulatory bodies, which may increase uncertainty and inefficiency.[86] Notwithstanding, it is arguable that uncertainty is likely to incentivise depositors to monitor banks. However, in fact, by the FSF's survey on deposit insurance, most depositors do not have the professional knowledge or willingness to do so.[87]

Moreover, the disparity created by implicit deposit insurance between small and large banks undermines competition within China's banking industry to a significant extent. On one hand, the current state of China's banking sector is dominated by the Big Four, the four largest state-owned commercial banks, which are considered too big to fail and too big to regulate. Consequently, the Chinese government tends to offer excessive protection to these large banks, prioritising financial and social stability. This makes depositors think that depositing money in the Big Four is much safer than saving in other banks, which is the reason why most depositors are willing to put their money in the Big Four rather than small banks with good services and low NPL ratios. As a result, it is reasonable to see that the Big Four, to date, are able to remain monopolies in the domestic banking market, whereas the marketplace for small and medium banks has shrunk amid limited financial resources, resulting in an unfair and concentrated domestic banking market with low competition that significantly undermines customers' interests.

On the other hand, the inequality that significantly reduces competition leads to an obvious moral hazard within the Big Four. The case of the Big Four discussed above demonstrates that, based on past practice, the Chinese government has long been the saviour of the Big Four by using massive public funding to offset nonperforming loans and losses of deposits, leaving the managers of the Big Four with an incentive to pursue high-return but risky investment portfolios. Moreover, risky banks that should be eliminated from the market and go insolvent with a negative balance sheet would still survive due to government backing.[88] It is to be said that this mirrors the ineffectiveness of banking regulation and the urgency of establishing an explicit deposit insurance scheme in China, as government bailouts are not sustainable options versus a systemic financial crisis.

It is undoubted that implicit deposit insurance cannot catch up with the rapid growth of China's banking sector despite its contribution to maintaining financial and social stability during the transition economy in China. Weaknesses exposed in implicit deposit insurance that directly hinder China's efforts to build a more market-oriented banking system are reflected in the following parts: first, taxpayers ultimately pay the giant costs of bank failures; second, uncertainty arising from implicit deposit insurance undermines public confidence and causes deposits to flow to large banks; finally, inequality incurs disequilibrium of competition between large, small, and medium banks, which simultaneously endangers moral hazard within big-name banks. Fortunately, the first formal deposit insurance scheme in China, announced by the State Council in May 2015, is the beginning of China's ambition to build up an efficient and modern financial sector safety net.

5.5 Unveiling the Features of China's Explicit Deposit Insurance Scheme

5.5.1 The Bumping Road of China's Deposit Insurance Scheme

In addition to implicit deposit insurance, China made numerous attempts and faced many challenges before launching its first explicit deposit insurance scheme. The first blueprint for establishing an explicit deposit insurance scheme was introduced with the release of the 'Decision of the State Council on Reform of the Financial System' in 1993, marking the beginning of China's efforts to develop a customised explicit deposit insurance system.[89] In 1997, the central government set out an agenda to implement an explicit deposit insurance system, outlining a detailed timetable, institutional architecture, and strategies for addressing moral hazard, etc. In contrast, the plan was ultimately halted when the central government decided to choose the option of bailouts at the onset of the 1997 Asian financial crisis.

Since the end of 2006, the PBOC emphasised that the banking sector in China was fully ready to launch an explicit deposit insurance system.[90] In 2007, the time seemed right to establish a deposit insurance system nationally, as the State Council assigned the CBRC and PBOC to lead the efforts to launch the Chinese deposit insurance scheme. However, the progress was halted for a second time due to strong lobbying from the large banks and the outbreak of the global financial crisis, which disrupted financial stability worldwide.[91] In 2013, the PBOC reaffirmed that China was fully prepared to implement an explicit deposit insurance scheme, viewing it as a crucial step toward reinforcing the financial safety net. In his 2014 Government Work Report, Premier Li Keqiang emphasised that 'the top priority for advancing China's financial reforms in that year was to ensure the successful establishment of the explicit deposit insurance scheme'.[92] China officially introduced its first explicit deposit insurance scheme on 1 May 2015, with the State Council issuing the Regulation on Deposit Insurance.

The launch of this explicit deposit insurance scheme is expected to drive the development of China's domestic banking industry, especially as China has to confront the recession of its economy following years of rapid economic growth. The slowing economy, which leads to the continuous increase in shadow banking activities and private lending, urges China to accelerate its pace in establishing an explicit deposit insurance scheme to prevent prospective systemic risks.

Furthermore, while China has made great efforts to eliminate excessive controls on its banking sector in order to liberalise and diversify the market, deposit insurance is still regarded as a long-awaited prerequisite to cement further financial reforms, including depositor protection, interest rate liberalisation, the entrance of private banks, and banking resolution regime.

As for the banking resolution regime, many high-profile officials publicly state that China will have real insolvent banks, and deposit insurance will be the major player countering failing commercial banks. For instance, Zhang Tao, the former deputy governor of the PBOC and the current deputy managing director at the IMF, says that 'Chinese commercial banks must be allowed to go insolvent, which is a significant symbol of becoming a market-based banking system'.[93] Zhou Xiaochuan, the former governor of the PBOC, adds that deposit insurance can be the ideal mechanism curtailing contagions and bank runs when a bank goes insolvent.[94] In other words, these reforms, as driving forces, compel deposit insurance to take immediate effect, presenting the urgency of deposit insurance in China. Finally, on 24 May 2019, the PBOC registered the Deposit Insurance Fund Management Corporation (DIFMC) with the capital of RMB 10 billion, and it is fully owned by the PBOC.[95]

5.5.2 Driving Forces for Starting an Explicit Deposit Insurance Scheme

5.5.2.1 Extremely High Household Savings in China

Traditionally, depositing money into banks has long been the most popular financial activity among Chinese citizens. In light of the latest statistics by the IMF, China has been retaining one of the highest national savings rates around the world since the 1980s. By the end of 2017, China's national savings, including household savings, corporate savings, and government savings, took up 45.9 percent of its GDP, which was ranked the second highest savings rate in comparison with the average of approximately 20 percent globally, just slightly falling behind Singapore.[96] Along with a high national savings rate, the household savings rate in China is also much higher than the global average level. By 2017, the global average household savings rate dropped to around 7 percent of GDP, whereas the household savings rate in China reached 23 percent of GDP and the outstanding balance of household savings in China amounted to RMB 60.26 trillion.[97] From Figure 5.5, it can be noticed that the outstanding balance of household savings in China has a close gap with its GDP, reflecting the giant importance of depositor protection in maintaining financial and social stability.

However, before China's explicit deposit insurance scheme came into effect, it was unreasonable that merely the Chinese Commercial Bank Law, the Chinese Enterprise Bankruptcy Law, and the Civil Procedure Law of the People's Republic of China set provisions arranging the order of creditors on bank insolvency, which placed depositors behind employees. Furthermore, the Chinese Commercial Bank Law defines that the relationship between depositors and banks is a debt contractual relationship that cannot secure a priority on bank insolvency. Therefore, an explicit deposit insurance scheme is urgently needed to protect Chinese depositors

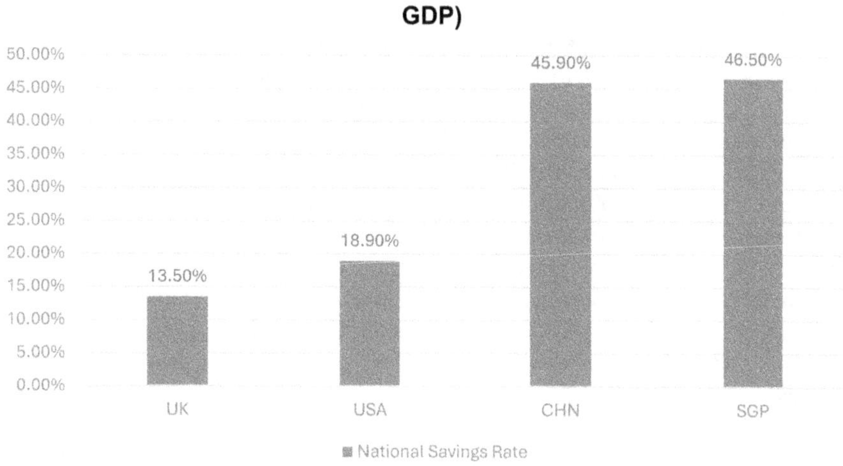

Figure 5.5 National Savings Rate in 2017 (in percent of GDP)
(Data Source: IMF and PBOC)

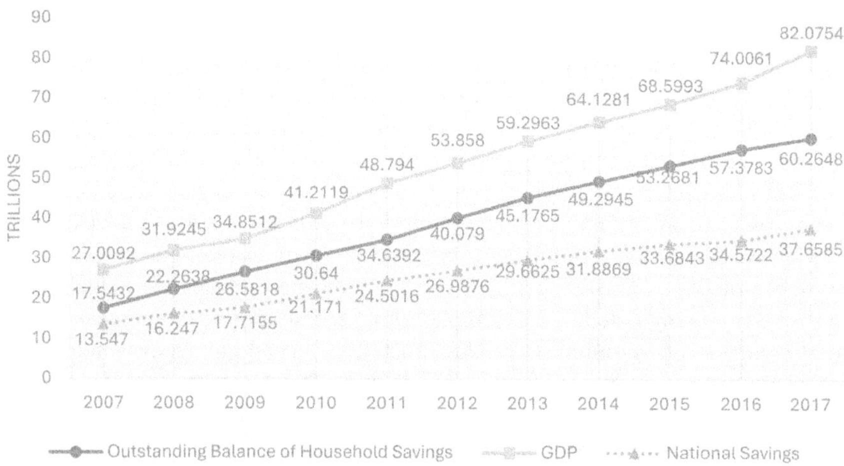

Figure 5.6 The Outlook of Savings in China
(Data Source: Wind Data, National Bureau of Statistics of China)

by creating a specific deposit insurance fund that collects premiums from insured banks to compensate depositors within a reasonable coverage limit. Most importantly, considering the giant amounts of Chinese household savings, a well-designed deposit insurance scheme is urgently needed to protect depositors (Figure 5.6).

5.5.2.2 Interest Rate Liberalisation

Interest rate liberalisation in China is a financial progress, indicating that the PBOC, which takes charge of monetary policy, relinquishes control over setting interest rates, thereby allowing market orientation to pinpoint domestic deposit and lending interest rates. In the past, Chinese commercial banks were subject to unified interest rates, and the right to adjust upper and lower caps on interest rates had long been tightly grasped by the PBOC. Admittedly, that was fair under the centrally planned economy, but when China initiated market-oriented overhauls that converted most commercial banks, including the Big Four, to a joint-stock ownership structure, fixed interest rates adversely impacted competition within China's banking market. The first move towards interest rate liberalisation was on 29 October 2004, as the PBOC removed the upper cap on lending interest rates and the lower cap on deposit interest rates, regarded as the start of progress.[98] The finale came on 24 October 2015, the PBOC repealed the upper limit on deposit interest rates with remaining administrative restrictions, symbolising that China has fundamentally realised interest rate liberalisation.[99]

Nevertheless, the US's experience has demonstrated that interest rate liberalisation might reversely undermine financial stability as riskier depository institutions are likely to pay higher interest rates than the rates at which healthy institutions could pay to attract deposits. Regulation Q was created by the Banking Act of 1933 to allow the Federal Reserve to impose interest rate ceilings on deposits honoured by depository institutions between 1933 and 1986.[100] However, since the 1970s, with the emergence of money market funds, investors rushed to these funds due to the absence of ceilings on interest rates, which hinted that investors might get higher yields than saving money in depository institutions. In order to boost the competitiveness of depository institutions confined by interest rate ceilings, the US Congress passed the Depository Institution Deregulation and Monetary Control Act in 1980, where interest rate ceilings within Regulation Q were planned to be phased out by 1986, signalling the beginning of interest rate marketisation in the US.[101]

However, since the proceeding of interest rate liberalisation, guaranteed by the existence of deposit insurance, high and volatile interest rates circulated in the market when many federally insured depository institutions unscrupulously began to offer higher deposit interest rates to attract deposits and put deposits into riskier investment portfolios in pursuit of high yields.[102] Consequently, the Savings and Loans Crisis erupted, leading to more than 1,500 insured depository institutions closed.[103] The US Congress took two steps in response to the crisis. First, Congress enacted the Financial Institution Reform, Recovery and Enforcement Act in 1989 to underpin the FDIC's powers on deposit insurance by creating the Savings Association Insurance Fund administered by the FDIC to resolve failed depository institutions.[104] Second, the US Congress passed the Federal Deposit Insurance Corporation Improvement Act of 1991 (FDICIA) to strengthen deposit insurance in an effective way. In response to the causes of the crisis, the FDICIA introduced three new measures – a risk-based premium system, prompt corrective action, and least cost resolution – to address dangers exposed during the crisis. As a result, the US finally overcame the crisis and returned to financial stability for years.

From the PBOC's perspective, deposit insurance is expected to be an effective measure to overcome the market turmoil triggered by volatile interest rates since China has basically freed interest rates.[105] In the meantime, interest rate liberalisation that benefits Chinese depositors is regarded as the destination for Chinese financial reform, although Chinese depositors have subsidised low and fixed deposit interest rates for a long time. Nonetheless, the lesson learnt from the US experience indicates that the revolution of interest rates can still can trigger market turbulence unless a well-designed deposit insurance scheme is comprehensively set up. Therefore, a well-designed deposit insurance scheme is the engine driving the marketisation of China's financial system.

5.5.2.3 The Entry of Private-Owned Banks

China has unveiled a pilot programme that allows privately owned banks to provide fundamental banking services to the public since March 2014. This move was aimed at breaking the monopolies of state-owned commercial banks, thereby promoting competition by diversifying financing channels and consumer choice. Since January 2015, backed by private capital, the first five privately owned banks started offering financial services. The eye-catching characteristic of Chinese privately owned banks is that the financial services they provide concentrate on financial inclusion, local communities, and SMEs by making use of internet finance and fintech through operating virtual branches based on their online platforms that can be downloaded from mobile app stores.

The first private bank, WeBank, can be an existing example demonstrating how a private bank works without any physical branch. WeBank, mostly owned by Tencent, a Chinese tech giant, has been offering traditional banking services coupled with emerging technology, like online payment systems, online loans and online savings, through Tencent's communication app 'WeChat', the most circulated mobile communication app in China. This is to say, anyone who has a smartphone can have access to banking services via WeChat just by a swipe of their fingers in few seconds. Simultaneously, regarding risk management, supported by big data, WeBank has a comprehensive credit rating system working for every user of WeChat who could be a potential client, and the maximum loan allowed for individuals, local communities, and SMEs is RMB 3 million.

To date, in the wake of the first five pilot private-owned banks, another 12 private-owned banks have been founded to operate fundamental banking services within a limited geographic scope. In the long run, these private-owned banks will be leading the way in China's blueprint to reshape the prospective bank market in China, which will definitely overhaul China's banking sector (Figure 5.7).

Although private-owned banks provide convenience for individuals and SMEs to deposit money and loan money out, it is dangerous to enable privately owned banks to run without having an explicit deposit insurance scheme in place. One view agrees that deposit insurance is the most important precondition for allowing privately owned banks to participate in China's banking market. As noted by Premier Li Keqiang:

> From international experience, establishing a deposit insurance scheme is compulsory precondition for developing private banks, small and medium

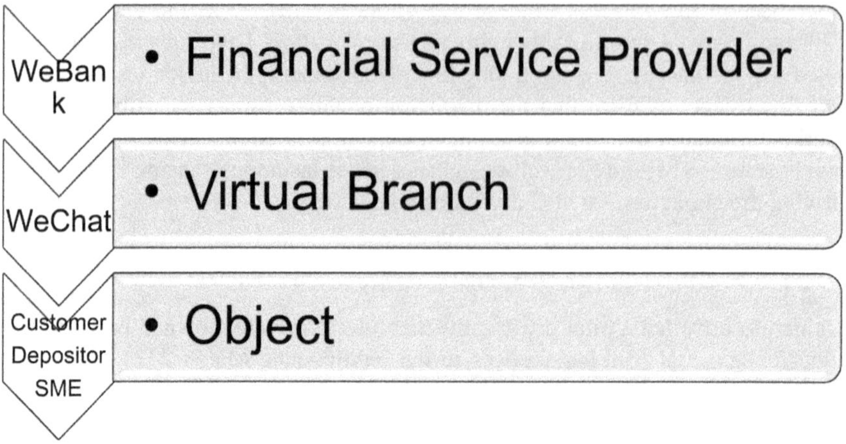

Figure 5.7 How WeBank Works?

> banks. Deposit insurance not only can promote fair competition with the financial market but also can strengthen the reliability of these banks, hence pushing financial reform forward towards real market-based financial system.[106]

The US's experience illustrates the importance of deposit insurance in keeping community banks competitive and resilient amid consolidation in the banking industry between 1980 and 2013. The function and market position of US community banks are quite similar to Chinese privately owned banks in accordance with the FDIC's definition of community banks, which provide fundamental banking services that target individuals, local communities, and SMEs.[107] Alongside a study on community banks by the FDIC, from 1985 to 2013, amid interest rate marketisation, the total number of banks significantly slumped from around 20,000 to 6,812, including 68 percent of total community banks that had failed, been acquired, or been consolidated in comparison with 94 percent of total non-community banks.[108] More straightforwardly, the ratio of FDIC-insured community banks had climbed to 93 percent, 6 percentage points ahead of 1985, reflecting the resilience and competitiveness of FDIC-insured community banks faced with long-term consolidation in the banking industry and two financial crises in the US.[109] It is clear that deposit insurance and the FDIC should be praised for keeping community banks competitive, which underscores the importance of implementing deposit insurance in an effective way that allows community banks to contend with larger and riskier banks on a level playing field, as deposit insurance implemented by the FDIC gives better protection to community banks' core business of 'small deposit, small lending'.[110]

Therefore, deposit insurance in China is urgently needed to create a level playing field for privately owned banks to contend with state-owned commercial banks. Unlike state-owned commercial banks, which are backed by the government credit, private banks founded through private capital are completely market-oriented and thus vulnerable to failure or mergers. The establishment of a deposit insurance scheme can reassure depositors that there is no difference between state-owned commercial banks and privately owned banks, ensuring that depositors of both privately owned banks and state-owned commercial banks are fairly treated under the same scheme. The experience of US community banks has proven that deposit insurance is one of the most important factors in ensuring small banks survive in a competitive market.

Opponents argue that, with deposit insurance, these privately owned banks might become financing channels for their shareholders to become involved in riskier investment portfolios.[111] Concerned by opponents, amid the concurrent implementation of deposit insurance and interest rate liberalisation, the sudden increase in costs comprising of deposit insurance premiums and higher interest rates may hit privately owned banks' revenues and force them to pursue high-yield but riskier portfolios, thereby placing them on the verge of danger. Nonetheless, in reality, all privately owned banks appear to deliver a decent performance rather than previous estimations. According to the figures released by the CBRC, as of the end of 2018, the average NPL ratio of privately owned banks just 0.53 percent, the lowest rate among China's banking industry.[112]

5.5.2.4 *Market-Based Banking Resolution Regime*

Along with the commencement of interest rate liberalisation and privately owned banks, bank collapses that were a taboo subject in the past will appear as a normal phenomenon in the near future. With accelerating reforms to further open up China's financial system, banks will encounter troubles when risks accumulate to a certain level, and the resilience of China's banking industry is in doubt. In reality, through studying the history of massive bailouts in the cases discussed above, China has not yet carried out any formal banking resolution regime to resolve failing financial institutions. Bailouts that waste huge amounts of taxpayers' contributions for remedying mistakes arising from state-owned commercial banks are no longer appropriate, especially when privately owned banks enter the market. Therefore, establishing an explicit deposit insurance scheme is set to be the foundation for integrating a specialised banking resolution regime on the agenda. [113]

Besides, under China's contemporary legal framework, existing laws including the Chinese Commercial Bank Law, the Chinese Banking Regulation and Supervision Law, and the Enterprise Bankruptcy Law leave a huge vacuum in mapping out rules for preventing risks and resolving troubled banks. Surprisingly, the most relevant rules, namely Regulations on the Cancellation of Financial Institutions, can be traced back to 2001. These regulations merely detailed responsibilities and mandates of the PBOC in revoking licenses and being involved in winding-up procedures.[114] However, both existing laws and regulations neglect the importance of depositor protection, exposing depositors to risks, which might increase the possibility of bank runs and panic.

The UK and the US's experiences illustrate deposit insurance in different ways to facilitate the effectiveness of banking resolution mechanisms. Focusing on the

US mechanism, the FDIC, which is well-equipped to resolve troubled banks, is undoubtedly a big name for banks that engage in risky financial activities. At an early stage, underpinned by the FDICIA in 1991, the FDIC can implement capital-based prompt corrective action to decide mandatory actions necessary to confront financial institutions placed in different capital categories.[115] For example, the FDIC shall be appointed as a receiver or conservator within 90 days when a bank is classified as 'critically undercapitalised' due to its tangible equity being equal to or less than 2 percent of its total assets, unless other better alternatives are approved by the FDIC.[116]

After that, the FDIC might, through various purchases and assumption transactions, look for potential buyers who will assume all or some liabilities. In addition, under the Federal Deposit Insurance Act, the FDIC has full authority and mandate to deal with assets and liabilities of a failed bank in pursuit of maximising the interests of depositors without any disruptions arising from the courts, creditors, and shareholders. Hence, focusing on the US approach, deposit insurance in the US is integrated into a banking resolution mechanism committed to keeping the financial market stable for both banks and depositors.[117] In contrast to the US approach, the UK has adopted a relatively simple way to run deposit insurance coupled with banking insolvency.

Under the UK banking resolution regime, the FSCS, the UK's deposit insurer and a member of the Liquidation Committee, is capable of engaging in decision-making to appoint a bank liquidator and work closely with the bank liquidator and relevant authorities to ensure that faster payouts with priority can be delivered as soon as possible. In order to achieve this goal, since 1 January 2011, the Single Customer View has been adopted by the FSCS to secure the accuracy of most individual deposit accounts, so as to compensate depositors immediately after accepting claims submitted by depositors.

Having drawn lessons from the UK and the US, it is obvious that deposit insurance is the starting point of the entire banking resolution process. With the further opening of China's financial market, China must build its own bank resolution mechanism before bank failures actually happen. Therefore, China's deposit insurance scheme that has been unveiled recently is paving the way towards initiating a progressive banking resolution mechanism. However, the only question that might reduce the effectiveness of a banking resolution regime in China is whether the PBOC or the CBRC should take the lead in the banking resolution process, as both of them appear to be entitled to run this mechanism, and regulatory overlaps would incur potential conflicts.

5.5.3 Features of the Chinese Deposit Insurance Scheme

5.5.3.1 Institution and Governance

On 1 May 2015, the State Council issued the Regulation on Deposit Insurance, consisting of 23 articles that establish the essential components of an explicit deposit insurance scheme, including governance, compensation limit, responsibilities, pricing system, and funding mechanism. To date, the China Deposit Insurance

Fund Management Corporation (DIFMC) of the PBOC serves as the deposit insurer in China, though Article 3 of the Regulation anticipates the creation of an entirely independent DIFMC in the near future in China. However, Chinese scholars express three different opinions on the institutional structure of the DIFMC.

First, some Chinese scholars argue that the DIFMC should be a subsidiary of the NFRA. Qingming Yan, the director of China Investment Corporation and a leading proponent of this view, believes that placing the deposit insurance function under the NFRA would enhance coordination and information sharing within the NFRA, given that the NFRA is the most authoritative and relevant regulatory body for banking oversight in China.[118] Fan supports Yan's idea, adding that integrating deposit insurance with banking regulation could greatly improve regulatory efficiency by diversifying supervisory tools in a cost-effective manner. This framework would allow the NFRA to impose differentiated deposit insurance premiums on banks engaging in risky activities and optimise the precision and timing of information sharing, while reducing regulatory costs.[119]

In the meantime, Article 1 of the Chinese Banking Regulation and Supervision Law states that the NFRA is responsible for protecting depositors, which suggests that the NFRA has the legal authority to oversee depositor protection, positioning it as the irreplaceable and primary authority in banking supervision.[120] However, critics argue that placing deposit insurance under the NFRA could lead to regulatory forbearance and capture, undermining its effectiveness.[121] They contend that because deposit insurance acts as the last ditch of the financial safety net, the NFRA might loosen its regulation of banks, knowing that deposit insurance will undertake all losses of bank failures, leading to regulatory forbearance. Additionally, if the DIFMC is a subsidiary of the NFRA, it could be subject to regulatory capture, where it might be used to cover up regulatory shortcomings, particularly concerning the management of its funding pool raised from premiums. In such a scenario, the DIFMC could shift its focus from protecting depositors to shielding banking institutions, thereby defeating its core goal.

Second, some proponents argue that the DIFMC should be overseen and managed by the PBOC. Historically, under implicit deposit insurance, the PBOC had acted as a safeguard for both depositors and banks, gaining significant experience in handling non-performing loans and executing bailouts to extend the survival of struggling banks. The Big Four case, for example, reveals the PBOC's involvement in rescuing technically insolvent banks back to normal. Wei, a supporter of this approach, favours the PBOC's control over deposit insurance, citing its extensive experience and deep understanding of deposit insurance as a key advantage over the NFRA.[122] In addition, Wei argues that deposit insurance and lender of last resort are two critical mechanisms for mitigating public panic during financial instability. Housing both functions within the PBOC could enable closer collaboration and better performance in risk prevention than if they were separated[123] Furthermore, with the PBOC's backing, deposit insurance, a relatively new concept in China, is more likely to gain trust and confidence.

However, Yan and Chen strongly oppose this institutional structure, arguing that placing deposit insurance under the PBOC would severely compromise the independence of monetary policy.[124] Yan elaborates that, in some cases, the PBOC might attempt to rescue struggling banks by printing additional currency, potentially leading to an oversupply of money and causing inflation, particularly during a significant banking crisis.[125] Moreover, the coexistence of deposit insurance and the lender of last resort function could blur the decision-making process regarding whether to allow failing banks to collapse. Bagehot's principle, which advocates for the lender of last resort to provide funds freely to solvent but illiquid institutions against good assets and securities at a high interest rate, would become less clear in such a scenario.[126]

Nevertheless, deposit insurance works in contrast with the lender of last resort, as the purpose of deposit insurance is to keep depositors – usually small and ordinary depositors – away from the losses in the event of bank failures. Garcia stresses that the undue use of lender of last resort will delay the timing of closure for a troubled bank, which should go insolvent, and increase the costs for deposit insurance. Therefore, it is fair to say that deposit insurance should not be together with the lender of last resort given the entirely different purposes and functions of each and the conflict of interest in practice.[127]

The third perspective, which aligns with international standards and consensus, strongly advocates for an independent deposit insurance agency, separate from both the PBOC and the NFRA. Nearly all major international organisations emphasise that a deposit insurer should be operationally independent and protected from external interference to avoid the aforementioned conflicts of interest. As yet, almost all influential international organisations underscore that a deposit insurer should be operationally independent and insulated from external intervention to maximally dodge aforementioned conflicts of interest.[128] The IADI surveys conducted between 2011 and 2018 show that the number of countries with independent deposit insurance agencies has doubled, with the majority of such agencies worldwide being operationally independent.[129] While there is no universally perfect approach to designing a perfect deposit insurance scheme, the trend of establishing independent deposit insurance agencies has become mainstream and is often considered the preferred option for newly created deposit insurance systems (Table 5.3).

Focusing on China's deposit insurance scheme, although the Regulation on Deposit Insurance has not given a clear definition regarding the governance and administrative structure, Articles 7 and 14 hint that the DIFMC will be directed by the State Council and independent from the PBOC and the NFRA.[130] The proposal

Table 5.3 Legal Structure of Deposit Insurance Agency Worldwide

Year		*Independent*	*Within the Central Bank*	*Within the Bank Supervisor*	*Others*
2011	Number	51	13	1	14
	Proportion	64.56%	16.46%	1.27%	17.72%
2018	Number	102	13	5	14
	Proportion	76.12%	9.70%	3.73%	10.45%

Data Source: IADI.

to create an independent deposit insurance agency is also supported by numerous domestic scholars, aiming to strengthen China's financial safety and incorporate a system of checks and balances within the country's financial regulatory architecture. This architecture would establish a tripartite mechanism within the financial safety net, where the PBOC would serve as the lender of last resort, the NFRA would handle prudential regulation, and the DIFMC would manage the deposit insurance function[131] Besides, like the FDIC and the FSCS, the board of the DIFMC can be made up of directors arising from the PBOC and the CBRC, aimed at fortifying coordination and information sharing among the participants of the financial safety net.

While this architecture may help China align with the global trend of implementing deposit insurance, the issue of funding – both in terms of initial capital and the deposit insurance fund – remains pressing. As of the end of 2023, China's deposit insurance fund had reached RMB 81.01 billion, which is inadequate when compared to the total banking assets of RMB 419.64 trillion and the total household savings of over RMB 147.13 trillion.[132] Therefore, the funding scale represents a critical weakness for the Chinese deposit insurance scheme, and the central government should provide necessary financial support to establish a robust deposit insurance fund capable of handling bank runs and failures. Given the current high volume of government debt, direct lending from the central government seems impractical. Instead, a more feasible option is for the government to raise funds for the deposit insurance fund by selling shares of state-owned commercial banks[133] This approach could significantly reduce the government's stake in the banking sector, potentially opening the door for more private capital and making banks more market-driven, with less political influence. However, the downside is that state-owned commercial banks, which traditionally focus on maintaining financial stability without the pressure to maximise profits, would face new financial and profit expectations after losing control, leading them to pursue riskier, high-yield investments.

Unfortunately, it seems like China has chosen the second view to place the deposit insurance agency into the PBOC. On 24 May 2019, the PBOC registered the DIFMC with registered capital of RMB 10 billion, which means that the DIFMC became an independent legal entity entirely owned by the PBOC.[134] Xiaolong Huang, deputy director of the Financial Stability Bureau of the PBOC, has officially become the first chairman of the DIFMC, indicating that deposit insurance will still be grasped by the PBOC in the following decades.

5.5.3.2 Obligations, Mandates, and Authority

According to the Regulation on Deposit Insurance, the DIFMC is primarily focused on protecting depositors and minimising losses in the event of bank failures.[135] While the Regulation does not clearly define the institutional structure or administrative framework of the DIFMC, it emphasises that unresolved matters will ultimately be decided by the State Council. However, the Regulation does outline several key responsibilities of the DIFMC, including:

- Formulating and issuing rules related to its duties;
- Setting and adjusting deposit insurance premium rates, subject to the State Council's approval;
- Determining the specific premium rates for each insured financial institution;
- Collecting deposit insurance premiums;
- Managing and utilising the deposit insurance fund;
- Implementing early corrective actions and managing risks;
- Timely compensation of depositors in accordance with the Regulation;
- Carrying out other tasks and responsibilities as assigned by the State Council.[136]

To fulfil its duties, the Regulation grants the DIFMC the authority to inspect insured financial institutions under specific conditions: (1) when changes in the institution's risk level render their premium rates unsuitable; (2) when there are concerns about the scale, structure, or accuracy of deposits at the institution; and (3) when the accuracy and reliability of information or documents submitted by the institution need verification.[137] If serious deficiencies are discovered during these inspections, the DIFMC is required to promptly notify the NFRA of its findings.[138] Additionally, the DIFMC has the authority to issue warnings to insured institutions facing capital shortfalls or other negative indicators that could endanger the deposit insurance fund and the insured deposits.[139]

Moreover, the Regulation allows the DIFMC to impose higher premiums on troubled institutions that fail to take corrective action to restore capital adequacy and meet other requirements after suffering significant asset losses or other events that could severely impact the deposit insurance fund and insured deposits.[140] The DIFMC can also require institutions to correct major issues if they: (1) fail to join the deposit insurance scheme; (2) fail to pay deposit insurance premiums; (3) provide inaccurate information or documents; (4) obstruct the DIFMC's inspections; (5) interfere with the use of the deposit insurance fund.[141] In addition to these mandates, the DIFMC is authorised to penalise directors or other responsible individuals. Notably, Article 19 of the Regulation highlights that the DIFMC has the power to take control of insured institutions and act as the liquidator in cases of bank insolvency.[142]

The decision to grant the DIFMC broad authority has sparked significant debate within academic circles. The IADI has classified mandates of deposit insurers into four categories – pay box, pay box plus, loss-minimiser, and risk-minister.[143] According to the classification by the IADI, the DIFMC operates between the loss-minimiser and risk-minimiser models. In contrast to the broad mandates granted to the DIFMC, some opponents argue that under the current financial regulatory architecture, the PBOC and the NFRA already possess sufficient authority to oversee banking supervision and regulation, making a pay box model deposit insurance scheme adequate for the Chinese banking system.[144] Kryzanowski further points out that having multiple financial regulatory bodies can lead to regulatory overlaps, reducing efficiency and wasting resources.[145] However, he underscores that a deposit insurer with clearly defined objectives, responsibilities, and powers can still function effectively within the financial safety net.[146] From a legislative standpoint, a potential conflict of interest already exists between the NFRA and the DIFMC. Article 1 of the Chinese Banking Regulation and Supervision Law identifies the protection of depositors as a key mission of the NFRA, while Article 1 of the Regulation on Deposit Insurance specifies that the DIFMC's primary goal is also to protect depositors.

Despite the debate, most Chinese scholars agree that the DIFMC should be granted sufficient authority. First, as economist John A. Weinberg from the Federal Reserve Bank of Richmond suggests, having multiple financial regulators can encourage competition, driving them to perform more efficiently, although it may also lead to regulatory forbearance.[147] Second, Wei argues that the creation of the DIFMC would not result in overlaps with the NFRA and PBOC, as each body has distinct policy objectives when taking action.[148] For example, unlike the NFRA and PBOC, the DIFMC's purpose in conducting on-site examinations and inspections is to set premium rates at appropriate levels and prepare for potential risks, ultimately to protect depositors. However, without a well-designed arrangement, insured institutions could become burdened by multiple regulators, facing repeated inspections from different agencies. As a result, many experts recommend the establishment of an effective coordination mechanism to minimise unnecessary on-site inspections and reduce the waste of regulatory resources.[149]

In addition to a well-designed coordination mechanism, a comprehensive overhaul of legislation is essential. This includes drafting enforceable rules that clearly define the responsibilities of each regulatory body, enhancing information collection and sharing, and incorporating interagency cooperation into laws and regulations. The recently established Financial Stability and Development Committee could be a potential solution to optimise China's financial safety net. Notably, this Committee is composed of leaders from relevant regulatory bodies, including the PBOC and the CBIRC, and is chaired by the Vice Premier. It has the potential to unify these regulatory bodies, address regulatory gaps and overlaps, and harmonise conflicting policies, thereby strengthening regulatory cohesion and improving coordination[150] (Table 5.4).

5.5.3.3 Membership of the Chinese Deposit Insurance Scheme

In theory, when a country establishes a new deposit insurance system, two critical issues must be considered: the types of financial institutions to be insured and

Table 5.4 Ideal Financial Safety Net in China

Institution	*Designed Role*	*Target*	*Measure*
NFRA	Prudential regulator	All banking institutions	On-site examination, revocation of banking licenses, enforceable punishments
PBOC	Lender of last resort	Troubled banking institutions	Emergency lending, liquidity support
DIFMC	Deposit insurer	Insolvent banking institutions	Depositor compensation, banking liquidator

whether membership should be voluntary or mandatory. Fortunately, many prominent international organisations and experts have reached a consensus on the membership structure for an effective deposit insurance scheme. For instance, the IADI, IMF, and Garcia strongly advocate for compulsory membership, recommending that all banks subject to prudential regulation and supervision be required to participate in the deposit insurance system.[151] The purpose of implementing compulsory membership in a deposit insurance scheme is to reduce adverse selection and ensure a level playing field for all banks.

Article 2 of the Regulation on Deposit Insurance addresses two key issues in line with the recommendations from the IADI and IMF. According to this article, all deposit-taking institutions established in China must participate in the deposit insurance scheme and pay the corresponding premiums, with the exception of overseas branches of Chinese banks and domestic branches of foreign banks, unless there is a bilateral deposit insurance agreement with China. Notably, 39 locally incorporated subsidiaries wholly owned by foreign banks, such as HSBC Bank (China) Limited and Citibank (China) Limited, are included in China's deposit insurance scheme. Additionally, Article 22 specifies that institutions identified by the CBRC for takeover or licence revocation, or those that have had bankruptcy petitions processed prior to the enactment of this Regulation, are also excluded from the scheme.

In past decades, China's banking system remained isolated from the global market, even with the implementation of reform and opening-up policies. The lack of competitiveness allowed state-owned commercial banks, which are the dominant form of bank in China, to accept deposits while offering consumers low interest rates. They would then lend these deposits to state-owned enterprises without conducting proper risk assessments, relying on the belief that the central government would act as the ultimate guarantor in the event of a banking failure. This situation created implicit subsidies supported by Chinese depositors and the government. Consequently, state-owned commercial banks and state-owned enterprises, being the primary beneficiaries of this implicit deposit insurance, have been the main lobbying force against the introduction of formal deposit insurance for many years.[152] Despite the rapid growth of a more diversified banking system and the easing of banking licence requirements, the market share of the Big Four banks still exceeded 40 percent by assets as of 2023. Thus, including these major banks in China's deposit insurance scheme represents significant progress, serving as a reminder to all banks that no institution is immune from risk, and they must prioritise risk management.

It is clear that China has kept the same pace as the US and the UK in managing membership for deposit insurance. In the US and the UK, only locally incorporated foreign banks can be fully insured by the FSCS and the FDIC, respectively. For example, ICBC has a New York branch and a US-incorporated subsidiary, namely ICBC (US), National Association. In accordance with the ICBC resolution plan submitted to the FDIC, only the deposits in the US-incorporated subsidiary of ICBC are insured and the New York branch is excluded.[153] As clarified by the relevant regulation, 'the FDIC will not insure deposits in any branch of a foreign bank unless that foreign bank agrees that every branch established or operated by the foreign bank in the same state that involves domestic retail deposit activity will be an insured branch'.[154]

The UK has learnt lessons from the GFC. In the collapse of Landsbanki, the Icelandic Depositors' and Investors' Guarantee Fund and Icelandic Financial Supervisory Authority merely decided to reimburse domestic depositors of Landsbanki, leaving 230,000 UK depositors of its UK branch 'Icesave' without their savings equal to around £3.5 billion.[155] Subsequently, in order to maintain financial stability and prevent bank runs during the global financial crisis, the FSCS and the UK government stepped in and determined to recover UK savers' deposits in 'Icesave', with full coverage and protection. However, after the UK savers' deposits had been recovered, the UK asked Iceland to repay in line with minimum deposit insurance guarantees in Iceland, whereas the Court of Justice of the European Free Trade Association States eventually objected to the UK's request and gave Iceland exemption from deposit guarantee obligations.[156] As a result, after the case, the UK altered and optimised its requirements on membership for foreign banks, as only UK-incorporated subsidiaries of foreign banks or branches of foreign banks authorised by the PRA are allowed to be covered under the FSCS.

Nevertheless, in light of China's concentrated banking market, extending membership to branches of foreign banks is expected to encourage more foreign banks to enter the Chinese market. This could help diminish the dominance of state-owned commercial banks and push them to improve their banking services. Nonetheless, it may be unrealistic and unnecessary to include foreign bank branches in the membership. In reality, these overseas branches primarily provide wholesale banking services to corporate clients rather than serving ordinary depositors. As a result, protecting corporate depositors may divert from the primary objective of deposit insurance, which is to safeguard regular depositors. Therefore, the existing membership structure of China's deposit insurance scheme, which aligns with those in the UK and the US, is sufficient to encompass the insured institutions.

5.5.3.4 Coverage in the Chinese Deposit Insurance Scheme

Coverage is a crucial aspect in balancing excessive depositor protection with market discipline. According to the IADI's Core Principle 8, an effective deposit insurance scheme should be thoughtfully designed with limited coverage that protects most depositors while still allowing a significant portion of deposits to be subject to market discipline.[157] While limited coverage may seem reliable during stable economic periods, financial crises often lead to calls for higher coverage levels or blanket guarantees to address public fears. For instance, during the global financial crisis, countries like the US and the UK significantly increased their coverage limits, while others, such as Germany, temporarily implemented blanket guarantees instead of traditional deposit insurance. Following the crisis, most deposit insurance schemes reverted to limited coverage but with revised and notably higher coverage limits.

Regarding coverage in China, the country, which established its deposit insurance scheme in 2015, has taken lessons from the global financial crisis into account when determining coverage levels. In line with international practices, Article 4 of the Regulation on Deposit Insurance extends coverage to foreign currency deposits while excluding interbank deposits and the deposits of senior management from insured institutions. Article 5 stipulates that depositors who maintain accounts in different insured banks are protected separately, with a maximum limit of RMB 500,000; any amounts exceeding this limit will be compensated according to winding-up procedures. Furthermore, the PBOC, in collaboration with other relevant ministries under the State Council, can adjust the coverage limit based on economic conditions, deposit structures, and risk levels, although any changes to the deposit insurance coverage must be approved by the State Council. After compensating insured deposits, the DIFMC will automatically assume the creditor's rights of insured depositors to pursue repayments from the insured institutions during the winding-up process.

When compared to coverage limits in the UK and the US, China's current deposit insurance limit, which covers 99.63 percent of depositors according to the PBOC, is notably high. This coverage is equivalent to 5.65 times the 2023 GDP per capita, in contrast to the US coverage limit, which is 3.06 times GDP per capita, and the UK's, which is 2.74 times GDP per capita.[158] Internationally, the average coverage limit typically ranges from 2 to 5 times GDP per capita.[159] Therefore, it is evident that China's deposit insurance scheme is heavily focused on protecting depositors rather than encouraging them to impose market discipline by monitoring banks' activities.

However, the PBOC takes a different stance and defends the decision to set a high coverage limit. It argues that, as a developing country, China lacks a comprehensive social welfare system, meaning its citizens must save extensively for education, healthcare, and pensions. This is one of the reasons China has the second-highest savings rate in the world. Therefore, establishing a high coverage limit to safeguard citizens' savings in support of social welfare is seen as both reasonable and necessary to maintain public confidence and financial stability, considering the country's specific circumstances.[160] However, in practice, the wealth gap in China means that wealthier individuals benefit most from the current coverage limit. For example, average individual savings in Beijing are over three times those in Hefei, and savings in Shanghai and Guangzhou are double those of the three lowest-ranked cities. Figure 5.8 illustrates significant wealth disparities and economic imbalances across regions, even though the coverage limit remains the same, highlighting that high coverage can be a double-edged sword in practice.

Besides, another gap in the Regulation on Deposit Insurance lies in Article 4, which only mentions that foreign currency deposits are protected but does not specify which types of deposits are covered or whether nonfinancial corporate deposits are excluded. In practice, it is likely that China will extend coverage to include demand deposits, time deposits, and even corporate deposits, particularly for SMEs, in both RMB and foreign currencies. This broad and inclusive coverage would facilitate the transition from implicit to explicit deposit insurance

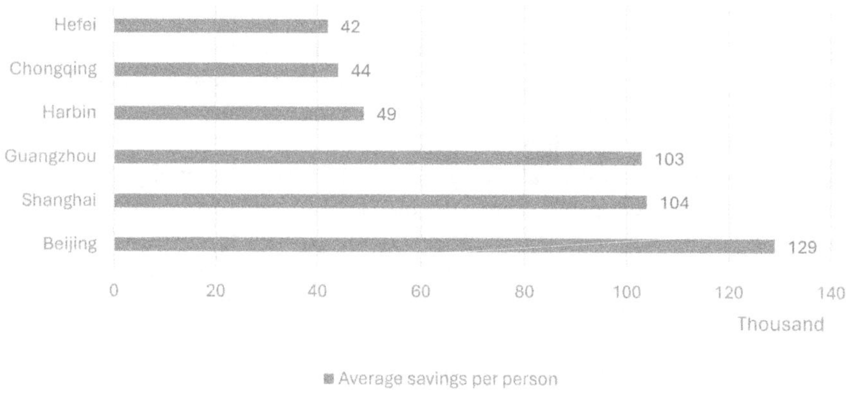

Figure 5.8 Three Highest Average Savings Comparing to the Three Lowest Average Savings in Provincial Capital Cities in China

(Data Source: National Bureau of Statistics of China)

in China's banking system. As the country opens its doors to private banks, the likelihood of bank failures increases, making it essential to establish clear deposit insurance coverage so that depositors are fully aware of the risks involved in financial activities.

5.5.3.5 The Deposit Insurance Premium Pricing Mechanism in China

In the aftermath of the global financial crisis, the ex-ante funding arrangement for accumulating deposit insurance funds has become a universally accepted standard, as recommended by the IADI, IMF, and FSB. Both the FSB and IADI emphasise that an ex-ante funding mechanism, which involves collecting premiums from member institutions in advance, is a crucial measure to ensure prompt deposit payoffs. Learning from international experience, China has established and implemented an ex-ante funding mechanism with compulsory membership since the Regulation on Deposit Insurance came into effect on 1 May 2015.

Article 6 of the Regulation on Deposit Insurance outlines the sources of China's deposit insurance fund, which include: (1) premiums contributed by depository institutions; (2) assets distributed from insured depository institutions after winding-up procedures; (3) returns generated from the use of the deposit insurance fund during stable periods; and (4) other legal income sources.[161] Article 8 specifies that existing depository institutions must begin paying premiums following the implementation of the deposit insurance scheme, while new banks licenced after 1 May 2015, are required to start contributing premiums within six months of their establishment.[162] According to Article 10, depository institutions must pay premiums every six months, with the amount calculated by the DIFMC based on periodic reports submitted by insured institutions, which detail their outstanding deposit balances, deposit structure, and other relevant information.[163]

The PBOC has provided three reasons for adopting an ex-ante funding mechanism.[164] First, unlike ex-post funding, which only requires contributions from surviving banks after a failure, ex-ante funding ensures fairness across China's banking system by requiring all member banks to pay premiums in advance, sharing the burden of potential bank failures. Second, an ex-ante funding mechanism insures the deposit insurance, allowing the DIFMC to respond swiftly to reimburse depositors and prevent panic. Third, the mechanism's anti-cyclical nature allows premiums accumulated during stable economic periods to cover losses during downturns when bank failures are more likely. However, as Blair et al. point out, a key drawback of ex-ante funding is its potential to reduce capital and liquidity in the banking system since the accumulated funds can only be invested in certain low-risk financial products as regulated by law.[165] By contrast, ex-post funding raises concerns because it only requires sound banks to contribute after a failure, leading to unfairness as these banks bear the financial burden.[166]

Interestingly, China's deposit insurance fund pricing mechanism consists of both flat-rate and risk-based premiums. According to Article 9 of the Regulation on Deposit Insurance, all depository institutions in China are required to pay both types of premiums at the same time. The basic flat-rate premiums for banks are determined using a specific formula:[167]

$$\text{Deposit Insurance Premiums} = \text{the Volume of Insured Deposits} \times \text{Fixed Rates } (\leq 0.016\%)$$

The PBOC initially set fixed rates for insured institutions ranging from 0.01% to 0.02%, ultimately capping the fixed rate at 0.0016%.[168] However, Zhou Xiaochuan, the former Governor of the PBOC, acknowledged that this rate, significantly lower than the international average, has a minimal impact on insured banks, leading to a lack of caution regarding risky assets.[169] Despite being lower than the global average, the lower fixed rate is understandable in light of the additional risk-based premiums. While flat-rate premiums simplify the fee structure for member banks, they overlook essential aspects of banks' risk management and overall stability.[170] Given the dominance of the Big Four banks in China's banking sector, even with flat-rate premiums, they would still end up paying more in premiums compared to other banks. Risk-based premiums are particularly effective at reducing moral hazard by addressing issues related to poor corporate governance and lending practices. However, establishing a comprehensive risk-based premium system in China poses challenges due to the need for a robust database and experienced personnel to verify information and assess risk levels accurately.[171]

Additionally, the PBOC has not provided any specific details on how the assessment of risk-based premiums operates in China. The presence of state-owned commercial banks poses a significant challenge for implementing effective risk-based premiums. Due to long-standing implicit subsidies from the government, these banks often have stronger balance sheets and lower non-performing loan (NPL) ratios, allowing them to pay lower premiums compared to their competitors, which creates an unfair advantage. However, since state-owned commercial banks are the primary beneficiaries of financial stability and implicit guarantees, they should contribute more to the deposit insurance fund, as these subsidies ultimately come from taxpayers. To gain public trust, China needs to establish a credible and equitable risk-based assessment system. This includes developing scientifically sound formulas for calculating premiums that accurately reflect the actual risk levels, creating detailed rules for assessing risk-based premiums, and ensuring fairness between large and small depository institutions.

Since the start of its deposit insurance programme in 2015, China has grappled with establishing an optimal size for its deposit insurance fund, alongside setting a suitable pricing mechanism. By the end of 2023, China's deposit insurance fund had grown to RMB 81.01 billion, representing about 0.1% of insured deposits.[172] However, compared to countries with well-established deposit insurance systems like the US, Canada, and the UK, China's ratio remains relatively low and is far from adequate to safeguard depositors.[173] The IADI advises that countries aiming to establish financially sustainable deposit insurance funds should begin by determining the fund's size, taking into account funding sources, risk exposures, and macroeconomic conditions.[174] As an example, since the Dodd-Frank Act came into effect in 2010, the FDIC has been authorised to set the Designated Reserve Ratio (DRR) for the deposit insurance fund above 1.35% of insured deposits. Since 2011, this ratio has remained at 2 percent of insured deposits.[175] As a newcomer in establishing a deposit insurance scheme, China should carefully consider the optimal size of its deposit insurance fund and incorporate this target size into laws or regulations, along with its pricing mechanism, to help close the gap with developed countries.

5.5.3.6 Compensation Mechanism in the Chinese Deposit Insurance Scheme

An effective deposit insurance scheme that ensures prompt reimbursement of depositors is regarded as one of the most powerful tools for preventing panic withdrawals.[176] Although deposit insurance laws or regulations should clearly define compensation procedures and timelines, China's Regulation on Deposit Insurance lacks detail in this area. The relevant clauses are fairly minimal, simply outlining the methods and conditions for compensating depositors.

Article 18 of the Regulation requires the DIFMC to compensate depositors using one of several methods, guided by the least-cost principle: (1) directly reimbursing insured depositors within a designated timeframe, (2) permitting other qualified insured institutions to handle reimbursements on behalf of the DIFMC, or (3) offering guarantees, loss-sharing, or cash flow to potential acquirers to support the transfer of some or all business, assets, and liabilities of a failing institution. Article 19 further specifies the conditions that trigger depositor compensation, mandating that the DIFMC reimburse insured depositors within seven working days, in line with IADI core principles. Beyond these essentials, the Regulation provides little additional detail on implementation, timelines, or information access. Nonetheless, the IADI emphasises that a credible deposit insurance scheme should include clear, thorough rules to outline each step in the compensation process.

Moreover, the absence of regulations granting the DIFMC access to information on insured depositors significantly hinders prompt reimbursement, as it is challenging to identify depositors eligible for compensation after a bank failure without accurate records. Currently, no supplementary article addresses access to insured deposit accounts. In contrast, jurisdictions like the US and the UK have the authority to regularly obtain updated insured deposit information from member banks, with the UK implementing the Single Customer View to ensure the FSCS can reimburse insured parties accurately and efficiently.

Learning from the global financial crisis and practices in other jurisdictions, the Regulation on Deposit Insurance would benefit from more specific rules and clarifications on the circumstances that trigger reimbursements, reimbursement timelines, and access to information for each insured account in the event of a bank failure. On information access, Article 10 of the Regulation grants the DIFMC authority to collect information on covered deposits, accounts, and relevant data for calculating deposit insurance premiums, suggesting the potential to expand this authority to include insured account data—facilitating timely and accurate compensation through targeted access to covered depositors' information.

5.5.3.7 *Prompt Corrective Action*

Although prompt corrective action, innovated by the US in response to the Savings & Loans crisis in the 1980s, has been deployed by the FDIC to intervene and correct troubled banks timely in order to minimise moral hazard and losses of the deposit insurance fund since 1991, an increasing number of jurisdictions now regard prompt corrective action as a favourable measure for clamping down on moral hazard and minimising losses of the deposit insurance fund. The IADI also incorporates prompt corrective action into its core principles and proclaims that 'a deposit insurer should be an essential part of the financial safety net that carries out the early inspection and timely intervention in problematic banks by way of safety and soundness indicators, including capital ratio, asset quality, and management *etc.*'.[177]

Striking a balance between moral hazard and financial stability is the biggest challenge for deposit insurance in the long run, as opponents of deposit insurance argue that deposit insurance that secures deposits from banks' investment activities exaggerates moral hazard in the banking sector due to generating reasonable incentives for bankers to pursue riskier assets without any scruple.[178] In this context, prompt corrective action is expected to help deposit insurance mitigate moral hazard, thereby keeping banks safe and sound as much as possible.

In China, Zhou Xiaochuan, the former Governor of the PBOC, in a press conference publicly expressed that the DIFMC will be responsible for functioning prompt corrective action independently. However, in fact, in light of the Regulation on Deposit Insurance, it is clear to see that the Regulation even does not give the DIFMC authority to carry out on-site examination to probe into banks' actual circumstances, restricting the DIFMC to implement prompt corrective action. Article 10 allows the DIFMC to capture necessary useful information used to work out each banking institution's premiums based on information and documents filed by insured institutions. Article 13 lists underlying situations where the DIFMC is entitled to further investigate the credibility of information and documents filed by insured institutions, these situations are: (1) changes to risk level of insured institutions that result in adjustments in deposit insurance premium rates; (2) doubtful deposit insurance premium rates based on deposit base and amounts of insured deposits; (3) serious flaws within information and documents filed by insured institutions. Most notably, the last clause in Article 13 underscores that the DIFMC must report to the CBRC when it finds out serious problems after inspecting information and documents of insured institutions, which hints that the NFRA is the ultimate player implementing prompt corrective action.

Besides, Article 14 of the Regulation requires the DIFMC to establish information sharing network with the NFRA and the PBOC, and, in turn, obtain on-site examination reports and ratings of insured institutions from the NFRA and the PBOC, revealing a weak role of Chinese deposit insurer within the financial safety net. Furthermore, Article 15 and Article 16 of the Regulation reveal the DIFMC's two prompt corrective measures against troubled banks. First, in light of Article 15, the DIFMC can issue warning to insured institutions which have capital adequacy ratio less than 8% or other situations where safety of deposits and the deposit insurance fund could be damaged. Second, Article 16 authorises the DIFMC to raise deposit insurance premium rates against insured institutions that have sharp decrease of capital adequacy ratio because of having suffered significant losses of assets with no sign of improvement. However, raising deposit insurance premium rates is the only weapon seemed to be enforceable and effective to threaten member banks. By and large, this is far from enough to make the DIFMC available to implement prompt corrective action.

Despite the Regulation on Deposit Insurance struggling to empower the DIFMC, it is obvious that the DIFMC is not capable of exerting prompt corrective action. Compared with the UK and US, the DIFMC has to confront two challenges – interrelationship with other participants of financial safety net and on-site examination. Regarding the first challenge, the IADI suggests that effective prompt corrective action that helps deposit insurers resist banking crises is based on accomplished coordination and an information sharing network through interrelationship with other participants of the financial safety net.[179] However, in practice, the DIFMC, a subsidiary under the PBOC, has a lower administrative status than the PBOC and the NFRA, which means it is hard to build reciprocal coordination and information sharing network among financial authorities with different administrative level and political ranking because of current political regime in China. Since 2023, China has set up the Financial CFC, a committee similar to the Financial Stability Oversight Council led by Vice Premier, which aims to provide a constructive platform for Chinese financial authorities at a ministerial level to coordinate and share information without the need to reshuffle existing structure.[180] Obviously, the DIFMC, a corporation totally owned by the PBOC, cannot reach this level and direct the PBOC and the NFRA to deliver key information required.

However, the IADI claims that all sorts of deposit insurers basically should have information access to information on insured banks' financial conditions, insured deposit accounts, outstanding amounts of insured deposits, and deposit bases, regardless of the pay box model or risk minimiser model.[181] Two ways to address the lack of information access and coordination have been put forward for China.

The first, which can be learned from the presence of the FDIC in the Financial Stability Oversight Council established after the global financial crisis for the sake of inter-agency information exchange and coordination, is to promote the DIFMC to ministerial level like the PBOC and the NFRA so that the DIFMC can join the Central Finanical Committee to prompt information gathering and facilitate inter-agency coordination against unresolved macro-prudential and systemic risk issues, but it currently seems like a daydream not a realistic proposal under contemporary China's political regime.

The second way, learnt from UK experience, encourages the DIFMC to sign memorandum of understanding with other participants of the financial safety net, ensuring timely access to information on insured deposits that enables the DIFMC's speedy involvement in early intervention and banking resolution to prevent weak insured banks from falling short. In this context, allowing the DIFMC to sign memorandum of understanding appears to be the most achievable way to remove barriers blocking the information exchange among Chinese financial authorities.

Another challenge for the DIFMC to take charge of prompt corrective action is the absence of the authority to implement on-site examinations. At present, in accordance with Article 13 of the Regulation on Deposit Insurance, the DIFMC can only inspect the credibility and authenticity of information and documents filed by insured banks but has to report serious issues arising from the inspection to the NFRA. One prominent feature of prompt corrective action is speed, but the current framework takes more time as the DIFMC has to report to the NFRA, and then the NFRA starts working on on-site examinations.

From a legal perspective, the NFRA is also seen as the ultimate player who runs prompt corrective action. According to Article 24 of the Chinese Banking Regulation and Supervision Law, the NFRA has the authority to implement on-site examinations on all businesses and the risk status of all banking institutions.[182] Article 38 and Article 39 of the Chinese Banking and Supervision Law add that when a bank is likely to have a credit trouble that harms the interests and rights of depositors, the NFRA can take over or restructure the bank in line with relevant laws and regulations; and when a bank violates laws and regulations or has seriously unsound and unhealthy management that poses a threat to financial stability and public interests, the NFRA is authorised to close the bank in line with relevant laws and regulations.[183]

Clearly, compared with the NFRA, though the PBOC insists that the DIFMC is responsible for implementing prompt corrective action, the only corrective action the DIFMC can do is to issue timely warning and threaten weak banks by raising deposit insurance premium rates, which are ineffective to urge them to boost key financial indicators.[184] This is to say, the DIFMC has a long journey to become a real deposit insurer that can perform all functions and responsibilities in terms of performing prompt corrective action.

5.6 Positive Influences for Maintaining Financial Stability by the Chinese Deposit Insurance Scheme

Interestingly, China launched a deposit insurance scheme at a sensitive time when its economic growth was at a 25-year low, less than 7 percent.[185] Despite various blueprints for China's financial overhaul arising from the reform and opening-up policy, China's financial system remains somewhat traditional, with expectations for increased diversification and further openness in its financial markets. The main goal of creating a deposit insurance scheme is to promote financial stability as China's banking sector transitions from a state-controlled model to a more liberalised and modernised system. In other words, with deposit insurance protection, Chinese depositors can feel secure and less anxious about potential bank failures, while commercial banks, now allowed to fail and close, are encouraged to reassess their profitability and corporate governance.

In past decades, the government was seen as all-powerful, often stepping in to rescue financially unstable banks and ensuring full recovery for depositors and creditors to preserve financial stability. Now, with the introduction of a deposit insurance scheme, the government signals a commitment to end bailouts for bank mismanagement, meaning that all banks, particularly state-owned commercial banks, must now face market discipline and its consequences. Cases like Hainan Development Bank, Zhengzhou Cooperative Bank, and the Big Four illustrate how the government ultimately bore the costs of poor corporate governance, risky lending practices, and even corruption. Thus, the establishment of a deposit insurance scheme is a significant step in promoting the modernisation and market-oriented reform of commercial banks, alongside measures like interest rate liberalisation, the pilot programme for privately-owned banks, and banking resolution reforms.

Nevertheless, building up a deposit insurance scheme to resolve all financial turmoil is not realistic. Some even argue that deposit insurance is a source of financial instability, as it resembles a form of social welfare from an economist's perspective.[186] Given the debate surrounding deposit insurance, a carefully designed scheme is essential to ensure it can effectively lessen market panics and bank runs, thereby supporting financial stability. Currently, China's deposit insurance scheme has several shortcomings due to limited practical experience, raising concerns about the potential impact it may have on China's developing banking system.

Many scholars emphasise that while deposit insurance aims to keep the financial system stable, it also introduces moral hazard.[187] This can happen in two ways: first, member banks may feel less motivated to adopt safer investment strategies; second, depositors may be less inclined to monitor banks because deposit insurance provides a safety net.[188] However, in China's banking context, compared to the previous implicit government guarantee, deposit insurance is expected to mitigate moral hazard by reducing taxpayer burden and challenging the traditional beliefs of Chinese depositors. With this new scheme, taxpayers are no longer responsible for a blanket guarantee; instead, all banks, including the Big Four, contribute premiums to a deposit insurance fund to compensate depositors of failed banks. Meanwhile, due to the Chinese preference for bank deposits, depositors, especially retail ones, may become more vigilant about monitoring bank performance as they understand that their protection is limited in case of bank failure. That said, moral hazard is indeed lower than in previous decades. However, as China's financial system and deposit insurance scheme mature, it is likely that China will face similar moral hazard issues to those currently experienced in the US and UK.

The introduction of a deposit insurance scheme can create a level playing field that allows private banks, locally incorporated foreign banks, and small and medium banks to compete with state-owned commercial banks in a friendly market environment where discrimination would be eliminated as depositors, either in state-owned commercial banks or in other banks, would be equally covered under the same deposit insurance scheme. Unlike large state-owned commercial banks lending giant amounts of loans to government favoured mega projects or state-owned enterprises, private banks, locally incorporated foreign banks and small and medium banks are more focused on lending to SMEs, which account for more than 50% of government tax revenue and more than 80% of urban employment.[189] Thus, deposit insurance, an effective mechanism jeopardising bank runs, is of great importance to strengthen smaller banks' competitiveness, resilience and viability in the wake of interest rate liberalisation and tariff war with the US.[190]

On the other hand, some argue that with interest rate liberalisation and the presence of deposit insurance, small and medium banks may raise interest rates to attract more deposits, potentially increasing their costs and placing strain on liquidity. Additionally, if depositors become aware of potential bank insolvencies, they may transfer their funds to larger or state-owned banks perceived as more stable, negatively impacting smaller banks. Given China's unique context, it may be beneficial to implement more flexible policies and standards for private banks, locally incorporated foreign banks, and small and medium banks, while applying stricter standards and requirements to larger or state-owned banks.

Under China's contemporary banking regulation, the emergence of deposit insurance may break up current regulatory architecture dominated by the PBOC and the NFRA, and fill regulatory gaps in regard of depositor protection, level playing field and banking resolution. Currently, the NFRA concentrates on prudential regulation, responsible for overseeing the constantly modernised banking system, and the PBOC, with no intention to undertake the function of deposit insurance, gives priority to macroeconomic control and stable monetary policy, not deposit insurance and relevant matters.[191] In accordance with the Regulation on Deposit Insurance, it is clear that the DIFMC's mandates between loss minimiser model and risk minimiser model indicate its potential to be a regulatory watchdog, thereby consolidating China's financial safety net and reshuffling China's regulatory architecture.

5.7 Conclusion

Since the reform and opening-up policy in 1978, China has been determined to build real commercial banks in its financial system. For a long period, before long-awaited deposit insurance was established in 2015, the government had long been a saviour rescuing troubled banks by various measures, including closure, merger, and blanket guarantees. The chapter first discusses China's banking regulatory architecture, which shows conflicting interests and mandates between the PBOC and the NFRA, as well as political intervention and involvement in China's financial system. Deposit insurance in China, aimed at moving commercial banks in line with market orientation and protecting depositors economically, is expected to accelerate financial reforms alongside interest rate liberalisation and the pilot programme of private banks.

Having encountered several financial distresses that resulted in massive losses of taxpayers' money and painful bailouts, the government eventually determined to launch China's own deposit insurance, which would be a landmark in China's banking reform history. During the financial distresses, it was obvious that the government demonstrated its faith in saving state-owned commercial banks first, incurring inequality and imbalance within the banking system. This article provides a comprehensive analysis of China's implicit deposit insurance with three selected cases to show how the government resolves troubled banks before the introduction of deposit insurance and what consequences are triggered by implicit deposit insurance in China.

With the consideration of high saving rates, the marketisation of the banking system, and the lack of banking resolution, China has established a formal deposit insurance scheme following the international principles and standards in terms of compulsory membership, limited but high coverage, and risk-based deposit insurance premium rates. Accordingly, in order to examine to what extent the Regulation on Deposit Insurance has pushed forward the deposit insurance scheme, the article seeks to explore the features of China's deposit insurance. It was found that although the Regulation on Deposit Insurance has outlined the fundamentals of deposit insurance, it is too ambiguous and somewhat exposes the awkward status quo of the current arrangement for deposit insurance.

There are several unresolved issues related to deposit insurance. First, without unified and consistent legislation, the DIFMC's interests and responsibilities conflict with those of the PBOC and NFRA, and the scope of deposit insurance remains unclear, as it is uncertain what will and will not be covered from a legal standpoint. Second, the Regulation has yet to provide detailed guidelines on risk-based premium rates, particularly regarding how the DIFMC will assess member institutions and vary premium rates among them. Third, under the Regulation, it is doubtful that the DIFMC can carry out genuine prompt corrective action, as envisioned by former PBOC Governor Zhou Xiaochuan, since the only measure it can enforce to penalise member institutions is imposing higher premiums, which falls short of prompt corrective action.

In addition to introducing deposit insurance, Chinese commercial banks must improve corporate governance, information disclosure, and compliance—essential elements for a banking market that is both market-oriented and regulation-driven. As a newcomer, the government should support the DIFMC in establishing effective coordination and information-sharing with other components of the financial safety net, quickly elevating the DIFMC to a critical role despite the rigid political hierarchy.

Rome was not built in a day. Objectively speaking, China has set deposit insurance on the right path, which is a correct direction to modernise its banking regulation. However, in reality, a serious obstruction ahead of building effective deposit insurance is that state-owned commercial banks still have roots in the state-owned economy and Chinese political hierarchy. Consequently, deposit insurance cannot be expected to kerb state-owned commercial banks' policy lending to unprofitable state-owned enterprises and government-favoured mega projects, nor to promote their corporate governance.

Notes

1 Siwei Cheng, *Financial Reforms and Developments in China* (World Scientific Publishing 2014) 279.
2 Although there were some specialised banks between 1949 and 1979, they were departments of the Ministry of Finance or business branches of the PBOC. For example, the People's Construction Bank of China was the de facto cashier of the Capital Construction Finance Department of the Ministry of Finance, and the Bank of China was the de facto international business department of the PBOC. All businesses related to money had to go through the PBOC. See Jinglian Wu, 'China's Economic and Financial Reform' in On Kit Tam (ed), *Financial Reform in China* (Routledge, 1995) 85.
3 Mingkang Liu, 'Retrospective Review and Prospect of the Banking Industry in China (2009) 19 *China Finance*, 14.
4 Under this reform, the Agricultural Bank of China (ABC) was re-established for rural financial services; the Bank of China (BOC) was separated from the PBOC for foreign business transactions and foreign exchange; the Construction Bank of China was separated from the Ministry of Finance to be responsible for long-term investment and loans; and the Industrial and Commercial Bank of China was opened to run credit and savings business.
5 Tianyong Guo, *Review, Rethink and Restart: China Financial Reform and Opening-up 40 Years* (Special Sciences Academic Press 2018), 27.
6 The eight joint-stock commercial banks are China Everbright Bank, CITIC Industrial Bank, China Merchants Bank, Guangdong Development Bank, Huaxia Bank, Industrial Bank Co. Ltd., Shanghai Pudong Development Bank, and Shenzhen Development Bank Co. Ltd.
7 Chunxia Jiang and Shujie Yao, *Chinese Banking Reform: From the Pre-WTO Period to the Financial Crisis and Beyond* (Palgrave 2017) 19.
8 Xiaoping Deng, *Works of Xiaoping Deng Vol 3: Enterprise Reform and Financial Reform* (People's Press 1993) 192. *Provisional Regulations of the People's Republic of China on the Control of Banks* then were expired and replaced by the Law of the People's Republic of China on Commercial Banks, Law of the People's Republic of China on Commercial Banks, and *Measures for Banning Illegal Financial Institutions and Illegal Financial Activities.*

9 Xiaoqiu Wu, *Reform of Financial Regulation in China: The Realistic Motivation and Theoretical Logic* (China Finance Publishing House, 2018) 136. China has implemented separate operation and separate supervision since 1995. Under the separate operation, non-banking financial institutions cannot carry out any deposit-taking activities, while commercial banks cannot engage in securities, trust, and insurance. For separate supervision, the PBOC is no longer the only financial supervisor in China, as China has established separate financial supervisors in banking, securities, and insurance.

10 Gongsheng Pan, *Evolution of China's Big Commercial Banks: The Road to Revival* (China Finance Publishing House, 2012), 23.

11 *Ibid.*

12 Four asset management companies, Cinda Asset Management Company, Great Wall Asset Management Company, Oriental Asset Management Company, and Hurong Asset Management Company, are responsible for offloading non-performing loans from the Big Four: Great Wall for Agricultural Bank of China; Huarong for Industrial and Commercial Bank of China; Cinda for China Construction Bank; and China Orient for Bank of China.

13 Xiaochuan Zhou, 'Retrospective Review and Expectation for China's Big Bank Reform' (2012) 6 *China Finance*, 10.

14 Jianhui Huang, Yifeng Wang, and Yan Ma, 'A Study and Analysis on Non-performing Loans of China's Commercial Banks (2017) 20 *China Mingsheng Bank Review*, 6.

15 Siwei Cheng, *Cheng Siwei on Financial Reforms* (Renmin University of China Press, 2006).

16 Justin Yifu Lin, 'WTO Accession and Financial Reform in China' (2001) 21 *Cato Journal*, 13.

17 Mark Tran, 'RBS Buys Stake in Bank of China' *The Guardian* (London, 18 August 2005) <https://www.theguardian.com/business/2005/aug/18/china.internationalnews> accessed 10 January 2018.

18 Michael Wines, 'China Bank IPO Raises $19 Billion' *The New York Times* (New York, 6 July 2010) <https://www.nytimes.com/2010/07/07/business/global/07ipo.htm>, and The Wall Street Journal 'AgBank Finally Takes IPO Crown' *The Wall Street Journal* (New York, 16 August 2010) <https://www.wsj.com/articles/SB10001424052748703960004575427192644180132> accessed 12 January 2024.

19 CBRC official website: http://www.cbrc.gov.cn/showyjhjjindex.do.

20 One bank refers to the PBOC, and three commissions refer to the CBRC, CSRC, and CIRC. Since March 2018, the CBRC has merged with the CIRC into the newly established China Banking and Insurance Commission in line with the 'State Council Institutional Reform Plan'. See State Council, 'State Council Institutional Reform Plan, (17 March 2018) <http://www.gov.cn/guowuyuan/2018-03/17/content_5275116.htm> accessed 10 December 2023.

21 Hui Huang, 'Institutional Structure of Financial Regulation in China: Lessons from the Global Financial Crisis' (2010) 10 *Journal of Corporate Law Studies*, 230.

22 See WeBank official website: https://www.webank.com/en/aboutus/about.html#page1.

23 These five private banks are Tianjin KinCheng Bank, Zhejiang MYbank, Shanghai Huarui Bank, Wenzhou Minshang Bank, and Qianhai WeBank.

24 CBRC, *2017 Annual Report* (China Finance Publishing House 2018) 96.

25 *Ibid.*

26 Bing Xu, Adrian V Rixter and Michiel V Leuvensteijn, 'Measuring Bank Competition in China: A Comparison of New Versus Conventional Approaches Applied to Loan Markets' (Bank for International Settlements, August 2013) <https://www.bis.org/publ/work422.htm> accessed 8 Jan 2024.

27 *Ibid* at 172-175.

28 Zhongfei Zhou and Jingwei Li, 'Independence and Accountability of the People's Bank of China: A legal Perspective' (2006) 17 *European Business Law Review*, 1313.
29 Regulation on Deposit Insurance, Article 7.
30 State Council, 'Reply of the State Council on Approving the Implementation Plan for Deposit Insurance System' (State Council, 2015) <http://www.gov.cn/zhengce/content/2015-04/01/content_9571.htm> accessed 10 Feb 2024.
31 Article 33 says that the PBOC may, according to the demands of implementing monetary policy and maintaining financial stability, request that the banking regulatory authority under the State Council supervise and examine financial institutions. The banking regulatory authority should respond to the request within thirty days. Article 34 states that when financial institutions have difficulties in honouring deposits that may incur financial risks, the PBOC shall, in the interest of financial stability, have the power to supervise and examine financial institutions after getting approval from the State Council.
32 Justin Yifu Lin, 'WTO Accession and Financial Reform in China' (n16).
33 Charles Goodhart and Dirk Schoenmaker, 'Should the Functions of Monetary Policy and Banking Supervision Be Separated' (1995) 47 *Oxford Economic Papers*, 545.
34 Weiping He, 'Banking Regulation in China: What, Why, and How?' (2012) 20 *Journal of Financial Regulation and* Compliance, 367, 384.
35 CBRC official website available at: http://www.cbrc.gov.cn/chinese/yjhjj/index.html.
36 Hui Huang, 'Institutional Structure of Financial Regulation in China: Lessons from the Global Financial Crisis' (n21).
37 MOF official website available at: http://www.mof.gov.cn/zhengwuxinxi/benbugaikuang/bbzn/.
38 Barry Naughton, *The Chinese Economy: Transitions and Growth* (MIT Press, 2007) 453.
39 Gang Yi, 'Following the Reform and Opening Up Policy to Pursue New Financial Achievement – To Commemorate the 40th Anniversary of Reform and Opening Up Policy and the 70th Anniversary of the People's Bank of China' (2018) 23 *China Finance*, 15.
40 Gregory T. Chin, 'Understanding Currency Policy and Central Banking in China' (2013) 72 *The Journal of Asian Studies*, 528.
41 Nicholas R. Lardy, *China's Unfinished Economic Revolution* (Brookings Institution, 1998) 175. Also see Law of the People's Republic of China on People's Bank of China, Article 2.
42 Leong Liew and Harry X. Wu, *The Making of China's Exchange Rate Policy* (University of Chicago Press, 2007), 163.
43 Victor Shih, *Factions and Finance: Elite Conflict and Inflation* (Cambridge University Press 2008) 32.
44 *Ibid* and Nicholas R. Lardy, *China's Unfinished Economic Revolution* (n41).
45 The Constitution of the CCP, Article 32.
46 The Constitution of the CCP, Article 10 (3).
47 The other six state-owned financial groups are: three policy banks, Bank of Communication, Everbright Group, and CITIC Group.
48 Kjeld E. Brødsgaard, 'Politics and Business Group Formation in China: The Party in Control (2012) 211 *The China Quarterly* 628.
49 Sebastian Heilmann, 'Regulatory Innovation by Leninist Means: Communist Party Supervision in China's Financial Industry' (2005) 181, *The China Quarterly*, 10, 17.
50 *Ibid* at 20.
51 For the IMF suggestion, see Christopher Crowe and Ellen E. Meade, 'Central Bank Independence and Transparency: Evolution and Effectiveness' (IMF, May 2008) <https://www.imf.org/en/Publications/WP/Issues/2016/12/31/Central-Bank

-Independence-and-Transparency-Evolution-and-Effectiveness-21903> accessed 20 Feb 2024.

52 Patrick Honohan, 'Protecting Depositors in China: Experience and Evolving Policy' in Asli Demirgüç-Kunt, Edward J Kane and Luc Laeven (eds), *Deposit Insurance around the World: Issues of Design and Implementation* (The MIT Press, 2008) 340.

53 Asli Demirgüç-Kunt, Baybars Karacaovali and Luc Laeven, 'Deposit Insurance around the World: A Comprehensive Database' (World Bank, April 2005) <http://siteresources.worldbank.org/INTRES/Resources/DepositInsuranceDatabasePaper_DKL.pdf> accessed 10 Feb 2024.

54 Shiyu Liu, 'China's experience in Small and Medium Financial Institution Resolution' (BIS, October 1999) <https://www.bis.org/publ/plcy07t.pdf> accessed 12 February 2024.

55 Five failing trust & investment companies were Funan Trust & Investment Company, Shuxing Trust & Investment Company, Zheqiong Trust & Investment Company, Huaxia Financial Company, and Sanya Jiya Trust & Investment Company.

56 The only operational company was Funan Trust & Investment Company.

57 Wenyong Wu, *Study on State Aid Legal Systems of Market Exit Mechanisms of Financial Institutions* (China University of Political Science and Law Press, 2012) 101.

58 Sina Finance, 'Hainan Development Bank: The First Closure in History' *Sina Finance* (Beijing, 26 June 2013) <http://finance.sina.com.cn/money/bank/20130626/072415917875.shtml> accessed 20 Feb 2024.

59 Lixin Ma et al, 'The Division of Powers in Resolving Commercial Bank Bankruptcy Risks' (2016) 10 *Financial Regulation Research*, 81.

60 *Ibid.*

61 Daniel L. McCullough, 'Feeling the Stone: Measuring the Potential of Deposit Insurance in China through A Comparative Analysis' (2007) 11 *North Carolina Banking Institute*, 425. Minggui Yu and Hongbo Pan, 'Government Intervention, Legal Enforcement, Financial Development and Bank Loans to State-Owned Enterprises' (2008) 339 *Journal of Financial Research* 1, 3.

62 Jianbo Lou, 'China's Bank Non-Performing Loan Problem: Seriousness and Causes' (2000) 34 *The International Lawyer*, 1147, 1192.

63 *Ibid.*

64 In an article, Zhou Xiaochuan, the Governor of the PBOC, said that the official ratio of non-performing loans to total outstanding loans was 25%. However, he admitted that the ratio might be higher than the official data. Because of undisclosed balance sheets of the Big Four, speculations of the ratio vary from 10% to 40%. For the ratio of 34%, the author collects data of total outstanding loans and GDP from the PBOC, 'China Financial Stability Report 2005" (PBOC, 15 September 2005) <http://www.pbc.gov.cn/jinrongwendingju/146766/146772/146776/2889089/index.html> accessed 20 March 2019. Moreover, RMB 3.2 trillion was estimated by the PBOC. Also see Charles Booth, "The 2006 PRC Enterprise Bankruptcy Law: The Wait Is Finally Over" (2008) 20 *Singapore Academy of Law Journal* 275, 278.

65 Ben Fund, Jason George, Stefan Hohl and Guonan Ma, 'Public Asset Management Companies in East Asia: Case Studies' (BIS, February 2004) <https://www.bis.org/fsi/fsipapers03.pdf> accessed 20 July 2019.

66 Jiangfeng Li, 'Non-performing Loans and Asset Management Companies in China: Legal and Regulatory Challenges for Achieving Effective Debt Resolution and Recovery' (2013) 1 *Peking University Transnational Law Review* 85, 122.

67 Ben Fund, Jason George, Stefan Hohl and Guonan Ma, 'Public Asset Management Companies in East Asia: Case Studies' (n65).

68 Nicholas R. Lardy, *China's Unfinished Economic Revolution* (Brookings Institution 1998) 83.

69 Gang Yi, *Thinking of China's Financial Reform* (Commercial Pressing, 2009) 291. The Resolution Trust Corporation was primarily set up to deal with the assets of failing savings and loans associations in Savings & Loans crisis in the 1980s. In 1995, the Savings Association Insurance Fund (SAIF) of the FDIC took charge of this responsibility. After SAIF and the Bank Insurance Fund merged into the Deposit Insurance Fund (DIF) in 2006, the DIF took over the responsibility.
70 Jing Leng, 'China's Banking Reform in the Context of Globalisation and Transition' (2006) 17 *European Business Law Review*, 1281.
71 PBOC, 'China Financial Stability Report 2005' (PBOC, 15 September 2005) <http://www.pbc.gov.cn/jinrongwendingju/146766/146772/146776/2889089/index.html> accessed 20 July 2024.
72 See CBRC's statistics on NPL ratio at: http://www.cbrc.gov.cn/chinese/home/docView/1391.html.
73 Guonan Ma, 'Who Pays China's Bank Restructuring Bill' (BIS, February 2007) <https://www.bis.org/repofficepubl/arpresearch_fs_200702.01.htm> accessed 12 Feb 2024.
74 See CBRC's statistics on recovery rate at: http://www.cbrc.gov.cn/chinese/home/docView/2456.html.
75 Yiyu Wang and Songling He, 'Corruption Caused by Financial Regulatory Forbearance: Structural Regime and Structural Reform (2018) 5 *Modern Law Science*, 117-129. Furthermore, there are many corruption cases related to the senior management of UCCs and RCCs.
76 See http://www.zzbank.cn/about/introduction/dsj/201711/t20171123_567.html.
77 Tianyu Wang, *Study on Deposit Insurance System in China* (China Financial Publishing House, 2015) 119.
78 *Ibid.*
79 *Ibid.*
80 Mai Qiao, 'Bank of Zhengzhou was on the Verge of Collapse 20 Years Ago' *China Fund* (Beijing, 19 September 2018) <http://stock.jrj.com.cn/2018/09/19193225115717.shtml> accessed 18 February 2020.
81 Law of People's Republic of China on Commercial Banks, Article 64.
82 Sohu Finance, 'Bank of Zhengzhou is Going to List in Hong Kong Stock Exchange, and Who are the Shareholders' *Sohu Finance* (Beijing, 9 October 2015) <http://money.sohu.com/20151009/n422778944.shtml> accessed 20 February 2024.
83 Samuel Talley, 'Deposit Protection and the Spread of Deposit Insurance: Some Guidelines for Developing Countries' (The World Bank, June 1994) <http://documents.worldbank.org/curated/en/190571468781531830/Deposit-protection-and-the-spread-of-deposit-insurance-some-guidelines-for-developing-countries> accessed 20 Feb 2024.
84 John R. LaBrosse and David G. Mayes, 'Promoting Financial Stability through Effective Depositor Protection: The Case for Explicit Limited Deposit Insurance' in Andrew Campbell, John Raymond LaBrosse, David G. Mayes and Dalvinder Singh (eds) *Deposit Insurance* (Palgrave Macmillan 2007) 5.
85 PBOC, 'China Financial Stability Report 2009' (PBOC, 2009) <http://www.pbc.gov.cn/jinrongwendingju/146766/146772/146776/2898290/index.html> accessed 21 Feb 2024.
86 Deposit Insurance Research Group of the PBOC, 'Some Thinking and Reflections on Establishing Explicit Deposit Insurance System in China' (2003) 5 *China Finance*, 18.
87 Financial Stability Forum Working Group Deposit Insurance, 'A Consultative Process and Background Paper' (Financial Stability Forum, June 2000) <https://www.iadi.org/en/assets/File/Core%20Principles/Consultation_Paper_English.pdf> accessed 23 Feb. 2024.
88 Lijun Wang and Xingxu Cai, 'A Study on Exit Mechanism under Implicit Deposit Insurance' (2019) 2 *Social Science Journal*, 119.

89 Tianyu Wang, *Study on Deposit Insurance System in China* (n77) 158.
90 PBOC, 'Financial Stability Report 2006' (PBOC, December 2006) <http://www.pbc.gov.cn/jinrongwendingju/146766/146772/146776/2899533/index.html> accessed 20 Feb 2020.
91 State Council, 'Notice of the State Council on Ratifying and Forwarding the Opinions of the National Development and Reform Commission on Deepening the Reform of Economic System 2009' (State Council, May 2009) <http://www.gov.cn/zwgk/2009-05/25/content_1323641.htm> accessed 20 July 2024.
92 Keqiang Li, 'Report on the Work of the Government of 2014' Xinhua News (Beijing, 14 March 2014) <http://www.gov.cn/guowuyuan/2014-03/14/content_2638989.htm> accessed 20 March 2024.
93 Tao Zhang, 'Global Challenge on the Economic Growth and Financial Reform' (Lujiazui Forum, Shanghai, June 2016).
94 Xiaochuan Zhou, 'An explanation on China's Deposit Insurance' *China Business News* (Shanghai, 28 April 2015) <https://www.yicai.com/news/4611472.html> accessed 30 March 2019.
95 Yujia Wu, Yuzhe Zhang and Denise Jia, 'PBOC Sets Up Deposit Insurance Fund Management Company' *Caixin Global* (Beijing, 29 May 2019) <https://www.caixinglobal.com/2019-05-30/pboc-sets-up-deposit-insurance-fund-management-company-101421410.html> accessed 22 Feb 2024.
96 Longmei Zhang et al., 'China's High Savings: Drivers, Prospects, and Policies' (IMF, December 2018) <https://www.imf.org/en/Publications/WP/Issues/2018/12/11/Chinas-High-Savings-Drivers-Prospects-and-Policies-46437> accessed 23 July 2024.
97 *Ibid.*
98 PBOC, 'Report on Steady Progress in Market-based Interest Rate Reform' (PBOC, January 2005) <http://www.pbc.gov.cn/english/130721/2831321/index.html> accessed 27 Sep 2024.
99 People's Daily, 'The PBOC Announces It Remove Cap on Deposit Interest Rates' *People's Daily* (Beijing, 25 October 2015) < http://cpc.people.com.cn/n/2015/1025/c64387-27737167.html> accessed 27 July 2024.
100 Christoffer Koch, 'Deposit Interest Rate Ceilings as Credit Supply Shifters: Bank Level Evidence on the Effects of Regulation Q' (2015) 61 *Journal of Banking and Finance*, 317.
101 R. Alton Gilbert, 'Requiem for Regulation Q: What It Did and Why It Passed Away' (1986) 68 *Federal Reserve Bank of St. Louis Review*, 22, 37.
102 Timothy Curry and Lynn Shibut, 'The Cost of the Savings and Loan Crisis: Truth and Consequences' (2000) 13 *FDIC Banking Review*, 27.
103 *Ibid.*
104 The Savings Association Insurance Fund was incorporated into the Deposit Insurance Fund in 2006. Ann M. Taylor, 'The FDIC's Enchanced Powers over Savings Associations: Does FIRREA Make It 'SAIF'? ' (1991) 59 *Fordham Law Review*, 384.
105 Financial Stability Bureau of the PBOC, *Deposit Insurance* (China Financial Publishing House, August 2015), 25.
106 Keqiang Li, 'Issues and Thoughts on Deepening Economic Reform' (2014) 9 *QiuShi*, 1.
107 In light of the FDIC Community Banking Study in 2012, community banks are defined as the most vital financing resources for small lending to US farms and SMEs, and banking service providers for local communities, rural communities, and underserved communities. See FDIC, 'FDIC Community Banking Study' (FDIC, December 2012) <https://www.fdic.gov/regulations/resources/cbi/report/cbi-full.pdf> accessed 14 August 2024.
108 Benjamin R. Backup and Richard A. Brown, 'Community Banks Remain Resilient amid Industry Consolidation' (2014) 8 *FDIC Quarterly*, 38.

109 Two financial crises in the US refer to the Savings and Loans Crisis in the 1980s and the Global Financial Crisis in 2008. Also see Ibid.

110 Council of Economic Advisers, 'The Performance of Community Banks over Time' (Council of Economic Advisers of the White House, August 2016) <https://obamawhitehouse.archives.gov/sites/default/files/page/files/20160810_cea_community_banks.pdf> accessed 20 August 2024.

111 Yi Zhou, 'Establishing A Deposit Insurance System in China: A Long-Awaited Move toward Deepening Financial Reform' (2016) 16 *Chicago-Kent Journal of International and Comparative Law*, 66.

112 CBRC, 'General Statistics of Commercial Banks in 2018' available at http://www.cbrc.gov.cn/chinese/home/docView/2ED43A31B3CA4071A1D76901502E3A7A.html.

113 Xiaochuan Zhou, 'An explanation on China's Deposit Insurance' *China Business News* (Shanghai, 28 April 2015) <https://www.yicai.com/news/4611472.html> accessed 30 March 2024.

114 Regulations on the Cancellation of Financial Institutions, Article 2.

115 Kenneth Spong, *Banking Regulation: Its Purposes, Implementation, and Effects* (Federal Reserve Bank of Kansas City, 5th ed., 2000) 91.

116 *Ibid* at 93.

117 Jerome J P. Deslandes, Marcel Magnus, and Cristina S P. Dias, 'Liquidation of Banks: Towards an 'FDIC' for the Banking Union' (European Parliament, 8 February 2019) <http://www.europarl.europa.eu/thinktank/en/document.html?reference=IPOL_IDA(2019)634385> accessed 30 March 2024.

118 Qingming Yan, 'Ideas for Establishing Deposit Insurance in China' (2003) 3 *Economic Theory and Business Management*, 27.

119 Jianjun Fan, 'The Urgency of Establishing Deposit Insurance in China since China's Interest Rate Liberalisation Started' (2013) 2 *Journal of Chongqing University of Technology* (Social Science), 27.

120 See Article 1 of the Chinese Banking Regulation and Supervision Law. This law is enacted for the purposes of improving banking regulation and supervision, standardising banking supervisory processes and procedures, preventing and mitigating financial risks in the banking industry, protecting depositors and customers, as well as promoting a safe and sound banking industry in China.

121 Yanhong Pan, 'Research on the Core Issues of Deposit Insurance System on the Establishment of Deposit Insurance Corporation' (2010) 11 *Journal of Shanghai Business School*, 18, 22.

122 Jianing Wei, *Deposit Insurance and Financial Safety Net* (China Economic Publishing House, 2014) 124.

123 *Ibid.*

124 Haipo Yan and Hucheng Chen, 'Six Important Relationships in the Establishment of Deposit Insurance in China' (2005) 2 *Journal of Henan College of Financial Management Cadres*, 7, 10.

125 Haipo Yan, 'Difficulty and Choice of Establishing Deposit Insurance in China' (2004) 11 *Journal of Financial Research*, 30.

126 Walter Bagehot, *Lombard Street: A Description of the Money Market* (Henry S. King & Co., 1873) 56, 57.

127 Gillian G. Garcia, 'Deposit Insurance: Actual and Good Practices' (IMF, 2000) <https://www.imf.org/en/Publications/Occasional-Papers/Issues/2016/12/30/Deposit-Insurance-Actual-and-Good-Practices-4043> accessed 20 Feb 2024.

128 According to core principle 3 that the IADI set for effectiveness, the deposit insurer should be operationally independent, well-governed, transparent, accountable, and insulated from external interference. Meanwhile, the FSB mentions that no matter what kind of model is applied, deposit insurance agencies should be entitled to have enough independence. The World Bank and IMF also express similar suggestions regarding

the governance of deposit insurance agencies. See IADI, 'Core Principles for Effective Deposit Insurance Systems' (IADI, 2014) <https://www.iadi.org/en/assets/File/Core%20Principles/cprevised2014nov.pdf> accessed 23 March 2024, and FSB, 'Thematic Review on Deposit Insurance Systems Peer Review Report' (FSB, 2012) <https://www.fsb.org/wp-content/uploads/r_120208.pdf?page_moved=1> accessed 23 March 2024, Claire McGuire and Yejin C. Lee, 'Deposit Insurance Systems' (World Bank, 2013) <http://siteresources.worldbank.org/EXTFINANCIALSECTOR/Resources/282884-1303327122200/VP340-Deposit-Insurance-Systems.pdf> accessed 23 March 2024.

129 IADI, 'IADI Annual Survey on Deposit Insurance' (IADI, 2011 and 2018) <https://www.iadi.org/en/core-principles-and-research/deposit-insurance-surveys/> accessed 10 April 2024.

130 In this context, Article 7 of the Regulation on Deposit Insurance states that the deposit insurer should be under the leadership of the State Council, and Article 14 regards the deposit insurer as an independent authority under the State Council to collaborate with the PBOC and CBRC in order to improve coordination and information sharing.

131 Yan Xing, 'Thoughts on the Establishment of Deposit Insurance Agency in China' (2016) 10 *Wuhan Finance*, 7.

132 The data was collected from the PBOC official statistics; see PBOC website at http://www.pbc.gov.cn/jinrongwendingju/146766/2165207/3794891/index.html.

133 Jianing Wei, *Deposit Insurance and Financial Safety Net* (n122).

134 Yujia Wu, Yuzhe Zhang and Denise Jia, 'PBOC Sets Up Deposit Insurance Fund Management Company' *Caixin Global* (Beijing, 29 May 2019) < https://www.caixinglobal.com/2019-05-30/pboc-sets-up-deposit-insurance-fund-management-company-101421410.html>.

135 Regulation on Deposit Insurance, article 3.

136 *Ibid*, article 7.

137 *Ibid*, article 13.

138 *Ibid*.

139 *Ibid*, article 15.

140 *Ibid*, article 16.

141 *Ibid*, article 21.

142 *Ibid*, article 19.

143 IADI, 'Core Principles for Effective Deposit Insurance System' (n128).

144 Haipo Yan and Qin Liu, 'International Experiences on Deposit Insurance' (2007) 3 *The Chinese Banker*, 28, 33.

145 Lawrence Kryzanowski, 'Organizational Design and Positioning of the Deposit Insurance Function in the Financial System Safety Net' in Andrew Campbell (eds) *Deposit Insurance* (Palgrave Macmillan, 2007) 102.

146 *Ibid*.

147 John A. Weinberg, 'Competition among Bank Regulators' (2002) 88 Economic Quarterly, 19, 33.

148 Jianing Wei, *Deposit Insurance and Financial Safety Net* (n122).

149 Min Liao, Tao Sun and Jinfan Zhang, 'IMF Working Paper on China's Financial Interlinkages and Implications for Inter-Agency Coordination' (IMF, August 2016) <https://www.imf.org/external/pubs/ft/wp/2016/wp16181.pdf> accessed 10 March 2024.

150 *Ibid*, and see Yu Liang, 'China Establishes Financial Stability Committee' *Xinhua News* (Beijing, 08 November 2017) <http://www.xinhuanet.com//english/2017-11/08/c_136737901.htm> accessed 20 March 2024.

151 Both Principle 7 of the IADI Core Principles for Effective Deposit Insurance Systems and the IMF Working Paper on Deposit Insurance: Actual and Good Practices written by Gillian G. Garcia suggest the necessity of compulsory membership for deposit insurance. See IADI, 'Core Principles for Effective Deposit Insurance System' (n128) and Gillian G. Garcia, 'Deposit Insurance: Actual and Good Practices' (n127).

152 Neil Gough, 'China Rethinks Safety Net for Its Banking System' The New York Times (New York, 30 April 2015) <https://www.nytimes.com/2015/05/01/business/dealbook/china-rethinks-safety-net-for-its-banking-system.html> accessed 20 Sep 2024.
153 ICBC, 'ICBC US Resolution Plan Public Section' (FDIC, December 2018) <https://www.fdic.gov/regulations/reform/resplans/plans/icbc-165-1812.pdf> accessed 22 March 2023.
154 12 CFR § 347.203.
155 Mathias Hanten and Marion Plaschke, 'EU Law Impact on Deposit Protection in the Financial Crisis: Icesave (2014) 51 *Common Market Law Review*, 299.
156 Simon Gompertz, 'Icesave: Icelandic Government Wins Compensation Ruling' BBC (London, 28 January 2013) <https://www.bbc.co.uk/news/business-21231535> accessed 22 Sep 2024.
157 See IADI, 'Core Principles for Effective Deposit Insurance System' (n128).
158 Xinhua News, 'Li Keqiang Signed on the Regulation on Deposit \insurance' *Xinhua News* (Beijing, 31 March 2015) <http://www.xinhuanet.com/politics/2015-03/31/c_1114827127.htm> accessed 20 March 2024.
159 IADI, 'Enhanced Guidance for Effective Deposit Insurance Systems: Deposit Insurance Coverage' (IADI, March 2013) <https://www.iadi.org/en/assets/File/Papers/Approved%20Guidance%20Papers/IADI_Coverage_Enhanced_Guidance_Paper.pdf> accessed 21 Sep 2023.
160 Financial Stability Bureau of the PBOC, *Deposit Insurance* (n105) 40.
161 Regulation on Deposit Insurance, Article 6.
162 *Ibid*, article 8.
163 *Ibid*, article 10.
164 Financial Stability Bureau of the PBOC, *Deposit Insurance* (n105) 44.
165 Christine E. Blair, Frederick Carns, and Rose M. Kushmeider, 'Instituting a Deposit Insurance System: Why? How?' in Andrew Campbell (eds) *Deposit Insurance* (Palgrave Macmillan, 2007) 79.
166 Wally Suphap, 'Toward Effective Risk-adjusted Bank Deposit Insurance: A Transnational Strategy (2004) 42 *Columbia Journal of Transnational Law*, 836.
167 The Ministry of Finance and the State Administration of Taxation, 'Notice of the Ministry of Finance and the State Administration of Taxation on Issues Concerning the Policies for the Deduction of Deposit Insurance Premiums of Banking Financial Institutions before Payment of Enterprise Income Tax' (2016) <http://www.chinatax.gov.cn/n810341/n810755/c2348847/content.html> accessed 20 Sep 2024.
168 *Ibid.*
169 Xiaochuan Zhou, 'An explanation on China's Deposit Insurance' (n94)
170 IADI, 'Enhanced Guidance for Effective Deposit Insurance Systems: Ex-ante Funding Guidance Paper' (IADI, June 2015) <https://www.iadi.org/en/assets/File/Papers/Approved%20Guidance%20Papers/IADI_Enhanced_Guidance_on_Ex-Ante_Funding_June_2015.pdf> accessed 20 Sep 2024.
171 *Ibid.*
172 See the financial statement of the deposit insurance fund in 2018 on the PBOC official website, available at: http://www.pbc.gov.cn/jinrongwendingju/146766/2165207/3794891/index.html accessed 20 Sep 2023.
173 Targeted reserve ratios of the deposit insurance fund in the US and Canada are 2% of insured deposits and 1% of deposit insurance, respectively. The UK adopts a different mechanism for determining the target level, which sets the highest limits for each category of financial institutions, accounting for approximately 2% of insured deposits.
174 IADI, 'Enhanced Guidance for Effective Deposit Insurance Systems: Ex-ante Funding Guidance Paper' (n170).

175 See every year's DRR on the FDIC official website, available at https://www.fdic.gov/deposit/insurance/fund.html accessed 21 Sep 2023.
176 Varadarajan V. Chari, 'Banking without Deposit Insurance or Bank Panics: Lessons from a Model of the US National Banking System (1989) 13 *Federal Reserve Bank of Minneapolis Quarterly Review*, 3, 19.
177 IADI, 'Core Principles for Effective Deposit Insurance System' (n128).
178 For a dissenting opinion against deposit insurance, Andreas Wesemann in the Centre for Policy Studies, a think tank in the UK, writes an article appealing to abolish deposit insurance that can be seen as representative of opponents. See Andreas Wesemann, 'The Abolition of Deposit Insurance: A Modest Proposal for Banking Reform' (Centre for Policy Studies, January 2016) <https://www.cps.org.uk/files/reports/original/160112130402-TheAbolitionofDepositInsurance.pdf> accessed 20 Sep 2024.
179 IADI, 'General Guidance on Early Detection and Timely Intervention for Deposit Insurance Systems' (IADI, June 2013) <https://www.iadi.org/en/assets/File/Papers/Approved%20Guidance%20Papers/2013-06_Early_Detection_Timely_Intervention-publication_final.pdf> accessed 20 Sep 2024.
180 Huiqiang Xing, 'Optimal Targets and Functions of the Financial Stability and Development Committee under the State Council' (2018) 3 *Law Review*, 88, 98.
181 IADI, 'General Guidance on Early Detection and Timely Intervention for Deposit Insurance Systems' (n179).
182 Law of People's Republic of China on Regulation and Supervision over the Banking Industry, article 24.
183 Law of People's Republic of China on Regulation and Supervision over the Banking Industry, article 38 and article 39.
184 Financial Stability Bureau of the PBOC, *Deposit Insurance* (n105) 87.
185 Alan Raybould, 'China to Bring in Bank Deposit Insurance, Step towards Liberalisation' Reuters (London, 31 March 2015) <https://www.reuters.com/article/china-economy-deposits/china-to-bring-in-bank-deposit-insurance-step-towards-liberalisation-idUSKBN0MR1KL20150331> accessed 25 Sep 2024.
186 Wei Shen, 'Is China's New Deposit Insurance Scheme a Panacea? And Why Now? A Functional Analysis' (2016) 31 *Journal of International Banking Law and Regulation*, 88.
187 Andrew Campbell and Peter Cartwright, 'Deposit Insurance: Consumer Protection, Bank Safety and Moral Hazard (1999) 10 *European Business Law Review*, 96, 102.
188 Harris Weinstein, 'Moral Hazard Deposit Insurance and Banking Regulation' (1992) 77 *Cornell Law Review*, 1109, 1104.
189 Caixin Global, 'China's Small Businesses Need Effective Support' *Caixin* (Beijing, 28 August 2018) <https://www.caixinglobal.com/2018-08-28/editorial-chinas-small-businesses-need-effective-support-101319746.html> accessed 1 October 2024.
190 Douglas W. Diamond and Philip H. Dybvig, 'Bank Runs, Deposit Insurance, and Liquidity' (1983) 91 *Journal of Political Economy*, 401, 419.
191 Haibo Yan and Ying Huang, 'Deposit Insurance and Banking Supervision in China: the Agenda Ahead' (2008) 33 *The Geneva Papers on Risk and Insurance. Issues and Practice*, 599.

6 Suggestions and Recommendations for China's Deposit Insurance Scheme

From a Comparative Perspective

6.1 Introduction

Deposit insurance, as an essential player in the financial safety net, has been absent in China, the world's second-largest economy, for years. Since 1 May 2015, China has finally commenced its own deposit insurance scheme with the government's ambition to build a deposit insurer like the FDIC. However, apparently, China's deposit insurance scheme, as a newborn system in China, is flawed. Before the establishment of the Deposit Insurance Fund Management Corporation (DIFMC) on 29 May 2019, the Financial Stability Bureau of the PBOC had temporarily fulfilled the function of deposit insurance.

Tracking China's reform of financial regulation after the GFC, it is clear that the US and the UK have hugely influenced China's financial regulation, not only because many Chinese financial reformers have undergone an educational background in both countries, but also because China has revamped its financial regulatory architecture similar to the UK and the US. After the GFC, the UK and the US, representing two totally different deposit insurance models, have refurbished their deposit insurance schemes, in full or in part, to pursue financial stability when bank failures occur. At the current stage, China's deposit insurance model is closer to the UK's model, but the ultimate objective for China is to transition to the US's model. Therefore, the UK and the US are good samples mirroring China's deposit insurance.

In this context, this chapter attempts to provide suggestions and recommendations to China's deposit insurance scheme from a comparative perspective by comprehensively comparing China with the UK and the US, with a focus on how China transitions its deposit insurance scheme from the UK's pay box model to the US's risk-minimiser model. This chapter consists of three parts. Part one provides a comprehensive study on how the UK and the US influenced China's financial regulation and deposit insurance. Part two provides a roadmap for prospective reforms of China's deposit insurance scheme, after drawing lessons from the FSCS and the FDIC. Finally, a conclusion will be drawn.

6.2 The Overhaul of Regulatory Structure and Deposit Insurance after the Global Financial Crisis: the US, the UK, and China

After the GFC, both the US and the UK revisited their regulatory frameworks and made significant alterations to their regulatory architectures. From a comparative

DOI: 10.4324/9781003612759-6

analysis of the US and the UK, it is clear that there are many similar developments consolidating banking regulation, showing the international trend of consolidating the banking regulatory framework.[1] Apparently, China has been influenced very much by US and UK movements in optimising banking regulation through structural reshuffles.[2]

6.2.1 The US: Continuously Consolidating Coordination and Banking Resolution

US financial regulatory architecture has long been criticised for its complex dual system and fragmented regulatory framework, in which financial institutions, comprising federal chartered and state chartered financial institutions, have to abide by regulators, either at the federal level or state level.[3] From the federal level, after the Dodd-Frank Act, coordination mechanisms and deposit insurance have been strengthened by establishing the FSOC, chaired by the Secretary of the Treasury, and introducing the Orderly Liquidation Authority to the FDIC, which extends the FDIC's responsibilities to large and complex financial institutions.

6.2.1.1 The Creation of the FSOC to Facilitate Coordination and Information Sharing

Before the GFC, each primary federal regulator just concentrated on its own supervisory objectives, and no primary regulator undertook responsibility for overseeing threats posed to the entire US financial system, which produced overlapping and conflicting mandates and interests among primary regulators, thereby triggering inefficiency and the waste of regulatory costs.[4] The FSOC, a super interagency committee created by the Dodd-Frank Act, was created to fill supervisory gaps and retain regulatory consistency, aimed at promoting coordination, information sharing and collection, and pinpointing non-bank financial companies that may pose threats to overall financial stability.[5]

The FSOC consists of ten voting members, including all primary federal regulators, and five nonvoting members. With a two-thirds vote, the FSOC can determine whether a systemically important non-bank financial institution should be subject to heightened supervision under the Federal Reserve.[6] While the FSOC does not have direct supervisory power over individual financial institutions, it is capable of recommending that primary financial regulators apply stricter standards on prudential supervision.[7] Most importantly, the FSOC provides an interagency connection to optimise coordination and information sharing and collection among multiple regulators.

6.2.1.2 The Strengthened and Powerful FDIC in the New Era of US Banking Resolution

The FDIC, created in 1933 in the wake of the Great Depression, has undertaken a broader resolution authority after the Dodd-Frank Act, namely the Orderly Liquidation Authority, which allows the FDIC to resolve entire large and complex bank holding companies defined as systemically important financial institutions (SIFIs). Orderly bankruptcy procedures are somewhat incapable of resolving large and complex financial institutions in a timely manner, leading to financial contagions. For example, in the case of the Lehman Brothers Holdings failure, the most well-known case during the GFC, more than $75 billion was unrecoverable under the Bankruptcy Code, and over $2.2 billion had been spent on legal services and other professional fees until 2013.[8] Thus, as an alternative, when it comes to SIFIs that cannot be disposed of by the Bankruptcy Code, the FDIC hence has resolution authority, as granted by the Dodd-Frank Act, to resolve failed SIFIs directly.

To carry out the Orderly Resolution Authority, the FDIC has prepared a specific plan called the 'single point of entry' (SPOE) strategy, where the FDIC would be appointed as the receiver of the biggest financial holding companies.[9] Under the SPOE, the FDIC is capable of establishing a bridge company to take over most of the assets from the failed holding company, as well as allowing all subsidiaries of the failed holding company to continue operations as usual, thereby eliminating financial disruptions as much as possible. Once recovered, the FDIC shall retreat from the bridge company, leaving the company to the private sector. In the meantime, although the FDIC would transfer most liabilities to the bridge company, shareholders and unsecured creditors of the failed holding company could still suffer losses without any compensation or returns.[10] Furthermore, if encountering inadequate private funding, the FDIC is entitled to borrow from the Orderly Liquidation Fund from the Treasury and then lend to the bridge company safely, whereas the FDIC should repay the fund as soon as possible when it obtains enough private funding.[11]

However, despite having a detailed and well-organised SPOE, the Orderly Liquidation Authority has not yet been implemented and has become more controversial amid vocal proponents and overwhelming opponents in the US. Academics from the Hoover Institution have strongly backlashed against the Orderly Liquidation Authority. As criticised by Kroener III, the FDIC selecting liabilities considered fitting to the bridge company seems like 'picking winners and losers among the creditors' and leaves a door open for political intervention, thereby unduly relying on the FDIC's discretion.[12] In addition to excessive discretion, supported by cheaper financing resources and government backing, the Orderly Liquidation Authority could trigger moral hazard by propping up a protective umbrella to tolerate so-called 'too big to fail' SIFIs, as the FDIC will eventually save SIFIs that are 'too big to fail' and continue their operations as usual.[13] Many also admit the gaps in the existing Bankruptcy Code in resolving large and complex financial institutions and suggest eliminating gaps by strengthening the Bankruptcy Code, referred to as Chapter 14, because meaningful judicial review and legal accountability contained in the Bankruptcy Code are important advantages over a powerful agency's discretion.[14]

Proponents of the Orderly Liquidation Authority reiterate that only the government has the capability to prompt decision-making that accelerates the process of bank resolution, with fewer administrative costs in comparison with court orders. Ben Bernanke, former Chairman of the Federal Reserve, defends the

Orderly Liquidation Authority, saying that financial regulators, because of their main responsibility to monitor the entire financial system, have better knowledge and information with respect to large financial institutions' operations and balance sheets, unlike the information conveyed to judges.[15] Furthermore, faced with large transnational financial institutions, the FDIC, unlike judges, has international liaisons with foreign financial regulators and central banks, which can collaborate with foreign financial regulators to jointly resolve financially nonviable transnational financial holding companies, thereby reducing US investors' and depositors' losses.[16] By and large, the Orderly Resolution Authority has long been controversial among US scholars and government officials since it was born after the Dodd-Frank Act.

6.2.2 *The UK: A Consolidated Bank of England, New Twin Peaks, and Slightly Enhanced Deposit Insurer*

6.2.2.1 A Consolidated Bank of England and New Twin Peaks Model

After the GFC, the UK introduced a brand-new regulatory hierarchy on 1 April 2013 in response to drawbacks that occurred during the crisis by fundamentally fortifying the role of judgement and expertise.[17] The new framework is composed of the FPC, a sub-committee of the Bank of England, to identify, monitor, and take action against systemic risks, as well as to promote the resilience of the UK financial system; the PRA, separated from the FSA and established as a subsidiary under the Bank of England, responsible for the prudential regulation and supervision of large banks, building societies, and other large financial firms;[18] and the FCA, split from the FSA, responsible for all firms' conduct of business and prudential regulation of remaining financial firms.

Under the new regulatory structure, the FPC, chaired by the Governor of the Bank of England with the Chief Executives of the PRA and the FCA, has become a powerful authority beyond twin peaks, overseeing the entire UK financial system and developing counter measures against financial instability. In the meantime, the FPC is capable of directing the PRA and the FCA to conduct specific macro-prudential tools.[19]

In contrast to US sectoral regulation, the UK has adopted twin peaks, in which both financial regulators monitor all financial services. The PRA, as a subsidiary of the Bank of England, is focused on supervising around 1,500 banks, insurers, and large investment firms that significantly threaten financial stability from a micro-prudential level.[20] The FCA, which is regarded as the narrower FSA, is responsible for overseeing the conduct of business of all financial service providers and being a prudential regulator for non-PRA-authorised firms. However, the twin peaks model inevitably creates regulatory overlap for around 2,000 UK financial firms that are subject to dual regulators, giving rise to increasing compliance costs.[21] In response to such a situation, the new UK regulatory system strengthens coordination, as both the PRA and FCA are required to fulfil their functions by way of legislative duty to coordinate, mutual consultation, information sharing, and cross-membership of boards.

6.2.2.2 A Slightly Strengthened Financial Services Compensation Scheme in UK Banking Resolution

The Northern Rock failure during the GFC reflected the outright failure of the UK deposit insurance scheme. In this case, in the wake of the liquidity crisis arising from the US sub-prime mortgage crisis, Northern Rock, the fifth-largest UK mortgage lender, became the first UK bank to experience a run since 1878.[22] Consequently, in order to stop long queues and mitigate public panic, the UK government eventually provided a blanket guarantee that all depositors of Northern Rock could get their savings back. After the crisis, the role of FSCS in participating in a bank insolvency was slightly enhanced to a pay box plus model.

Since the Banking Act 2009 came into effect, the FSCS's capability to prompt compensation has significantly strengthened. In accordance with the Banking Act 2009,

> a bank liquidator has two objectives: Objective 1 is to work with the FSCS so as to ensure that as soon as reasonably practicable each eligible depositor (a) has the relevant account transferred to another financial institution; or (b) receives payment from (or on behalf of) the FSCS; and Objective 1 is prior to Objective 2.[23]

Coupled with the amended Financial Services and Markets Act 2000 (FSMA 2000), which grants the FSCS additional powers to examine information collected by a banking liquidator in pursuit of paying off depositors within seven days of a bank failure, the FSCS, as a member of the Liquidation Committee, has been a key element proceeding bank insolvency.[24]

Besides, after 1 January 2011, the FSCS has implemented the 'Single Customer View' (SCV), a system to capture most individual deposit accounts by requiring each deposit-taking institution to submit precise and updated information associated with personal deposit accounts within 24 hours after the FSCS sends a request.[25] After testing and verification, the FSCS is capable of paying off individual depositors in line with the SCV files, aiming to pay SCV-captured accounts in seven days and remaining eligible accounts in 20 working days.[26] Having finalised depositor compensations, the FSCS will automatically take over depositors' rights to claim the amount of the SCV accounts and other insured accounts as a creditor.[27]

In a positive view, the FSCS's new improvements could accelerate depositor compensation, enhancing the capability and influence of the FSCS in preventing what happened in Northern Rock during the crisis. However, despite speedy payoffs, the FSCS still has to overcome some difficulties that obstruct the way forward. First, the faster payoff overwhelmingly relies on the SCV, which allows the FSCS to have precise information on individual deposit accounts. The big question is that, given the current legal framework, there is no enforceable, hard rule requiring deposit-taking institutions to report changes as fast as possible, especially when something emergent occurs. The second issue, which is labelled as the lack of effective mechanisms, is that without cohesive and comprehensive regulatory collaboration, communication, and coordination it is hard for the FSCS to work together with various parties to achieve a faster payoff.

6.2.3 China: Lessons Learned from the US and the UK

6.2.3.1 Unveiling a New Super Powerful Committee, the Central Financial Committee (CFC), following the FSOC and the FPC

Following the establishment of the FSOC and the FPC, China subsequently initiated a super committee, namely the Financial Stability and Development Committee, which has been renamed the CFC since 8 November 2017.[28] The CFC, which consists of all financial regulators and relevant ministries, is committed to strengthening coordination in financial regulation, identifying and preventing systemic risk, and further deepening China's financial reform. The CFC, led by the Vice Premier, has the capability to give directions to all financial regulators and relevant ministries, even though there is no legislation authorising mandates.[29] It is clear that the CFC, which combines the functions of the FSOC and the FPC, has been significantly influenced by the UK and the US's experience after the GFC.[30]

6.2.3.2 China's Long-Awaited Deposit Insurance Scheme: A Long Way from the UK Model to the US Model

After the first proposal of deposit insurance in 1993, China finally unveiled its deposit insurance scheme in 2015, after the global financial crisis.[31] In accordance with the Regulation on Deposit Insurance and the 'Reply of the State Council on Approving the Implementation Plan for Deposit Insurance', the destination of China's deposit insurer is to become an independent deposit insurer with broad mandates under the leadership of the State Council.[32] Before 29 May 2019, the Financial Stability Bureau of the PBOC had temporarily been responsible for operating deposit insurance and implementing functions authorised by the Regulation on Deposit Insurance. After 29 May 2019, the DIFMC, incorporated in the PBOC with a total capital of RMB 10 billion, became China's deposit insurer responsible for managing the deposit insurance fund and dealing with the assets of troubled banks. However, the DIFMC has to abide by the leadership of the PBOC, as the legal person is the Deputy Director of the Financial Stability Bureau of the PBOC.[33]

However, in reality, building up an ideal deposit insurance scheme is not a one-stop, simple process, and there is no one-size-fits-all deposit insurance model, so China, as a beginner, has a long way to go towards its destination of having an independent and multi-functional deposit insurer.[34] Despite registration information and the Regulation on Deposit Insurance implying that the DIFMC will have broad mandates with a resolution authority in managing deposit insurance and resolving troubled banks, at the present stage, the DIFMC, admittedly, is more like a pay box model rather than a risk-minimiser model due to the absence of experience, skill, human resources, and limited start-up funding. It is to be said that the current China's deposit insurance scheme seems closer to the UK arrangement rather than the US model, the goal for China's deposit insurance.

In the UK, the Bank of England, designated as a UK resolution authority with extended powers for information gathering, is responsible for conceiving and conducting bank resolution mechanisms through bail-in, a private sector purchase of a failed bank's business, the continuation of essential financial services of a failed bank via the establishment of a bridge bank controlled by the Bank of England, the acquisition by a separate asset management vehicle controlled by the Bank of England, and the bank insolvency process;[35] the PRA coordinates with the Bank of England and the FCA to exert prompt corrective action, referred to as the Proactive Intervention Framework in the UK;[36] and the FSCS mainly concentrates on implementing faster payouts within seven working days. Thus, apparently, the FSCS, as the UK's deposit insurer, is absent in the UK banking resolution regime, as it just has the single purpose of reimbursing depositors in a timely manner, without any other substantial powers and functions in the bank resolution process.

Similar to the UK, currently, the PBOC, China's central bank, is responsible for executing prompt correction and banking resolution in coordination with the NFRA, China's prudential regulator, despite China's ambition to build a deposit insurer like the FDIC.[37] Although many Chinese high-profile officials in banking and finance have hyped that China will establish an omnipotent deposit insurer with broad mandates similar to the FDIC, it can be anticipated that, in the near future, China's deposit insurance scheme will be mainly focused on managing China's deposit insurance fund and reimbursing depositors on time, considering the lack of an integrated legal framework, skilled human resources, and experience in running a deposit insurance system.[38]

Notably, by comparing Figures 6.1 and 6.2, it is obvious that both the UK banking market and China's banking market are highly concentrated, as several banks occupy over half of the market shares in the UK and China by total assets. After the State Council announced its 'Institutional Reform Plan' in 2023, China transitioned to a twin peaks era with one central bank – the PBOC – and two regulatory bodies – the NFRA and the China Securities Regulatory Commission.[39] Clearly, the UK's model, faced with the current situation in China where deposit insurance has just stepped into a highly concentrated banking market, is more suitable for China's deposit insurance, rather than the US's model.

Besides, admittedly, China is not capable of building up a perfect deposit insurance scheme immediately. Both Zhou Xiaochuan and Pan Gongsheng, the former Governor and the Deputy Governor of the PBOC, have acknowledged that China is unprepared to have an independent deposit insurer with broad mandates due to the absence of well-trained employees and adequate start-up funding.[40] For example, the most recent case of Inner-Mongolia-based Baoshang Bank, a medium-sized commercial bank on the verge of collapse due to bad lending practices in making use of wholesale funding, demonstrates that the PBOC and the NFRA jointly took over Baoshang Bank to pay out depositors and secured creditors from their own pockets based on their agency discretion, revealing China's helpless deposit insurance scheme against bank failures at present.

In sharp contrast to China's present model and the UK's model, the FDIC, undoubtedly the most advanced and leading pioneer in deposit insurance, has very

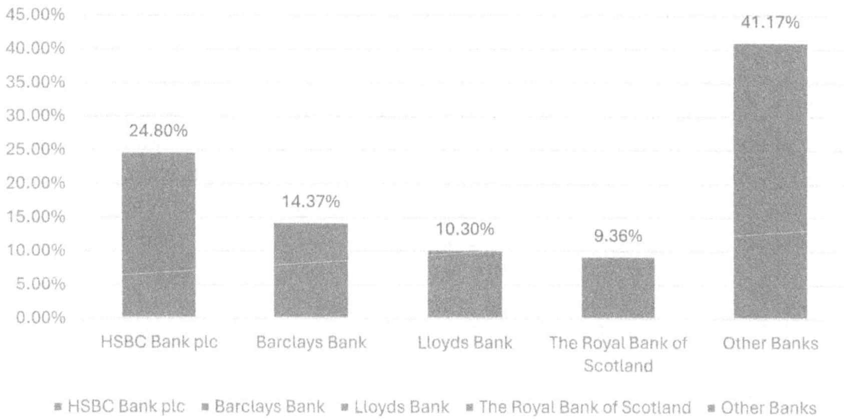

Figure 6.1 Market Share by Total Assets for Banks in the UK 2017
(Data Source: Statista and Bank of England)

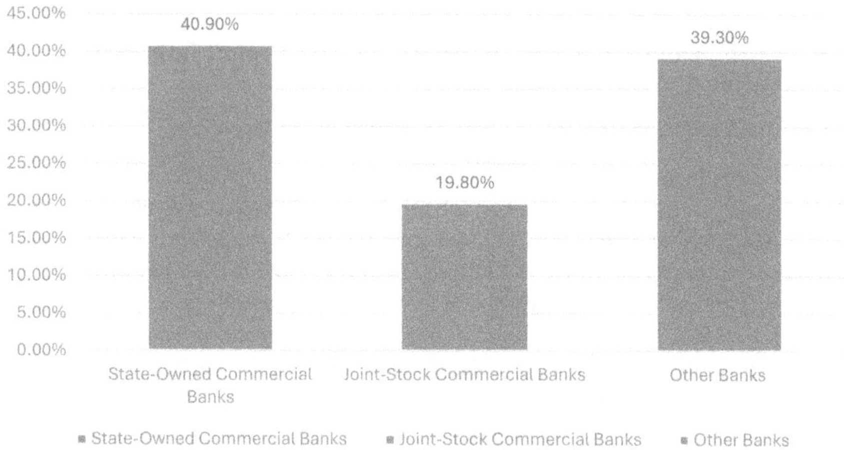

Figure 6.2 Market Share by Total Assets for Banks in China
(Data Source: NFRA)

broad mandates and powerful agency discretion in dealing with troubled financial institutions, especially through the Orderly Resolution Authority to resolve large, complex, significantly important financial institutions after the promulgation of the Dodd-Frank Act. In the meantime, the FDIC unequivocally plays an indispensable role in US banking regulation, as the FDIC has been a vital member of the FSOC, devoted to implementing prompt corrective action and preventing systemic risks. Through retrospective appraisal of the rise of the FDIC, it can be found that the FDIC has been significantly strengthened with major breakthroughs in prompt corrective action and risk-based premiums until the Federal Deposit Insurance Corporation Improvement Act (FDICIA) of 1991, 58 years after the commencement of the FDIC.[41] It is to be said that the rise of the FDIC is a noteworthy lesson teaching China how to effectively build a powerful deposit insurer with broad mandates.

Therefore, during the transition period, the UK's pay box model might be the most realistic and proper deposit insurance model for China, as both nations have similar banking markets and high-level interagency committees that exclude deposit insurers. Furthermore, the pay box model does not need vast amounts of start-up funding and skilled staff, which seems suitable for the development of China's deposit insurer. China should start reforming its deposit insurance scheme towards the FDIC when it has accumulated extensive experience and skilled personnel in deposit insurance. Despite having a highly concentrated banking market similar to the UK, from another angle, the number of deposit-taking institutions and the market scale of China's banking industry are following the US banking industry, especially with further openings of private-owned banks and foreign banks.[42] This is to say, while regarding the FDIC as a reasonable goal for China's deposit insurance scheme, it takes a long time to construct an influential deposit insurer like the FDIC.

6.3 A Roadmap for Reform: Optimising China's Deposit Insurance Scheme

6.3.1 The Need for an Integrated Legal System of Deposit Insurance

After the commencement of China's deposit insurance scheme, it is necessary for the Chinese government to optimise the relevant legal system, as well as to ensure the implementation, transparency, and clarity of China's deposit insurance scheme. Currently, China's Enterprise Bankruptcy Law and Civil Procedure Law have set out orderly procedures for dealing with liquidation and creditors, but both of them target enterprises with their creditors, not banks and depositors. Therefore, neither the Enterprise Bankruptcy Law nor the Civil Procedure Law can be applied to bank insolvency and depositor protection.

Although the Law of the People's Republic of China on Regulation and Supervision over the Banking Industry (Chinese Banking Regulation and Supervision Law), the Law of the People's Republic of China on People's Bank of China (PBOC Law), and the Law of the People's Republic of China on Commercial Banks (Chinese Commercial Bank Law) have set out information and procedures in association with banking resolution, these principles regarding information and procedures are too ambiguous to clarify the detailed procedures for resolving banks. For example, in light of Articles 28 and 29 of the Chinese Banking Regulation and Supervision Law, the NFRA should report emergent banking crises that might result in systemic risks and social instability to the State Council and relevant ministries like the PBOC and the Ministry of Finance, and then the NFRA should work with the PBOC, the Ministry of Finance, and other related ministries to finalise contingency plans, banking resolution measures, and procedures. The words written in other clauses with respect to banking resolution are parallel to these two articles; hence, it is hard to find functional and realistic procedures because all procedures and plans for banking resolution depend on agency discretion and multilateral agreement among relevant authorities.

Despite having commenced a deposit insurance scheme since 2015 in China, to ensure the effectiveness of China's deposit insurance scheme, the Chinese government should immediately put forward China's deposit insurance law based on the Regulation on Deposit Insurance to clarify objectives, responsibilities, rationales, and mechanisms, thereby enhancing the authority, credibility, and consistency of the DIFMC. Apart from enacting a deposit insurance law, the DIFMC and deposit insurance should be incorporated into the PBOC Law, Chinese Commercial Bank Law, and Chinese Banking Regulation and Supervision Law to create harmonisation and consistency with other participants of the financial safety net. In the meantime, banks and other banking institutions, subject to insured institutions under China's deposit insurance scheme, should be explicitly excluded from the Enterprise Bankruptcy Law and the Civil Procedure Law's definitions and targets.

In this regard, the US is a remarkable model, teaching the world how to strengthen a consistent and well-defined legal system in support of its deposit insurance system and deposit insurer. From the Banking Act of 1933 to the Dodd-Frank Act in 2010, there have been various legislations, in the wake of crises, driving the US deposit insurance scheme and the FDIC forward, especially when the FDICIA authorised the FDIC with the functions to prompt corrective action, least cost tests, and risk-based premiums to thwart the Savings and Loans Crisis in the 1980s.[43] In the meantime, the UK also has an integrated legal system for the FSCS, as everything related to the FSCS can be found in various acts and handbooks. Therefore, China, a beginner in deposit insurance, should first accelerate its progress in consolidating and specifying legislation for deposit insurance by drawing lessons from international experiences.

6.3.2 The Need for a Unified Bank Credit Rating System

Currently, China's deposit insurance premiums consist of flat-rate premiums and risk-based premiums, indicating that banks first have to contribute premiums based on a unified benchmark rate set by the DIFMC with the approval of the State Council, and then pay additional premiums in line with the DIFMC's risk-based assessment of each bank. However, China seems unprepared to start risk-based premium rates due to the absence of a banking rating system, which might be a giant barrier stopping the implementation of risk-based premium rates.[44] In 2004, the NFRA issued the 'Measures for Risk Ratings on Risk Level of Joint-Stock Commercial Banks (for trial implementation)', a similar method to the CAMELS rating system, to assess risks of Chinese joint-stock commercial banks.[45] Along with capital adequacy, asset quality, management, earnings, and liquidity under the CAMELS rating system, the NFRA added safety as an indicator into its risk ratings, which is similar to sensitivity under CAMELS. In accordance with the measures, every indicator in this assessment has a score, from the worst 0 to the best 100, and an overall weighted score demonstrating the ultimate assessment result would be calculated.[46] Table 6.1 details the weights of each indicator and the

Table 6.1 Calculation of Assessment Score

Indicator	*Weight (Percent)*
Capital Adequacy	20
Asset Quality	20
Management	25
Earnings	20
Liquidity	15

Table 6.2 Classification of Final Ratings

Ratings	*Scores*
Rating 1 (Well)	85–100
Rating 2 (Good)	75–85
Rating 3 (Pay Attention)	60–75
Rating 4 (Not Good)	50–60
Rating 5 (Bad)	0–50

calculation of a weighted score for each insured institution. Eventually, assessment scores could be divided into five classes illustrated in Table 6.2, from the best to the worst amid decreasing scores.

Although this was the first time China introduced a banking rating assessment, it was not successful and circulated due to the absence of applicable computing methods, and enforceable and effective action against big banks. Furthermore, the in-depth reason why this assessment has not taken effect so far is that China's banking industry has undergone significant overhaul amid the establishment of joint-stock state-owned banks, foreign banks, and privately owned banks, so the measures that concentrate on joint-stock commercial banks are outdated and do not reflect the accurate circumstances of banks, misleading the market and depositors.

Barring the measures set by the NFRA, the PBOC declares that it has completed risk assessments for all 3,969 banking institutions in the first quarter of 2018 in order to put risk-based premium rates on the agenda. The final assessment result has been divided into 10 categories, starting from level 1 (the worst) to level 10 (the best).[47] According to the PBOC's investigation, the final result of risk assessments for 3,969 banking institutions is demonstrated by Figure 6.3, which shows that 76 banking institutions between level 1 and level 2 occupy 1.91 percent, 3,473 banking institutions between level 3 and level 7 take up 87.5 percent, and 420 banking institutions between level 8 and level 10 account for 10.58 percent.[48] However, related information has not yet been disclosed, and the PBOC has not disclosed further details related to methodology, standards of classification, or data source, especially how these data can be used in calculating risk-based premium rates.

In order to ensure fair and accurate risk-based premium rates, China's banking rating system should be established in a dynamic and scientific way that can give a comprehensive outlook of banks' risk levels in consultation with capital adequacy, asset quality, management, earnings, and liquidity. The CAMELS rating system,

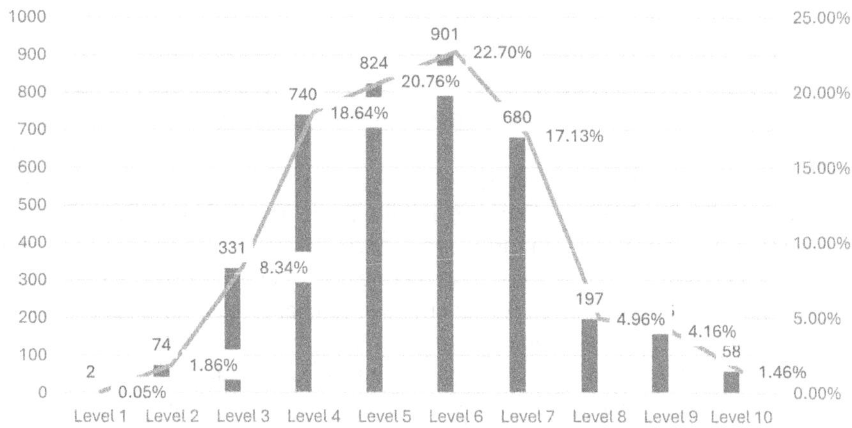

Figure 6.3 Distribution of Risk Level of 3,969 Banking Institutions by the PBOC (Data Source: PBOC)

deployed by the FDIC for years, is a great example to guide China's prospective banking rating system, showing the great importance of having a reliable banking rating system. The UK's approach to risk-based premiums also can be learnt by China, not only because both the UK and China have similar banking markets and banking regulatory frameworks but also because it is comparatively simple to work out final scores that reflect the risk level of depository institutions.

In addition, owing to having subsidised state-owned commercial banks with a giant amount of government guarantees, China's prospective banking rating system should set higher standards for state-owned commercial banks, along with slightly higher, risk-based premium rates in pursuit of fair competition with privately owned banks and locally incorporated foreign banks, as large state-owned commercial banks are the biggest beneficiaries from having a stable and effective deposit insurance scheme.

6.3.3 Liaison between the Deposit Insurer and Other Participants of the Financial Safety Net in China

While the establishment of a deposit insurance scheme in 2015 has accomplished the last segment of China's financial safety net, it has brought some unresolved issues. In theory, all participants of the financial safety net have the same ultimate purpose of maintaining financial stability, but, in detail, they have different regulatory objectives based on their de facto functions and responsibilities. For example, alongside the conception of China's financial safety net, the PBOC is mainly responsible for the lender of last resort; the NFRA shoulders the function of prudential regulation; and the DIFMC works as a deposit insurer.[49]

Nonetheless, as argued by Kahn and Santos, inappropriate institutional allocation of regulatory powers that may lead to overlapping supervision and regulation on banks can compel banks to confront conflicting rules and principles arising from an overregulated regulatory framework.[50] Schich also stresses that the difference between deposit insurance and lender of last resort is that deposit insurance focuses on paying out depositors after closing an insolvent bank, while the lender of last resort seeks to rescue banks that are solvent and just have temporary difficulties with liquid funds.[51] Carr found that conflicting rules and principles also may appear between deposit insurance and prudential regulation as the prudential regulators usually are unwilling to close a troubled bank because of the adverse reputation brought by a bank failure, triggering regulatory forbearance that raises the costs of deposit insurance.[52] However, Kahn and Santos also hold another view that, without good regulation and proper monitoring of the misconduct of relevant financial authorities, conflicts between their objectives inevitably will burst, which ultimately threatens banks by imposing increasing compliance costs and regulatory burden.[53] In addition, Goodhart adds that, indeed, it is hard to separate illiquidity and insolvency as illiquidity is the beginning stage of insolvency, indicating the interconnected and interactive liaison between deposit insurance and lender of last resort.[54]

Therefore, relevant legislation and a Memoranda of Understanding that define and distinguish objectives, responsibilities, and functions among the DIFMC, the PBOC, and the NFRA are urgently needed to be enacted for the reduction of regulatory overlaps and the improvement of regulatory efficiency in China. More essentially, China should clarify the boundary between deposit insurance and lender of last resort, optimising coordination mechanisms for banking resolution and information sharing. Despite deposit insurance being capable of resolving several bank failures, it cannot solely handle an entire financial system crisis without effective coordination with other participants of the financial safety net. After drawing lessons from international experience, China should maintain a high degree of transparency into its coordination mechanism so as to mitigate potential conflicts among the participants of the financial safety net.

Focusing on China's current legal framework, the mandates of the DIFMC between the pay box model and the risk-minimiser model do not contain the power to exert on-site examination for information collection and sharing, and the NFRA, China's prudential regulator and supervisor in the banking sector, is mainly responsible for implementing on-site examination, with broad mandates.[55] In good times, the DIFMC just needs information to calculate risk-based premiums, whereas when facing a bank failure, vast bundles of information are required to prompt depositor compensation, bank resolution, and the liquidation process in pursuit of financial stability. In practice, the NFRA has the power to exercise on-site examination, indicating that it can capture outright information on each bank which is desired by the DIFMC for the sake of implementing fast payouts. Hence, establishing swift information sharing among China's financial safety net is suggested to be specified by law or by relevant Memorandum of Understanding.

Article 14 of the Regulation on Deposit Insurance requires the DIFMC, the NFRA, and PBOC to build a tripartite information-sharing network, and if necessary, the DIFMC is allowed to request further information needed to prompt depositor payoffs and pinpoint risk-based deposit insurance premium rates. An effective information-sharing network among the participants of the financial safety net has been more imperative since the introduction of risk-based premium rates, an accurate and fair mechanism based on loads of information captured by all financial authorities.

Along with codifying legislation, one assumption that makes China's deposit insurance more efficient is to promote the DIFMC to the CFC, where a super-powerful inter-agency committee, including the PBOC and NFRA, led by the Vice Premier, dedicates itself to supervising monetary policy, preventing systemic risk, and strengthening coordination mechanism.[56] However, indeed, the DIFMC is currently a subsidiary of the PBOC specialising in deposit insurance, which indicates that under China's nomenklatura political regime, the DIFMC must obey the instructions and objectives from the PBOC and the NFRA, China's lender of last resort and prudential regulator, leading to conflicting mandates that weaken the DIFMC.

However, hosted and supported by the CFC, the DIFMC can engage in direct communication with the PBOC and the NFRA, forming a straightforward coordination mechanism that significantly improves regulatory efficiency by facilitating bank resolution and lowering overlaps and conflicting mandates. Apart from the coordination mechanism, promoting the DIFMC to the CFC is of great importance to accelerate China's ultimate pursuit of having an independent deposit insurer, as this assumption provides a level playing field for the DIFMC to equally work with the PBOC and the NFRA in advance.[57] However, in fact, it is very hard to promote the DIFMC to that high administrative level without long-standing preparation and political promotion, despite the assumption suggesting a shortcut.

Focusing on the US and the UK, establishing effective coordination between the participants of the financial safety net is also a headache troubling both countries for years. In the wake of the global financial crisis, the US set up the FSOC to strengthen coordination among various federal primary regulators, and the UK established the FPC without the FSCS. Unlike China and the UK, with fewer financial regulators, the US financial regulatory architecture has long been criticised for its complexity, overlap, and duplication, which enhance the difficulty of coordination among multiple regulators, resulting in higher regulatory costs and regulatory forbearance.[58]

6.3.4 The DIFMC's Involvement in Banking Resolution

With the further marketisation and liberalisation of China's banking industry, deposit insurance in China is expected to play an irreplaceable role in resolving troubled banks in a market-oriented way to eliminate over-reliance on the government. Proven by the several cases in China discussed in previous chapters, it is unequivocal that the government leading the way to resolve troubled banks via mergers, capital injections, and closure based on political trade-offs has consumed enormous amounts of taxpayers' contributions, which is overwhelmingly perceived as an adverse effect, devastating banks' efficiency, profitability, and stability. Though, from a positive aspect, government intervention might accelerate the resolution process because the government is capable of utilising administrative power to take charge of business transactions and liabilities.[59]

However, in the opposite view, political interference totally ignores the efficiency of market-based decision-making and managerial operations, resulting in increasing costs, as the government pursues overall stability of the macro economy, society, and entire financial system rather than well-performed business development and operation revenue.[60] Since an increasing number of foreign banks and privately owned banks have entered China's banking market, government involvement and political intervention should no longer be involved in bank insolvency and banking resolution, as state-owned commercial banks and joint-stock commercial banks with government ownership, supported and subsidised by the government, could have unfair subsidiaries and more favourable policies in competition with foreign banks and privately owned banks, which impair the progress of deposit insurance and China's effort to steer toward a market-oriented banking system.

To date, China's effort to establish market-based bank insolvency and bank resolution through the introduction of a deposit insurance scheme has proven to be ineffective, owing to conflicting legislation and chaotic mandates provided by the DIFMC, the PBOC, and the NFRA. Looking into the current legal framework, there is no specific law or regulation governing bank insolvency and banking regulation, and only the Chinese Commercial Bank Law, the Chinese Banking Regulation and Supervision Law, and the Enterprise Bankruptcy Law set out related rules regarding bank insolvency and bank resolution in separate provisions subject to a special resolution regime.

In accordance with Article 134 of the Enterprise Bankruptcy Law, the NFRA should request the courts to proceed with the reorganisation and winding-up procedures, which are totally different from normal insolvency procedures triggered by creditors or debtors. Nevertheless, the Chinese Commercial Bank Law and the Chinese Banking Regulation and Supervision Law require the courts to declare bank insolvency only after obtaining consent from the NFRA and empower the NFRA to take over and restructure financially non-viable banking institutions directly when these banking institutions suffer credit crises that could affect the interests of depositors.[61] In 2015, regulation pertaining to bank insolvency and banking resolution, the Regulation on Deposit Insurance, was unveiled, which literally makes the DIFMC become a liquidator, receiver, or conservator in charge of resolving troubled banks.[62] On 9 May 2017, the NFRA announced a legislative plan to enact the Regulation on Commercial Bank Insolvency and Resolution, a new banking resolution regulation, which is still underway with no exact date of issuance.[63]

In this context, as shown in Table 6.3, barring the clarity of lender of last resort, it is confusing that there is no specific division of powers and mandates in resolving troubled commercial banks in the stage of ex-post measures, particularly neither in law nor in regulation. In ex-post measures, both the NFRA and the DIFMC are entitled to claim that they are receivers or conservators for taking over troubled banks, and the only difference is that the NFRA acts on the behest of laws drafted

Table 6.3 China' Current Arrangement for Banking Resolution

Procedure	*Mandates*	*Main Player*	*Legal Basis*
Ex-ante	Issuing warning based on risk monitoring	PBOC	The PBOC Law
		NFRA	Chinese Banking Regulation and Supervision Law
		DIFMC	Regulation on Deposit Insurance
Intermediate	Lender of last resort (through deposit reserves or emergency liquidity support)	PBOC	Notice of the PBOC on Strengthening the Administration of Deposit Reserves; Interim Measures for Emergency Loans
Ex-post	Receiver or conservator	NFRA	Chinese Commercial Bank Law; Chinese Banking Regulation and Supervision Law
	Receiver or conservator	DIFMC	Regulation on Deposit Insurance
	Bankruptcy application	NFRA	Enterprise Bankruptcy Law; Chinese Banking Regulation and Supervision Law
	Adjudication of bankruptcy	The courts	Enterprise Bankruptcy Law

by the Standing Committee of the National People's Congress whilst the DIFMC accords with regulations formulated by the government that are subordinated to the laws under China's legislation hierarchy, implying that the NFRA, accordingly, has priority over the DIFMC. Notwithstanding the upcoming issuance of the Regulation on Commercial Bank Bankruptcy Resolution by the NFRA, it will become more complicated and difficult to say who should be the first option to be appointed as the receiver or conservator of troubled banks due to the absence of clear clarification of responsibilities, mandates, and powers under relevant laws and regulations among the DIFMC and the NFRA.

Focusing on international practices, in light of Table 6.4, it is clear that, except for Spain, almost all deposit insurers with the loss-minimiser model and the risk-minimiser model play the role of receiver or conservator, pointing out a way for China's prospective overhaul of banking resolution, especially for clarifying the DIFMC's role in resolving troubled banks.

After the DIFMC formally became incorporated on 29 May 2019, considering the DIFMC's mandates and powers beyond the loss minimiser model, it is reasonable to follow international practices to establish the DIFMC's authority in bank insolvency and bank resolution, while developing further market-based measures including purchase and assumption, bridge banks, and open assistance. However, in the most recent case of the Baoshang Bank collapse that occurred in May 2019, the DIFMC was silent and invisible during the entire resolution process.

Table 6.4 The Function of Deposit Insurers within the FSB Members

National and District	*Deposit Insurance Model*	*Deposit Insurer as a Receiver or Conservator*
Argentina	Loss-Minimiser	Yes
Australia	Pay box	No
Brazil	Loss-Minimiser	Yes
Canada	Loss-Minimiser	Yes
France	Loss-Minimiser	Yes
Germany	Loss-Minimiser	Yes
Hong Kong	Pay box	No
India	Loss-Minimiser	Yes
Indonesia	Loss-Minimiser	Yes
Italy	Loss-Minimiser	Yes
Japan	Loss-Minimiser	Yes
Korea	Risk-Minimiser	Yes
Mexico	Loss-Minimiser	Yes
Netherland	Pay box	No
Russia	Loss-Minimiser	Yes
Singapore	Pay box	No
Spain	Loss-Minimiser	No
Switzerland	Pay box	No
Turkey	Loss-Minimiser	Yes
UK	Pay box	No
US	Risk-Minimiser	Yes

(Data Source: IADI and relevant deposit insurers)

On 24 May 2019, the government takeover of Baoshang Bank was jointly announced by the PBOC and the NFRA, as the PBOC has been responsible for repaying all individual depositors and corporate and interbank debt holders with no more than RMB 50 million of liabilities, whilst the NFRA has mainly embarked on restructuring the bank.[64] Accordingly, it is clear that the DIFMC has not yet had the capability to resolve troubled banks because of its absence in this case.

Nevertheless, China still has time to formulate and specify bank insolvency and banking resolution into a new banking resolution law that clarifies authority, mandates, powers, and responsibilities among the PBOC, the NFRA, as well as the DIFMC, so as to unify and eliminate conflicting and chaotic rules across various laws and regulations with respect to overlapping functions undertaken by different financial authorities, consolidating a specialised law governing all matters of banking resolution and bank insolvency.

Through a retrospective look at China's bank collapses since the commencement of banking reform in 1979, it is noteworthy that China has had an overwhelming tendency to depend on agency discretion to cope with troubled banking institutions. Almost all cases have seen the PBOC and the NFRA's broad involvement in maintaining financial stability and protecting depositors through a few methods including bailouts, closures, and mergers. Accordingly, following the preference for utilising agency discretion to deal with troubled banks, the DIFMC is projected to be a powerful deposit insurer in the long run.

However, many US academics hold an antagonistic attitude towards excessive reliance on powerful agency discretion that results in low transparency and absent legal accountability, and call for exerting bank resolution under bankruptcy law.[65] They defend that judicial procedures attempt to provide fair treatment to creditors in comparison with decisions made at the agency's discretion, as there are clear and strict rules on priority, preference, and authority under bankruptcy law.[66]

From an opposite view, financial authorities have good oversight to monitor risks, and relying on financial regulators' discretion is time-saving compared to waiting for court orders. In addition, financial authorities, indeed, employ specialised staff with unrestricted on-site access to updated and accurate information and circumstances of banks. Some reflections of the Hainan Development Bank collapse, in which bank runs doomed and devastated the bank in a very short time, suggested that financial regulators, including the deposit insurer, should reassure depositors promptly and that deposit insurance is a prerequisite to counter market rumours and panics.[67] However, admittedly, everything has two sides; the presence of low transparency and uncertainty in agency discretion, undoubtedly, are indisputable facts.

Besides, by comparing the FDIC and the FSCS's performance during the global financial crisis, it should be admitted that the US's risk-minimiser model is more efficient than the UK's pay box model. Notably, since the global financial crisis, the FDIC has resolved approximately 500 failed depository institutions and spent around $73 billion of the Deposit Insurance Fund, without any bank runs.[68] The landmark case demonstrating the important functions of the FDIC was the failure of Washington Mutual Bank (WaMu), the largest US savings and loan bank, with total assets of $307 billion and deposits of $188 billion.[69] On 25 September 2008, the Office of Thrift Supervision determined to close WaMu, which was on the brink of collapse due to the burst of housing bubbles in the US mortgage market, and appointed the FDIC as the receiver. On the same day, the FDIC sold the deposits and branches of WaMu to JPMorgan Chase for $1.9 billion by way of a purchase and assumption agreement.[70] As a result, customers of WaMu continued their financial services in JPMorgan Chase without any disruption.

In contrast to the US, the Run on the Rock mirrored the total failure of the UK deposit insurance scheme. When bank runs erupted during the Northern Rock crisis, the FSCS was silent and did nothing effective to stop the long queues outside each branch of Northern Rock. Eventually, massive withdrawals and long queues disappeared only when the UK government promised to provide blanket guarantees. This landmark case clearly revealed the limitations of the pay box deposit insurance model, as the FSCS, the UK's deposit protection scheme manager, became a spectator during the Northern Rock run. After profound lessons learnt from the Northern Rock run, the FSCS has been strengthened with the SCV to capture insured individual accounts as much as possible, despite no given resolution authority. The UK's move to consolidate the FSCS testifies that it is inevitable that deposit insurance, in the long run, will become a crucial player involved in bank resolution.

From comparisons between the UK and the US, it is evident that a deposit insurer with broad mandates in dealing with troubled banks is more efficient and effective than a pay box model, although some critics argue that broad agency discretion could introduce unfairness in picking the acquirer.[71] Objectively speaking, China's plan to build up a powerful deposit insurer like the FDIC in coping with troubled banks is on the right track because the UK is also moving forward in that way by promoting the FSCS's role in coordination with bank liquidators.

6.3.5 Accelerating Marketisation of State-Owned Commercial Banks

After massive bailouts, while the state-owned commercial banks have undergone a flurry of modernisation overhauls, they still have been influenced by political intervention, helping the government and the CCP achieve political, economic, and social objectives.[72] At present, state-owned commercial banks, for example, still have to provide massive financing resources to government-favoured projects, such as the One Belt One Road Initiative and Supply-Side Structural Reform, which, however, increase the NPL ratios. Besides, in accordance with the Basel Committee, both board members and senior management should manage the bank in line with good corporate governance, business strategy, and policies.[73] In contrast to the Basel Committee, board members and senior members of state-owned commercial banks exert their responsibilities and decision-making in consistency with the nomenklatura system and government policies, and their pursuits are political achievement and political promotion in lieu of profitability and market performance.

The introduction of a deposit insurance scheme in 2015, however, has signalled the exit of blanket guarantees and government intervention in upcoming bank crises, especially when state-owned commercial banks are trapped in financial difficulties. This is to say, the Chinese government would no longer provide comprehensive and consistent subsidies in due course, and state-owned commercial banks must facilitate their corporate governance just like that of joint-stock commercial banks, foreign banks, and privately owned banks. But, in other words, the effectiveness of deposit insurance simultaneously needs to be underpinned by modernising corporate governance inside state-owned commercial banks, as state-owned commercial banks have been dominant and influential in China's financial system. As of today, the government has already paid over RMB 3.4 trillion to remove NPLs, which is a giant number compared to China's deposit insurance fund.[74] Although grasping control over financing resources is very meaningful for the government to reach its economic, social, and political objectives, it risks profitability and risk management. Therefore, accelerating the marketisation of state-owned commercial banks is an important step to ensure that China's deposit insurance can be implemented in an effective and market-based way.

However, on the one hand, China has made a great effort to build a modern deposit insurance scheme in line with international standards, aimed at protecting depositors, accelerating marketisation, and creating a level playing field among the participants in China's banking industry. On the other hand, the CCP is persistent in consolidating its leadership in both state-owned commercial banks and the entire banking sector. This is to say, it is a paradox that the government and the CCP are willing to see state-owned commercial banks become profitable with good risk management and corporate governance, but they are reluctant to retreat from controlling personnel appointments and interfering in state-owned commercial banks. As a result, it is likely that China's deposit insurance scheme is just like a rubber-stamp mechanism for state-owned commercial banks, with the Chinese government standing behind state-owned commercial banks.

6.3.6 Public Awareness

In the case of Northern Rock, it can be seen that public awareness, which refers to depositors' understanding of deposit insurance and its features, is of great importance to maintain financial stability by reducing public panic towards bank failures. Like the FSCS during the Northern Rock run, public awareness has been a big challenge since the implementation of a deposit insurance scheme in China in 2015. Currently, public awareness of China's deposit insurance scheme is quite low, as the Chinese government has not promoted the scheme to the public with further notice and advertisement. Though there is no official survey or statistics available to see the level of public awareness in China, it is clear that the publicity of deposit insurance is far below the normal level. For instance, browsing the PBOC website reveals that only five documents that explain China's deposit insurance have been posted since the commencement of China's deposit insurance scheme.[75] Therefore, after the DIFMC was incorporated on 24 May 2019, applicable means to prompt public awareness, in particular, should be devised with an advertising team to ensure that depositors become familiar with China's deposit insurance scheme as quickly as possible.

Most significantly, the DIFMC and the PBOC should begin embarking on running public awareness campaigns to popularise benefits and limitations of deposit insurance. Considering the compulsory membership mechanism China has adopted, both the general public and depositors, defined as target audiences, should be incorporated into deposit insurance education by deploying various ways to help target audiences obtain information and learn about deposit insurance. Ironically, every physical branch of Chinese commercial banks has recently embarked on holding training sessions to promote public understanding of deposit insurance in place of the DIFMC and other participants of the financial safety net, but this is not a sustainable measure in the long run.

China should follow what the FDIC and the FSCS have done in promoting public awareness of their deposit insurance schemes. The FDIC has set up a series of measures to promote public awareness, for example, broadcasting advertisements, providing training sessions for bankers, academics, and depositors, and distributing specific leaflets in multiple languages. The FSCS, after the global financial crisis, has attempted to overturn its previous underachieving performance in educating the public about deposit insurance. For instance, insured institutions currently are required to provide stickers, posters, and leaflets regarding deposit insurance, as well as to inform new and existing customers that they are covered by the FSCS.[76]

According to the IADI's guidelines, a deposit insurer should mainly undertake the responsibility to promote public cognition of deposit insurance, equipped with communication tools and resources applicable to widen the reach of public education.[77] Apparently, the DIFMC should hold seminars or workshops to deliver all key information in relation to China's deposit insurance scheme, such as the scope of coverage, depositor compensation, risk-based premiums, and contingency plans. In essence, at the current stage, the DIFMC should make full use of various communication tools to spread the knowledge of deposit insurance as much as possible, as China is still a developing country where information and messages are difficult to be conveyed to all social classes, especially the population in remote areas.

6.4 Conclusion

After waiting for years, China finally has its own deposit insurance system since 2015, with an integrated financial safety net. In the meantime, the UK and the US, two countries that have leading financial systems in the world, are experienced in operating deposit insurance schemes to combat bank runs. This chapter provides a comprehensive study of how China can draw lessons from the UK and the US to build an effective deposit insurance system and to continue further reforms.

After learning lessons from the global financial crisis, the UK and the US set up high-level interagency committees, the FPC and the FSOC respectively, to facilitate coordination among regulatory bodies and consistency of regulatory objectives that were absent during the crisis. Unlike the FDIC, as an essential member of the FSOC, the FSCS is excluded from the FPC, demonstrating that they represent two completely distinct deposit insurance models. As of the end of 2017, China launched the CFC, combining the functions and objectives of the FSOC and the FPC, whilst China's deposit insurer was not able to engage in the CFC.

Despite having the ambition to set up a deposit insurer like the FDIC, in reality, China, as a beginner, appears to commence operating its deposit insurance based on the UK's deposit insurance model, the pay box model, which is relatively simpler to initiate compared to the FDIC. It is reasonable for China, at the outset, to follow the UK's pay box model because this model can be easily achieved without large amounts of start-up funding and skilled personnel. Thus, China can phase in its progress to build a deposit insurer with broad mandates, like the FDIC, as the deposit insurance fund and experienced staff grows. Notably, even the UK has transitioned the FSCS from the pay box model to pay box plus, implying the significant importance of a deposit insurer's involvement in coping with troubled banks. Hence, building a multifunctional and broad deposit insurer represents the symbol of the prospective direction for expanding the function of deposit insurance.

Unlike the US and the UK with their stable deposit insurance systems, China has many problems to be resolved, from building an integrated legal system to promoting public awareness. This chapter gives a roadmap for China to evolve its deposit insurance scheme toward its ultimate goal of establishing a deposit insurer with broad mandates, aimed at providing conducive suggestions and recommendation based on lessons learnt from the UK and the US's experiences. Although the DIFMC targets the FDIC, in reality, it has to start up like the FSCS and needs a long time to adapt to the FDIC's model after overcoming many difficulties.

Overall, what the DIFMC's role will be in the future of banking regulation is clearly in line with the Chinese government's plan, but it is doubted how long it will take. Meanwhile, while this chapter provides suggestions and recommendations in theory, the reality is that the government is still tightly grasping the financial market. Consequently, without comprehensive marketisation, it is hard to fulfil the full function of deposit insurance, especially when facing state-owned commercial banks whose administrative level is higher than the DIFMC.

Notes

1 He Liu, *Comparative Study on the Two Global Crisis* (China Economic Publishing House, 2013) 138.
2 *Ibid.*
3 Marc Labonte, 'Who Regulates Whom? An Overview of the US Financial Regulatory Framework' (Congressional Research Service, 17 August 2017) <https://fas.org/sgp/crs/misc/R44918.pdf> accessed 15 May 2024.
4 Michael Schillig, *Resolution and Insolvency of Banks and Financial Institutions* (Oxford University Press, 2016) 157.
5 12 USC § 5323.
6 12 USC § 5321.
7 12 USC § 5330.
8 Maureen Farrell, 'Five Years Later, Lehman Bankruptcy Fees Hit $2.2 Billion' *CNN* (New York, 13 September 2013) <https://money.cnn.com/2013/09/13/news/companies/lehman-bankruptcy-fees/> accessed 20 May 2024.
9 The Department of The Treasury, 'Orderly Liquidation Authority and Bankruptcy Reform' (Treasury, 21 February 2018) <https://home.treasury.gov/sites/default/files/2018-02/OLA_REPORT.pdf> accessed 25 October 2023.
10 12 USC § 5381 (a) (3).
11 12 USC § 5384 (d) (2) and § 5390.
12 William F. Kroener III, 'Comment on Orderly Liquidation under Title II of Dodd-Frank and Chapter 14' in Kenneth E. Scott and John B. Taylor (eds), *Bankruptcy Not Bailout: A Special Chapter 14* (Hoover Institution Press, 2012).
13 Aaron Klein, 'A Primer on Dodd-Frank's Orderly Liquidation Authority' (Brookings Institution, 5 June 2017) <https://www.brookings.edu/blog/up-front/2017/06/05/a-primer-on-dodd-franks-orderly-liquidation-authority/> accessed 23 May 2024.
14 Kenneth E. Scott, 'A Guide to the Resolution of Failed Financial Institutions' in Kenneth E. Scott and John B. Taylor (eds), *Bankruptcy Not Bailout: A Special Chapter 14* (Hoover Institution Press, 2012).
15 Ben S. Bernanke, 'Why Dodd-Frank's Orderly Liquidation Authority Should be Preserved' (Brookings Institution, 28 February 2017) <https://www.brookings.edu/blog/ben-bernanke/2017/02/28/why-dodd-franks-orderly-liquidation-authority-should-be-preserved/> accessed 24 May 2024.
16 FDIC and Bank of England, 'Resolving Globally Active, Systemically Important, Financial Institutions' (FDIC and Bank of England, 10 December 2012) <https://www.fdic.gov/about/srac/2012/gsifi.pdf> accessed 25 May 2024.

17 HM Treasury, 'A New Approach to Financial Regulation: The Blueprint for Reform' (HM Treasury, June 2011) <https://assets.publishing.service.gov.uk/government/uploads/system/uploads/attachment_data/file/81403/consult_finreg__new_approach_blueprint.pdf> accessed 26 May 2024.
18 In accordance with the Bank of England and Financial Services Act 2016, since 1 March 2017, the Prudential Regulation Committee has replaced the PRA Board to make supervisory and policy decisions. See https://www.bankofengland.co.uk/news/2017/february/prudential-regulation-committee-replaces-pra-board.
19 BBC, 'UK Financial Regulation Overhauled' *BBC* (London, 1 April 2013) <https://www.bbc.co.uk/news/business-21987829> accessed 25 May 2024, and Bank of England Act 1998, s 9.
20 See PRA 'What is the Prudential Regulation Authority' available at https://www.bankofengland.co.uk/knowledgebank/what-is-the-prudential-regulation-authority-pra.
21 Andrew Godwin, 'Introduction to Special Issue – the Twin Peaks Model of Financial Regulation and Reform in South Africa' (2018) 11 *Law and Financial Markets Review*, 151.
22 Dominic O'Connell, 'The Collapse of Northern Rock: Ten Years on' *BBC* (London, 12 September 2017) <https://www.bbc.co.uk/news/business-41229513> accessed 19 June 2024.
23 Banking Act 2009, s 99.
24 FSMA 2000, s 200 and s 201A.
25 COMP 17. 2. 4R and COMP 17. 2. 3R(2)
26 FSCS, 'Faster Payout Questions and Answers' (FSCS, 16 July 2014) <https://www.fscs.org.uk/uploaded_files/faster_payout_qa_update_-_full_v4_2.pdf> accessed 20 June 2024.
27 *Ibid.*
28 State Council, 'China Establishes Financial Stability and Development Committee' (State Council, 9 November 2017) <http://english.www.gov.cn/news/top_news/2017/11/08/content_281475936107760.htm> accessed 21 June 2024.
29 Xinhua News, 'The Establishment and First Meeting of the FSDC' *Xinhua News* (Beijing, 8 November 2017) <http://www.xinhuanet.com//fortune/2017-11/08/c_1121926062.htm> accessed 20 June 2024.
30 A study jointly conducted by the Tsinghua University PBC School of Finance, the National Institute of Financial Research, the British Embassy, the London School of Economics and Political Science, and the Financial Markets Group Research Centre recommends the FSDC follow the FPC. See <https://assets.publishing.service.gov.uk/government/uploads/system/uploads/attachment_data/file/701846/financial_regulatory_regime_reform.pdf>.
31 The first proposal of deposit insurance in China can be traced back to the Decision of the State Council on Reform of the Financial System in 1993. Due to vigorous lobbying by state-owned commercial banks, China's deposit insurance was delayed for years.
32 Regulation on Deposit Insurance, Article 7.
33 Junling Wang, 'The PBOC Registered Deposit Insurance Corporation' *People's Daily* (Beijing, 1 June 2019) <http://www.xinhuanet.com/fortune/2019-06/01/c_1124570236.htm> accessed 19 July 2019
34 Nicholas J. Ketcha Jr, 'Deposit Insurance System Design and Considerations' (BIS, 15 February 2016) <https://www.bis.org/publ/plcy07o.pdf> accessed 20 June 2024.
35 Banking Act 2009, ss 8, 11, 12, and Bank of England, 'The Bank of England's Approach to Resolution' (Bank of England, October 2017) <file:///C:/Users/lwny/Downloads/the-bank-of-england-approach-to-resolution%20(1).pdf> accessed 20 July 2024.
36 PRA, 'The Prudential Regulation Authority's Approach to Banking Supervision' (PRA, October 2018) <https://www.bankofengland.co.uk/-/media/boe/files/prudential-regulation/approach/banking-approach-2018.pdf?la=en&hash=3445FD6B39A2576ACCE8B4F9692B05EE04D0CFE3> accessed 21 June 2024.

37 Law of People's Republic of China on Commercial Banks, Articles 64, 65, 66, 67, 68, 69, and Law of the People's Republic of China on Regulation and Supervision over the Banking Industry, Articles 23, 27, 28, 29.
38 State Council, 'State Council Routine Policy Briefing on Deposit Insurance in China' (State Council, 3 April 2015) <http://www.scio.gov.cn/32344/32345/32347/20150403/index.htm> accessed 20 June 2024.>
39 State Council, 'The State Council Institutional Reform Plan' (State Council, 17 March 2018) <http://www.gov.cn/guowuyuan/2018-03/17/content_5275116.htm> accessed 20 July 2024.
40 Xiaochuan Zhou, 'Interpretation on China's Deposit Insurance' *Tencent Finance* (Beijing, 23 April 2015) <https://finance.qq.com/zt2015/focus/zxc.htm> accessed 20 June 2024, and ibid.
41 George J. Benston and George G. Kaufman, 'FDICIA after Five Years' (1997) 11 *Journal of Economic Perspective*, 139, 158.
42 Peiyu Xu, 'The FSDC Announces 11 New Policies to Further Open Up China's Financial Industry' *People's Daily* (Beijing, 22 July 2019) <http://paper.people.com.cn/rmrbhwb/html/2019-07/22/content_1937225.htm> accessed 25 July 2024.
43 George J. Benston and George G. Kaufman, 'FDICIA after Five Years' (n41).
44 Delong Huang, Fei Lu, and Xiaoguang Yang, 'A Comparative Study of the Risk Rating of Commercial Banks between Watchdogs in the USA and China' (2006) 11 *Finance Forum*, 51.
45 NFRA, 'Measures for Risk Ratings on Risk Level of Joint-Stock Commercial Banks (for trial implementation) (CBRC, 5 February 2004) <http://www.gov.cn/gongbao/content/2004/content_62974.htm> accessed 19 July 2024.
46 *Ibid.*
47 PBOC, 'China Financial Stability Report 2018' (PBOC, 2 November 2018) <http://www.gov.cn/xinwen/2018-11/04/5337137/files/48b31c0c3cec41ac977b18a2b6b9590a.pdf> accessed 20 April 2024.
48 *Ibid.*
49 Caixin, 'Building Effective Financial Safety Net in China' *Caixin Weekly* (Beijing, 8 July 2019) <http://weekly.caixin.com/2019-07-05/101436002.html> accessed 20 July 2019.
50 Charles M. Kahn and Joao A. C. Santos, 'Allocating Bank Regulatory Powers: Lender of Last Resort, Deposit Insurance and Supervision' (BIS, August 2001) <https://www.bis.org/publ/work102.pdf> accessed 20 April 2024.
51 Sebastian Schich, 'Financial Crisis: Deposit Insurance and Related Safety Net Aspects' (*OECD*, December 2008) <https://www.oecd.org/finance/financial-markets/41894959.pdf> accessed 20 August 2024.
52 Winston K. Carr, 'Measures to Promote Effective Interrelationships among Financial Safety Net Participants' in Andrew Campbell, John Raymond LaBrosse, David G. Mayes, and Dalvinder Singh (eds), *Deposit Insurance* (Palgrave Macmillan, 2007) 188.
53 Charles M. Kahn and Joao A. C. Santos, 'Allocating Bank Regulatory Powers: Lender of Last Resort, Deposit Insurance and Supervision' (2005) 49 *European Economic Review*, 2107, 2136.
54 Charles Goodhart, *The Evolution of Central Banks* (MIT Press, September 1988).
55 Law of the People's Republic of China on Regulation and Supervision over the Banking Industry.
56 Xin Zhou, 'China's Super Financial Regulator Headed by Vice Premier More Powerful than Ministries' *South China Morning Post* (Hong Kong, 8 November 2017) <https://www.scmp.com/news/china/economy/article/2119001/chinas-super-financial-regulator-headed-vice-premier-more> accessed 26 July 2024.
57 Sina Finance, 'China Will Establish an Independent Deposit Insurer in the Future to Safeguard Chinese Depositors' *Sina* (Beijing, 15 March 2019) <https://finance.sina.com.cn/stock/stockzmt/2019-03-15/doc-ihrfqzkc4180732.shtml> accessed 20 August 2024.

58 Raymond S. Sczudlo, 'Consolidation of US Banking Regulation Proposed' [1994] 13 *International Financial Law Review*, 20.
59 Tianyu Wang, *Study on Deposit Insurance System in China* (1st edn, China Financial Publishing House 2015) 197.
60 Justin Yifu Lin and Guofu Tan, 'Policy Burdens, Accountability, and the Soft Budget Constraint' (1999) 89 *American Economic Review* 426, 429.
61 Law of People's Republic of China on Regulation and Supervision over the Banking Industry, Article 38, and Law of the People's Republic of China on Commercial Banks, Article 64 and Article 71.
62 Regulation on Deposit Insurance, Article 19.
63 The CBRC Announcement on 9 May 2017 states the Regulation on Commercial Bank Bankruptcy Resolution is being drafted. See CBRC, 'Legislative Plan in 2017' (9 May 2017) <http://www.cbirc.gov.cn/chinese/home/docView/2017D188DE4B4FBABA4EE1F3A3519899.html> accessed 21 August 2024.
64 Benjamin Roberson et al., 'China's Central Bank Says Baoshang Takeover Is an Isolated Case' *Bloomberg* (London, 2 June 2019) <https://www.bloomberg.com/news/articles/2019-06-02/china-s-central-bank-says-baoshang-takeover-is-an-isolated-case> accessed 7 July 2024.
65 Kenneth E. Scott, 'A Guide to the Resolution of Failed Financial Institutions' in Kenneth E. Scott and John B. Taylor (eds), *Bankruptcy Not Bailout: A Special Chapter 14* (Hoover Institution Press, 2012) 3, 24.
66 *Ibid.*
67 Sina Finance, 'Hainan Development Bank, the First Bank Insolvency in China' *Sina Finance* (26 June 2013) <http://finance.sina.com.cn/money/bank/20130626/072415917875.shtml> accessed 20 April 2024.
68 FDIC, *Crisis and Response: An FDIC History, 2008–2013* (FDIC, 2017) 181.
69 Elinor Comlay and Jonathan Stempel, 'WaMu Is Largest US Bank Failure' *Reuters* (London, 26 September 2008) <https://www.reuters.com/article/us-washingtonmutual-jpmorgannews1/wamu-is-largest-u-s-bank-failure-idUSTRE48P05I20080926> accessed 21 July 2024.
70 Christopher Palmeri, 'JPMorgan Chase to Buy Washington Mutual' *Bloomberg* (London, 26 September 2008) <https://www.bloomberg.com/news/articles/2008-09-26/jpmorgan-chase-to-buy-washington-mutualbusinessweek-business-news-stock-market-and-financial-advice> accessed 21 July 2024.
71 Thomas W. Merrill and Margaret L. Merrill, 'Dodd-Frank Orderly Liquidation Authority: Too Big for the Constitution?' (2014) 163 *University of Pennsylvania Law Review*, 174, 189.
72 Longjie Lu, 'Bankers' Remuneration and Political Incentives in Chinese State-Owned Commercial Banks: Regulation and Practice' (2019) 19 *Journal of Corporate Law Studies*, 487.
73 Basel Committee on Banking Supervision, 'Guidelines of Corporate Governance Principles for Banks' (BIS, July 2015) <https://www.bis.org/bcbs/publ/d328.pdf> accessed 20 August 2024.
74 Guonan Ma, 'Who Pays China's Bank Restructuring Bill' (2007) 6 *Asian Economic Papers*, 46, 71.
75 See PBOC official website, available at http://www.pbc.gov.cn/jinrongwendingju/146766/index.html.
76 PRA, 'Depositor and Dormant Account Protection' (PRA, April 2015) <https://www.bankofengland.co.uk/-/media/boe/files/prudential-regulation/policy-statement/2015/ps615> accessed 26 August 2024.
77 IADI, 'Public Awareness of Deposit Insurance System Guidance Paper' (IADI, 6 May 2009) <https://www.iadi.org/en/assets/File/Papers/Approved%20Guidance%20Papers/Public%20Awareness%20Final%20Guidance%20Paper%206_May_2009.pdf> accessed 29 August 2019.

7 Conclusion

7.1 Introduction

This chapter is the final chapter summing up the studies on deposit insurance in this thesis, from comparative, interdisciplinary, and transnational perspectives. It provides a summary of the findings, the prospects of deposit insurance, the limitations of this thesis, and the recommendations for further tentative research.

7.2 Findings of the Research

Despite the earliest known deposit insurance appearing in 1829 in the US, at the end of the Great Depression, the US government, led by President Roosevelt, formally incorporated deposit insurance into the Banking Act of 1933, aimed at maintaining financial stability by safeguarding depositors' savings and promoting public confidence against bank runs. After the successful trial of deposit insurance by the US, there has witnessed the increasing recognition of its importance, with many prominent international organisations like the Financial Stability Board (FSB), the International Monetary Fund (IMF), the World Bank, the Bank for International Settlements (BIS), and the International Association of Deposit Insurers (IADI), etc., putting forward principles for building an effective deposit insurance system amid more and more countries establishing their own deposit insurance schemes in pursuit of financial stability. Notably, the US and the UK are demonstrable examples showcasing two of the most popular deposit insurance models – the pay box model and the risk-minimiser model – in the world, based on their country specifics after having undergone various financial crises. China, the world's second-largest economy, initiated its own deposit insurance scheme in 2015, illustrating the Chinese government's determination to reform an old-fashioned banking industry. To date, research on how to build a functional deposit insurance system in China, based on comparative studies, has been significantly undeveloped by legal scholars, especially comparisons between the UK and the US, which have largely influenced China's banking regulation and the rise of China's deposit insurance. Therefore, this research is principally focused on providing a comprehensive comparative study beyond the existing research limitations, through analyses of regulatory frameworks, relevant laws, and regulations associated with deposit insurance. The underlying parts demonstrate the research outcomes of this thesis.

DOI: 10.4324/9781003612759-7

7.2.1 The Nature, Features, and Good Practices of Effective Deposit Insurance

Chapter 2 conveys a comprehensive study on how to establish effective deposit insurance, aimed at finding good practices for building an effective deposit insurance scheme and providing a vital foundation for further exploration in the following chapters. Notably, deposit insurance is becoming more and more essential for maintaining financial stability and safeguarding ordinary depositors. Therefore, this chapter is going to explore the rationale, features, and good practices of deposit insurance based on international standards with the following findings.

First of all, this chapter attempts to clarify the rationale and objectives of deposit insurance. Deposit insurance, regarded as a guarantee against depositors' losses, aims to maintain financial stability by providing protection for depositors' savings so as to reduce depositors' incentives to trigger bank runs, which is one of the main causes of contagions in the banking industry because of the interconnected nature of the banking market. At present, there are two mainstream objectives of deposit insurance: the first is to maintain financial stability, and the second, which is labelled as depositor protection, concentrates on consumer protection in terms of safeguarding ordinary and unsophisticated depositors. Apart from the two principal objectives, this chapter suggests an additional objective of deposit insurance in promoting fair competition between small and large banks. However, there is a question regarding which objective should be privileged. This chapter argues that each of these three objectives is mutually reciprocal and can be fulfilled by a well-functioning deposit insurance scheme.

Good practices and design features of deposit insurance can be regarded as effective solutions against financial instability in terms of bank runs and public confidence. At the present stage, the FSB, the IMF, and the IADI have issued well-defined guidance and recommendations in pursuit of building an effective deposit insurance scheme. In light of these recommendations and guidelines, various design features and standards have to be worked out in consideration of country specifics and policy objectives. This chapter sets out discussion and consideration pertaining to universally agreed upon good practices and design features of deposit insurance.

Next, this chapter unveils the mandates of deposit insurance schemes. Regarding the mandates of deposit insurance, there are generally two classifications relating to the mandates of deposit insurers. The first, which can be classified as privately run or government-run deposit insurance, demonstrates that government-run deposit insurance, backed by the government, has adequate financial resources to fight against systemic risks, whereas privately run deposit insurance is economical without massive political intervention and a waste of taxpayers' contributions. The second classification is to identify whether the mandates of deposit insurers are broadly defined or narrowly defined within laws or regulations. The government's determination to decide the mandates of deposit insurers is mainly based on what objectives and public policies the government expects deposit insurance to achieve. Supported by many academics, deposit insurance agencies, and authoritative international organisations, a deposit insurer is better off having proper powers and mandates granted by legislation to achieve its objectives in pursuit of financial stability. The institutional structure of deposit insurance should consider the mandates of the deposit insurer and country specifics. It is suggested that a deposit insurer should be independent and separate from other financial regulatory bodies to avoid potential conflicts of interest.

Third, this chapter demonstrates a general outlook on deposit insurance from the perspective of comprehensive banking regulation. Prompt corrective action or early intervention, which may prevent systemic risks and mitigate massive costs of resolution, plays a vital role in achieving the success of deposit insurance. Deposit insurance is significantly involved in banking resolution, aimed at resolving failed banks promptly and ensuring that depositors can withdraw their savings without any disruption. In some countries, such as the US, the Federal Deposit Insurance Corporation (FDIC), the US deposit insurer, is mainly responsible for resolving troubled banks, including large and complex financial institutions. As stressed by the FSB, three resolution measures – closure, purchase and assumption, and open bank financial assistance – are generally used to resolve troubled banks. Ring-fencing, currently enacted by the UK, is a new solution to insulate retail deposits from the adverse impact made by bankers' risky investments. Under ring-fencing architecture, a retail bank incorporated in a universal bank should be legally independent from investment activities that are naturally equipped with risks and speculation. However, the practical function of ring-fencing still needs time to be proven, despite being an ideal hypothesis for protecting retail deposits.

Fourth, moral hazard is an intrinsic feature of deposit insurance that brings adverse impacts on the insuree's behaviour from an economist's view. Under a deposit insurance scheme, all parties involved have incentives to pursue risks that trigger financial instability because of the coverage and protection provided by the deposit insurance scheme. Therefore, to mitigate excessive risks posed by moral hazard, setting up an explicit deposit insurance scheme, coupled with establishing limited coverage, has become a mainstream solution to stifling moral hazard arising from deposit insurance. As argued by the IADI and the IMF, an explicit deposit insurance scheme with limited coverage might mitigate moral hazard by providing certainty and incentives for depositors and bankers to monitor banks' management on a basis of market discipline. In addition, the IMF recommends that the coverage limit of deposit insurance should be one or two times per capita GDP; however, in reality, the majority of countries do not follow the standard issued by the IMF according to the data collected by the author. It is to be said that most countries, under the current situation where financial services have become more and more complex and unfriendly to depositors and consumers, are inclined to increase the coverage limit accordingly. Co-insurance is an alternative but controversial measure targeting moral hazard, aimed at encouraging depositors to discipline banks by way of letting them share losses with bankers. However, the collapse of Northern Rock was a landmark case demonstrating the total failure of co-insurance, as the first bank run since 1878 in the UK's history. Owing to information asymmetry and the absence of professional knowledge, it is unfair and unreasonable to expect ordinary depositors to exert market discipline against banks' risky investment portfolios.

Fifth, this chapter has presented design features devoted to avoiding adverse selection. Establishing compulsory membership is an effective solution to resolving adverse selection, as all deposit-taking institutions should cover the costs of deposit insurance under the same conditions. The only imperfection is that large and sound member institutions may impose cross-subsidisation to cover the funding gap of a deposit insurance scheme. To reduce cross-subsidisation, risk-based premiums assessment appears to be a functional measure diminishing cross-subsidisation and moral hazard in pursuit of fairness among member institutions. However, it is possible that undercapitalised and risky member institutions are unable to pay premiums. At present, it is obvious that more and more countries have employed risk-based assessment to strengthen their deposit insurance schemes.

Finally, this chapter discusses good practices for funding deposit insurance. The funding resource is one of the determining components for the effectiveness of deposit insurance, as a deposit insurance scheme demonstrating formidable financial viability may promote public confidence against bank failures. Two patterns of raising funding – ex-post funding and ex-ante funding – are generally used by most deposit insurers. Compared with the ex-post funding pattern that charges premiums from surviving member institutions after a failure, the ex-ante funding model is considerably more credible and reasonable in raising the funding of a deposit insurance scheme before the failure to cover prospective losses and expenses. In addition, a deposit insurer is responsible for setting a rational level of the deposit insurance fund, collecting deposit insurance premiums, and managing the deposit insurance fund and assets safely. However, the recent financial crisis has proven that government guarantees are still supplementary funding resources for deposit insurance, as the IADI found that, during the global financial crisis, 19 member countries temporarily utilised government guarantees to ensure financial stability.

7.2.2 Deposit Insurance in the US: Experience, Country Specifics, and Institutional Structure and Reform

After having an overview of good practices and designs of deposit insurance in Chapter 2, Chapter 3 principally focusses on the development and features of deposit insurance in the US, in order to answer whether the US deposit insurance scheme is sufficient and effective, and provide a comprehensive view of the pioneer in exploiting deposit insurance. This chapter finds that the US has had a prominent impact on the global trend of deposit insurance, from the commencement of the FDIC after the Great Depression to the bold reform after the GFC. Therefore, it explores the historical development, contemporary characteristics, and new reform of the US's deposit insurance programme.

First, through a retrospective analysis of deposit insurance in the US, the chapter demonstrates the significance of deposit insurance to the US financial system. Prior to the formal commencement of the FDIC by the Banking Act of 1933, the earliest known deposit protection scheme in the world appeared in New York State in 1829, perceived as a preliminary architecture of modern deposit insurance. From 1829 to 1933, there were several unsuccessful depositor protection schemes attempting to establish integrated deposit insurance schemes at the state level. When it came to the Great Depression, under massive pressure arising from the real economy and financial industries, the US Congress eventually passed the Banking Act of 1933, with consent to establish federal-level deposit insurance to promote financial stability. The FDIC, since 1933, has assisted the US in overcoming severe financial crises and maintaining financial stability on several occasions. It is clear from the US experience that bank runs have generally been resolved by having a reliable and efficient deposit insurance scheme. Following lessons learnt from several financial crises, the FDIC has gradually become a federal regulator and a receiver or conservator of failing financial institutions with multiple measures, like prompt corrective action and risk-based premiums, and responsibility to cope with complex and large financial institutions.

Second, this chapter identifies the prominent significance of deposit insurance in US banking regulation, as deposit insurance is an irreplaceable component forming the US's banking regulation. It is noteworthy that the FDIC, as a US deposit insurer, also has broad mandates and discretion in implementing prudential regulation. Subsequently, this chapter elaborates on major primary federal regulators in US banking regulation and identifies problems that exist in US banking regulation regarding conflicting decisions, regulatory competition, complexity, overlap, and duplication.

Third, Chapter 3 comprehensively unveils the present operating mechanisms and characteristics of the FDIC from a comprehensive perspective. The principal characteristics and features considered in this chapter are listed below.

1. **(1) Institutional Structure:** FDIC is an independent deposit insurer and a federal primary regulator administered by a board of directors that consists of five members. To dodge potential political intervention, since 1993, members of the board from the same party must be less than three. The FDIC is now managing three funds – the Orderly Liquidation Fund, the Federal Savings and Loan Insurance Corporation Resolution Fund, and the Deposit Insurance Fund (DIF). In addition, the FDIC is obliged to submit an annual report approved by Congress.
2. **(2) Funding Mechanism:** the FDIC, since its establishment, has always employed an ex-ante funding mechanism. Before the Federal Deposit Insurance Corporation Improvement Act (FDICIA) in 1993, all member institutions paid deposit insurance premiums using the same ratio. After the FDICIA, the FDIC raised the DIF through risk-based premiums assessment. Having failed to meet depositors' claims because of the shortage of the DIF during the 1980s, Congress, in 1989, commenced the Designated Reserve Ratio (DRR) designated to pinpoint the optimal fund size. The DRR had long remained at 1.25 percent until 2006, when the Dodd-Frank Act increased the minimum DRR to 1.35 percent with no upper limit cap.

(3) **Risk-based Premiums Assessment:** the US risk-based premiums assessment, aimed at differentiating premiums among insured banks in consideration of banks' risk levels, is one of the most complicated risk-based assessments in the world. This system has been significantly revamped since 2006, as targeting groups have been divided into three classifications: highly complex, large, and small insured institutions. Unlike insured small institutions that are pinpointed by the combination of financial ratios and supervisory ratings on the basis of CAMELS Composite Ratings, the FDIC currently applies two slightly different scorecards assessing large institutions and highly complex institutions with different focuses.

(4) **Coverage:** after the Dodd-Frank Act in response to the global financial crisis, the coverage of deposit insurance in the US was enhanced to $250,000 per depositor, per bank, for eight specific categories of accounts, 100 times the $2,500 in 1933. Through a retrospective look at the development of US deposit insurance, raising deposit insurance coverage is always regarded as an effective panacea to boost savings, strengthen public confidence, and promote competition during financial turbulences.

Finally, this chapter investigates the FDIC's rising powers in banking resolution, as the FDIC also acts as a receiver or conservator with a core mission to resolve bank failures. By drawing lessons from the GFC, US financial regulators and academics reached an agreement that 'too big to fail' institutions should be allowed to go bankrupt without any bailout. As a result, Title II of the Dodd-Frank Act has authorised the FDIC to cope with systemically important and complex financial institutions with a new resolution authority, namely, the Orderly Resolution Authority. Under this authority, even if a complex financial institution gets into the receivership process, the FDIC is legally capable of continuing qualified financial contracts by transferring them to either a solvent financial institution or a bridge financial institution managed by itself. However, enacting the Orderly Resolution Authority has provoked massive criticism from scholars as they argue that excessive reliance on boundless agency discretion may incur low transparency and abuses of authority, leaving room for political interference. From another perspective, it is admitted that financial markets, especially banking markets, are highly interconnected so that any failure could trigger a domino effect for entire financial markets. Therefore, financial regulators should have enough discretion to implement prompt action, and getting through court orders, which is time-consuming, may miss the best opportunity to resolve troubled institutions. At present, the FDIC is generally using two resolution measures – Purchase and Assumption transactions (P&A) and deposit payoffs – to resolve failing financial institutions. Since the FDICIA came into effect, P&As, considered to be the least interruptive but flexible measure, have long been favoured by the FDIC and have evolved into three ramifications, namely whole bank P&A transactions, P&A transactions with optional shared losses, and bridge bank P&A transactions, to satisfy different interests of potential acquirers and changing financial markets. Deposit payoffs, including straight deposit payoffs, insured deposit transfers, and deposit insurance national bank are subordinate options behind P&As in accordance with the FDIC's practice.

7.2.3 Deposit Insurance in the UK: Experience, Country Specific, Institutional Structure and Reform

Opposite to the US's risk-minimiser approach in functioning a deposit insurance scheme, the UK has applied a pay box model for years. Chapter 4 mainly concentrates on the development and characteristics of the deposit protection scheme in the UK after the global financial crisis, in order to find out deficiencies and benefits that exist and deepen understanding of the UK's way to improve its deposit insurance scheme by drawing lessons from the Northern Rock run. This chapter also finds that the UK's model is easier for newcomers to deposit insurance to establish a basic deposit protection scheme. Thus, this chapter discovers the historical development, contemporary features, and especially the reforms and recommendations for the FSCS after studying the case of Northern Rock.

First of all, this chapter looks into two phases of the deposit protection scheme in the UK through a historical perspective. At the first stage, the Deposit Protection Scheme, the earliest formal deposit protection scheme in the UK, was introduced by the Banking Act 1979 in response to the secondary banking crisis of 1973–75 and the first European Economic Community Banking Directive of 1977. However, this scheme led to hostile attitudes from large and sound banks because they thought flat-rate contributions might benefit risky institutions, as contributions paid by deposit-taking institutions ranged from a minimum £2,500 to a maximum £300,000 and financial institutions were eligible to stop contributing once the premiums they paid reached 0.3 percent of their deposit base. Eventually, the failure of the Bank of Credit and Commerce International led to reconsideration of the Deposit Protection Scheme. After the FSMA 2000, which significantly changed UK banking regulatory architecture, the FSCS stepped in and replaced the old Deposit Protection Scheme. The Northern Rock run in the global financial crisis mirrored the flaws of the FSCS, in terms of co-insurance, low coverage, and public awareness, resulting in the abolishment of co-insurance and an increase in coverage limit.

Second, Chapter 4 demonstrates the contemporary rationale and features of the FSCS from a comprehensive perspective. The major rationale and characteristics discussed in this chapter are summarised below.

(1) **Institutional Structure:** the FSCS has been a non-profit-making deposit insurance scheme manager in the UK since the promulgation of the FSMA 2000. To date, the FSCS is accountable to the PRA, the FCA, and the Treasury, instead of the FSA, as any removal and appointment of directors should be determined by the PRA and the FCA whilst the chairman and chief executive need to be approved by the Treasury. Section 217 of the FSMA 2000 notes that all board members are limited

to 'public interest representatives', to mitigate conflicts of interest. In order to promote efficiency, the FSCS is now working closely with the FCA and the PRA with a detailed memorandum.

(2) **Funding Mechanism:** the present funding scheme of the UK's deposit insurance is a hybrid funding mechanism comprising the co-existence of ex-ante levies and supplementary levies against contingency, supported by the amended FSMA 2000 and the Banking Act 2009. Unlike the US setting the target size for the deposit insurance fund, the UK calculates the funding size based on management expenses levies, specific costs levies, and compensation costs levies with allocating proportions of the funding size into eight broad classes and nine sub-schemes in line with the FCA and PRA's classifications. It is noteworthy that only the FCA sub-schemes can subsidise each other when the costs of a class exceed the limit.

(3) **Risk-Based Premiums Assessment:** since July 2017, the UK has formally installed risk-based levies for compensation costs levies paid to the FSCS. Under this new system, the PRA is responsible for calculating the aggregate risk score; the FSCS takes charge of calculating the risk-based levies based on the final score and the adjustment factor suggested by the PRA; and the FCA is focused on collecting levies from financial institutions. After the PRA works out an aggregate risk score, the FSCS will determine each institution's risk-based levies based on the PRA's result. This new system seems similar but simpler than the US's scoreboard measure, which weights each risk indicator into a total score. As a nascent assessment in the UK, it still needs to be further developed with time and experience.

(4) **Coverage:** before the global financial crisis, co-insurance was a prominent feature of the UK's deposit protection scheme, as the UK government expected co-insurance to jeopardise moral hazard by incentivising depositors to monitor banks. Nevertheless, the Northern Rock run delivered a blow to the implementation of co-insurance and led to the ceasation of co-insurance. Subsequently, in order to follow the Deposit Guarantee Schemes Directive, coverage in the UK has been ultimately raised to £85,000 for deposits. However, back to reality, in light of statistics released by UK Finance and the Office for National Statistics, the current limit of £85,000 for deposits appears to be high enough to protect ordinary depositors and helpless to increase market discipline, resulting in huge benefits paid to wealthy groups. It is suggested that the UK might abide by the IADI in line with 80/20 rule.

(5) **Compensation:** the FSCS is only responsible for promptly paying out compensation claims and undertaking depositors' legal rights within UK banking resolution framework. The FSCS has super-preferred priority over covered deposits in winding-up procedures, implying that covered deposits will be first paid. To achieve this objective, Section 99 of the Banking Act 2009 requires banking liquidators to work closely with

> the FSCS. In addition, the FSCS has ultilised 'Single Customer View', an approach to capture individual deposit accounts and accelerate the speed of compensation, but, in fact, hard rules and regulatory coordination between various regulators are needed to ensure that the 'Single Customer View' is enforceable and workable.

Third, this chapter discusses lessons learnt from the Northern Rock run, which is said to have had a significant impact on the UK regulatory architecture and deposit insurance scheme. Viewed from the UK's regulatory perspective, during the collapse of Northern Rock, the tripartite regulatory framework or single regulator regime failed to function in prudential regulation and liquidity support, which eventually led to the overhaul of the regulatory framework and the start of twin peaks. Most notably, the Northern Rock run clearly reflected the UK's deposit protection scheme's weaknesses in terms of co-insurance, inadequate coverage, and public awareness. First, the banking sector is too skilled and professional, so it is unrealistic to expect normal depositors to oversee banks; thus, co-insurance should be removed, and financial regulators should take full responsibility to monitor banks as they have powers and mandates authorised by legislation and the government, most importantly, with budgets contributed by taxpayers. Second, the UK's coverage limit, before the global financial crisis, was too low to protect UK depositors who maximally could get £31,700 protection under that coverage limit coupled with co-insurance. Therefore, setting a dynamic deposit insurance scheme or reviewing coverage periodically would be a good solution, despite raising costs. Third, public awareness was another deficiency of the UK's deposit insurance scheme, given anxious depositors queueing outside every branch of Northern Rock. By and large, it is clear that the pay box model is not capable of dealing with failing banks.

Finally, this chapter gives bold recommendations and suggestions for the future reform of the FSCS. As stressed in this chapter, the FSCS should be empowered in banking resolution and regulation, with discretion to carry out real regulatory action to protect depositors, not just the function of compensating depositors. The Northern Rock run shows that the FSCS did nothing to actively stop the run, even though it was a UK deposit insurer. Therefore, the UK could start a provocative revolution of deposit insurance, giving the FSCS powers to implement prompt corrective action and resolve troubled banks. Compared with the US's banking industry, the UK's banking industry is smaller and more concentrated, indicating that it is easier for the FSCS to implement prompt corrective action. In the US, the implementation of prompt corrective action has so far, been considered successful. More boldly, the FSCS can shoulder the obligation of being a banking liquidator in the UK. Modern banks, until today, have become so special and influential for social stability. Allowing the FSCS to become a banking liquidator may be time-saving and more efficient, as Section 99 of the Banking Act 2009 gives the FSCS a natural advantage over other options. As for public awareness, the FSCS still needs to keep up with various advertising tools in order to promote public understanding of deposit insurance, which is a long-term project.

7.2.4 Deposit Insurance in China: Experience, Country Specific, Institutional Structure and Reform

This chapter answers questions about why China needs deposit insurance and how to build an effective deposit insurance scheme in China by investigating into China's recent financial reforms in deposit insurance from a transnational, comparative, and interdisciplinary perspective. In addition, this chapter provides in-depth data and understanding in relation to China's significant progress in setting up the first formal deposit insurance.

First of all, this chapter demonstrates the evolution of China's banking system since 1949. Before the 'reform and opening up' policy in 1978, due to the far-left administration's ideology, the People's Bank of China (PBOC), also the central bank of China, was the only bank serving all banking functions, services, and activities. After 1978, along with the 'reform and opening up policy', the Chinese government started operating four state-owned commercial banks and stripped off commercial banking functions from the PBOC. In the beginning stage, the four state-owned commercial banks only provided financing resources to state-owned enterprises and policy-driven projects. Later, with the developments and further opening of China's banking market, joint-stock commercial banks were allowed to provide banking services and related services to the public. However, without effective banking regulation, many commercial banks were largely engaged in non-banking activities, which led to chaos in the financial markets. In response to this situation, in 1995, two laws regarding China's banking regulation, the Law of the People's Republic of China on People's Bank of China (PBOC Law) and the Law of the People's Republic of China on Commercial Banks, were enacted to assure the PBOC's role as China's central bank, the PBOC's responsibility for regulating commercial banks, separate operation, and separate supervision. Having witnessed financial bubbles by the end of the 1990s, China started introducing international standards in line with the Basel Capital Accord, which, however, did not stop loans from flowing to policy-driven projects and unprofitable state-owned enterprises. By 2003, in order to integrate banking regulation, the Chinese government set up the China Banking Regulatory Commission, later the NFRA, responsible for implementing prudential regulation, leaving the PBOC focused on monetary policy and macro-prudential regulation. Unfortunately, massive non-performing loans were still the biggest headache for the government, which paid amounts of money into the state-controlled banking industry in order to drag China's banking industry back from the verge of collapse. Since 2008, China has further deepened its reform of the banking sector by allowing private capital and foreign banks to operate in China, however, resulting in extensive concerns over depositor and consumer protection in China.

Second, this chapter elaborates on China's current banking regulatory framework to provide a detailed overview of how banking regulators work in China. Since the establishment of the NFRA, the PBOC has turned its attention to monetary policy and macro-economic objectives, coupled with temporarily administering China's deposit insurance since May 2015. The NFRA has been responsible for conducting prudential supervision and conduct supervision instead of the PBOC since 2003, in order to mitigate conflicts of interest between monetary policy and banking supervision. However, it is evident in this chapter, that there are huge overlaps and ambiguity between the PBOC and the NFRA due to conflicting legislation. Moreover, this chapter also points out that the nomenklatura regime, which has existed for a long time, has significantly devastated the effectiveness and efficiency of banking regulation and supervision in China.

Third, this chapter probes into China's implicit deposit insurance, aimed at revealing problems and weaknesses through studying China's measures against troubled banks. Under the implicit deposit insurance scheme in China, there were generally three resolution measures: government bailout after the closure, capital injection and non-performing loan disposal, and mergers used to resolve troubled banks. Apparently, implicit deposit insurance that exposes taxpayers to massive costs of saving banks is costly, as the Chinese government, before 2008, had spent RMB 3.8 trillion rescuing troubled banks, accounting for approximately one-tenth of GDP in China. Furthermore, from China's experience with implicit deposit insurance, it can be seen that, under implicit deposit insurance, the government is undoubtedly more likely to save large banks rather than small banks, which may introduce inequality between large and small banks that substantially threatens competition and gives rise to moral hazard. It concludes that implicit deposit insurance should no longer take effect in China's banking industry.

Fourth, this chapter unveils China's long-awaited deposit insurance scheme, discussing the reasons behind this move, and the features and deficiencies of China's new deposit insurance. China first proposed a deposit insurance scheme in the Decision of the State Council on Reform of the Financial System in 1994, but vigorous lobbying from state-owned commercial banks led to the suspension of China's deposit insurance scheme for years. Since 2004, China has further opened its banking market with several bold reforms, such as liberalising interest rates, allowing private banks to enter the market, and setting up market-orientated banking resolution. These changes urged the government to accelerate the establishment of an explicit deposit insurance scheme. Eventually, China commenced its first explicit deposit insurance scheme, despite having many flaws and weaknesses. The characteristics and problems of China's deposit insurance scheme are summarised as follows.

(1) **Institutional Structure and Governance:** at present, the Financial Stability Bureau of the PBOC temporarily plays the role of China's deposit insurer, whereas in light of Article 3 of the Regulation on Deposit Insurance, China's deposit insurer should be independent from the PBOC or the NFRA, revealing the destination of China's deposit insurance scheme. Currently, there are three mainstream proposals among scholars: first, China's deposit insurer should be placed into the NFRA; second, some suggest that China' deposit insurer should be undertaken by the PBOC, under the Financial Stability Bureau; last, China should follow international standards and common sense to set up an

independent deposit insurance. In reality, China has selected the second suggestion by registering China's Deposit Insurance Fund Management Corporation (DIFMC) under the Financial Stability Bureau, which is inconsistent with Article 3 of the Regulation on Deposit Insurance.

(2) **Responsibilities and Mandates:** the DIFMC, at the present stage, only has responsibilities relating to deposit insurance premiums. In order to achieve these responsibilities, the DIFMC, under the Regulation on Deposit Insurance, is capable of inspecting documents and information regarding deposit insurance premiums. Apart from charging deposit insurance premiums, the DIFMC, surprisingly, can be a receiver and a liquidator of insolvent institutions. However, China's deposit insurance is, clearly, a pay box model so far, not consistent with the Regulation on Deposit Insurance and initial agenda.

(3) **Membership:** China has set up compulsory membership for all deposit-taking institutions, following the IADI's core principles on membership that all financial institutions accepting deposits should automatically become members of deposit insurance to avoid adverse selection. It is clear that China's arrangement on membership is consistent with the US and the UK's mechanisms.

(4) **Coverage:** having seen the US and the UK's movement to sharply increase the coverage limits of their deposit insurance schemes, China has formulated a high but limited coverage, with maximum protection of RMB 500,000 excluding interbank deposits and savings of senior management of insured banks. However, faced with the UK and the US between 2 times GDP per capita and 4 times per capita, China's coverage reached over 5 times per capita, which is prominently higher than the IADI and IMF recommendations of a coverage limit between of 2 to 5 times GDP per capita. In addition, given the wealth gap, such a high coverage may just benefit a few rich people.

(5) **Funding Mechanism:** like the US and the UK, China has also initiated an ex-ante funding arrangement with the combination of flat-rate premiums and risk-based premiums. China has a fixed mathematic formula for charging flat-rate premiums that is capped within 0.0016 percent of total insured deposits, whereas, as for risk-based premiums, any related details and calculating information have not yet been given. It is suggested that China should conceive a credible and rational risk-based assessment, between state-owned commercial banks and other banks, to promote fairness and win public trust. Apart from pricing premiums, setting an optimal size for the deposit insurance fund is a big challenge for China's deposit insurance scheme, as the current deposit insurance fund has reached RMB 81.01 billion, just 0.1 percent of total insured deposits, which is much lower than the US and the UK levels.

(6) **Compensation:** prompt compensation, which plays an essential role in maintaining public confidence, is another issue that needs to be resolved as soon as possible in China. The Regulation on Deposit Insurance

highlights three ways to compensate Chinese insured depositors, and reiterates that the DIFMC should pay off within seven working days. However, the Regulation on Deposit Insurance does not provide adequate discretion and authority for the DIFMC to implement fast payouts.

(7) **Prompt Corrective Action:** although China's high-profile financial officials, on many occasions, claim that the DIFMC would be capable of implementing prompt corrective action, the Regulation on Deposit Insurance, which is subordinate to Chinese laws under the Chinese legal system, has failed to grant the DIFMC enough power to carry out prompt corrective action. The only punitive approach the DIFMC can take is to raise premium rates against insured banks, which is likely to be enforceable and effective. Under the current situation where the DIFMC is closer to the pay box model, the PBOC and the NFRA still lead to prompt corrective action in financial markets.

Finally, despite having many unresolved issues in place, this chapter finds that the implementation of deposit insurance brings positive influences to China's financial markets. First, this move shows China's determination to create a completely market-oriented banking market, as bank failures will become possible and normal in the future. Second, China's deposit insurance could create a level playing field that enables privately owned, small, and medium banks to contend with state-owned commercial banks in a friendly environment where depositors choose host banks based on their service quality. However, just establishing a deposit insurance scheme is not a panacea addressing all problems in China's financial markets, as more improvements in banking regulation are still needed to optimise China's banking industry.

7.2.5 Suggestions and Recommendations for China's Deposit Insurance Scheme

Chapter 6 aims to provide suggestions for China's policymakers regarding building up an effective deposit insurance scheme from a comparative and transnational perspective. The goal is to safeguard depositors, facilitate market discipline, accelerate the marketisation of the banking industry, and promote financial stability. Therefore, this chapter provides some essential recommendations for China's future reforms on its deposit insurance scheme based on the lessons drawn from the UK and the US.

At the beginning, this chapter, through a comparative study, demonstrates the post-crisis reforms of deposit insurance and banking regulation between the UK, the US, and China, unveiling China's step forward towards its banking regulation and deposit insurance scheme. From the study, it is clear that China is a good apprentice, committed to learning the UK's and the US's experiences in reforming banking regulation, especially in promoting deposit insurance. At present, China's deposit insurance scheme has just started its operation based on the pay box model, which is easier for newcomers and has long been used by the UK. However, China has solid determination to build up a risk-minimiser style deposit insurance scheme like the FDIC, aimed at accelerating marketisation, protecting ordinary depositors, increasing competition, and setting up consistent banking resolution. This chapter explains how China will transition from the UK's pay box model to the US's risk-minimiser model.

Second, this chapter gives out some important recommendations for prospective reforms of China's deposit insurance scheme as follows.

(1) **Codify an Integrated Deposit Insurance Legislation:** integrated legislation is essential in China, whose judicial practice is mainly based on a civil law system. Thus, drawing lessons from the US and the UK's progress in integrating deposit insurance into their legislation, China's legislature (the National People's Congress or its standing committee) should re-arrange current laws associated with deposit insurance and enact a specialised deposit insurance law. An integrated architecture of legislation can not only mitigate the inconsistencies between different laws, but also provide coherent and particular instructions for legal practitioners, market participants, and depositors who will be frequently influenced by such rules. The recommendations are listed to resolve underlying issues:
   - A clear and detailed deposit insurance law, empowering DIFMC with the same powers as the PBOC and the NFRA in resolving troubled banks, should be enacted as, in China, regulations are subordinate to laws;
   - Conflicting rules within the current legal arrangement should be scratched, as there are many conflicting rules among various laws that confuse the allocation of responsibilities.

(2) **Introduce a Unified Bank Rating System:** learned from the experience of risk-based premium assessment in the UK and the US, China can install a unified national banking rating system to assess depository banks amid the implementation of deposit insurance, which will ultimately benefit all involved parties.

(3) **Promote Interconnection between the DIFMC and the other Participants of the Financial Safety Net:** according to Article 3 of the Regulation on Deposit Insurance, putting the DIFMC into the PBOC is just an expedient and the DIFMC finally will become an independent deposit insurer, separating from the PBOC. Thus, China should set up a tripartite network to assist the DIFMC to achieve faster payouts and risk-based premium rates, when determining to build functional deposit insurance. Facing the current financial regulatory regime, the feasible approach to accelerate China's tripartite system is to promote the DIFMC to the CFC led by Vice Premier of China, a super interagency committee similar to the Financial Policy Committee in the UK and the Financial Stability Oversight Council in the US, aimed at preventing systemic risks and facilitating coordination.

(4) **Widen the DIFMC's Role in Banking Resolution:** China's long-awaited deposit insurance scheme is expected to fill a blank space of market-oriented banking resolution. By doing a comparative study between the US and the UK,

it is clear that the global trend is that deposit insurers, as an ex-post resolution, are playing an indispensable role, especially when troubled banks become insolvent. Therefore, China should formulate and specify the DIFMC's responsibility into deposit insurance law or a new banking resolution law to consolidate the DIFMC's authority in resolving failed depository institutions.

(5) **Deepen the Reform of State-Owned Commercial Banks:** apparently, the Chinese government shall keep its promise to further open the banking market by allowing qualified foreign and private investors to start running brand-new commercial banks, without imposing any restrictions. Therefore, long-standing government bailouts or blanket guarantees, which severely devastate market discipline and competition, are no longer needed to subsidise state-owned commercial banks amid the introduction of deposit insurance. In addition, to the introduction of intensified competition, bank insolvency may become real in China's banking market in the near future, urging profit-driven, state-owned commercial banks to have good corporate governance and risk management, which could impact the effectiveness of China's deposit insurance scheme.

(6) **Facilitate Public Awareness:** the US and the UK's experience during the global financial crisis suggests that public awareness also cannot be neglected in promoting the effectiveness of deposit insurance. Therefore, the DIFMC and the PBOC should set up a specific advertising department to convey the knowledge of deposit insurance through various means, including leaflets and media that people can easily access. The FDIC and the FSCS's current advertising measures over deposit insurance can provide a good opportunity to learn.

7.3 Limitations of This Research

This research is not perfect, and there are still many limitations existing in this thesis. One limitation within this thesis is the research method. It is regretful, due to the limited time and the availability of official data related to China, that the author is unable to conduct empirical studies based on first-hand data and resources, such as interviews with bankers, policymakers, officials in financial authorities, depositors, and judges, which can provide distinct perspectives on deposit insurance and how relevant reforms can be put forward. Despite making use of secondary resources in this research, the author has made a great effort to collect reliable and integrated materials and resources. Another limitation is the shortage of Chinese official data. For instance, the author cannot access the outcomes regarding bank risk assessments conducted by the PBOC to identify the standards used to calculate deposit insurance premiums in China. This can only be achieved when the PBOC releases the total outcomes.

7.4 Recommendations for Further Research

There is no specific research concentrating on China's first deposit insurance scheme through a comparative, interdisciplinary, and transnational perspective. This research, therefore, first makes an original contribution to the academic literature and debate in this field. However, further studies are necessary to explore other areas beyond this thesis, and the recommendations are as follows:

- Although China has established its deposit insurance scheme, it remains uncertain as to how this scheme fits into the current financial regulatory architecture, which requires further studies.
- New Zealand has become the first country to abolish the deposit insurance scheme; further studies should come out to explore how depositors could be protected without an explicit deposit insurance scheme.
- This thesis has singled out that systemic risks can be prevented by deposit insurance, due to its positive effects on stopping bank runs and promoting public confidence. It would be an opportunity for researchers to probe into the interconnection between deposit insurance and bank performance, in pursuit of finding out relevant risks and designing a more functional banking regulation.

7.5 Final Remarks

This research elaborates on deposit insurance in China, the UK, and the US, as well as how China can learn from both the US and the UK. In addition, it provides recommendations for China's prospective financial reforms in terms of building an effective and functional deposit insurance scheme. This research adds substantive knowledge to existing studies regarding banking regulation, Chinese studies, as well as banking resolution and depositor protection.

Bibliography

A. Statutes and Regulations

People's Republic of China

Civil Procedure Law 2012
Constitution of the China Communist Party
Decision on People's Bank of China in Specifically Exercising the Function of the Central Bank (1983)
Decision on Reform of the Economic Structure (1984)
Decision on strengthening Socialist Market Economy (2003)
Enterprise Bankruptcy Law 2007
Law of the People's Republic of China on Commercial Banks
Law of the People's Republic of China on People's Bank of China
Law of the People's Republic of China on Regulation and Supervision over the Banking Industry
Notice of the Ministry of Finance and the State Administration of Taxation on Issues Concerning the Policies for the Deduction of Deposit Insurance Premiums of Banking Financial Institutions before Payment of Enterprise Income Tax (2016)
Provisional Regulations of the People's Republic of China on the Control of Banks (1987)
Regulations on Deposit Insurance
Regulations on the Cancellation of Financial Institutions
State Council, 'Notice of the State Council on Ratifying and Forwarding the Opinions of the National Development and Reform Commission on Deepening the Reform of Economic System 2009' (2009)
State Council, 'Reply of the State Council on Approving the Implementation Plan for Deposit Insurance System' (2015)

United States

Banking Act of 1933 (the Glass-Stegall Act)
Dodd-Frank Wall Street Reform and Consumer Protection Act 2010
Federal Deposit Insurance Act 1950
Federal Deposit Insurance Corporation Improvement Act of 1991
Federal Deposit Insurance Reform Act of 2005
Financial Institutions Reform, Recovery and Enforcement Act of 1989

United Kingdom

Banking Act 1979
Banking Act 1987
Banking Act 2009
Financial Conduct Authority Handbook, Compensation (COMP)
Financial Conduct Authority Handbook, Fee 6
Financial Services Act 2012
Financial Services and Markets Act 2000
Prudential Regulation Authority Rulebook: Depositor Protection

European Union

Directive 2014/49/EU of the European Parliament and of the Council of 14 April 2014 on Deposit Guarantee Schemes

B. Books

Bagehot, Walter, *Lombard Street: A Description of the Money Market* (Henry S. King & Co., 1873)
Barth, James R., *The Great Savings and Loan Debacle* (American Enterprise Institute Press, February 1991)
Bliss Robert R. and Kaufman, George G. (eds), *Financial Institutions and Markets: 2007–2008 The Year of Crisis* (Springer, 2009)
Buckle, Mike and Thompson, John, *The UK Financial System: Theory and Practice* (Manchester University Press, 2004)
Campbell, Andrew, LaBrosse, John Raymond, Mayes, David G. and Singh, Dalvinder, *Deposit Insurance* (Palgrave Macmillan, 2007)
Campbell, Andrew and Cartwright, Peter, *Banks in Crisis: The Legal Response* (Ashgate, 2002).
Cartwright, Peter, *Consumer Protection in Financial Services* (Kluwer Law International, 1999)
Cheng, Siwei, *Cheng Siwei on Financial Reforms* (Renmin University of China Press, 2006)
Cheng, Siwei, *Financial Reforms and Developments in China* (World Scientific Publishing, 2014)
Cranston, Ross, *The Single Market and the Law of Banking* (Lloyds of London Press, 1995)
Demirgüç-Kunt, Asli, Kane, Edward J. and Laeven, Luc (eds), *Deposit Insurance around the World: Issues of Design and Implementation* (The MIT Press, 2008)
Deng, Xiaoping, *Works of Xiaoping Deng Vol 3: Enterprise Reform and Financial Reform* (People's Press, 1993)
Financial Stability Bureau of the People's Bank of China, *Deposit Insurance* (China Financial Publishing House, August 2015)
Gardener, Edward P. M. (eds), *UK Banking Supervision: Evolution, Practice and Issues* (Allen & Unwin, 1986)
Goodhart, Charles, *The Evolution of Central Bank* (MIT Press, September 1988)
Guo, Tianyong, *Review, Rethink and Restart: China Financial Reform and Opening-up 40 Years* (Special Sciences Academic Press, 2018)
Jiang, Chunxia and Yao, Shujie, *Chinese Banking Reform: From the Pre-WTO Period to the Financial Crisis and Beyond* (Palgrave, 2017)
Kane, Edward J., *The S & L Insurance Mess: How did it Happen?* (Urban Institute Press, 1989)
Kaufman, George G., *Prompt Corrective Action: 10 Years Later* (JAI/Elsevier Science, 2002).

Lardy, Nicholas R., *China's Unfinished Economic Revolution* (Brookings Institution, 1998)
Liew, Leong and Wu, Harry X., *The Making of China's Exchange Rate Policy* (University of Chicago Press, 2007)
Liu, He, *Comparative Study on the Two Global Crisis* (China Economic Publishing House, 2013)
Oditah, Fidelis, *Insolvency of Banks: Managing the Risks: A Specially Commissioned Report* (FT Law & Tax, 1996)
Pan, Gongsheng, *Evolution of China's Big Commercial Banks: the Road to Revival* (China Finance Publishing House, 2012)
Rosenfeld, James, *The Selected Works of George J Benston, Volume 1: Banking and Financial Services* (Oxford University Press, 2010)
Scott, Kenneth E. (eds), *Bankruptcy Not Bailout: A Special Chapter 14* (Hoover Institution Press, 2012)
Shih, Victor, *Factions and Finance: Elite Conflict and Inflation* (Cambridge University Press, 2008)
Singh, Dalvinder, *Banking Regulation of UK and US Financial Markets* (Ashgate Publishing, 2007)
Tam, On Kit (ed), *Financial Reform in China* (Routledge, 1995)
Wang, Tianyu, *Study on Deposit Insurance System in China* (China Financial Publishing House, 2015)
Wei, Jianing, *The Research of Deposit Insurance and Financial Safety Net* (China Economic Publishing House, 2014)
Wu Wenyong, *Study on State Aid Legal Systems of Market Exit Mechanisms of Financial Institutions* (China University of Political Science and Law Press, 2012)
Wu, Xiaoqiu, *Reform of Financial Regulation in China: The Realistic Motivation and Theoretical Logic* (China Finance Publishing House, 2018)

C. Speeches, Conference Papers, Policy Reports, Periodical Reports and Guidance Papers

Ayadi, Rym, 'Deposit Insurance Systems during and after a Systemic Crisis (Conference of European Forum of Deposit Insurers and Federal Deposit Insurance Corporation, 2009)
Bank of England, HM Treasury and FSA, 'Financial Stability and Depositor Protection: Further Consultation' (July 2008) https://assets.publishing.service.gov.uk/government/uploads/system/uploads/attachment_data/file/243379/7436.pdf
Basel Committee on Banking Supervision, 'Core Principles for Effective Banking Supervision' (Basel Committee on Banking Supervision, September 2012)
Basel Committee on Banking Supervision, 'Guidelines of Corporate Governance Principles for Banks' (July 2015) https://www.bis.org/bcbs/publ/d328.pdf
Basel Committee on Banking Supervision and International Association of Deposit Insurers, 'Core Principles for Deposit Insurance System' (June 2009)
Bernet, Beat and Walter, Susanna, 'Design, Structure and Implementation of a Modern Deposit Insurance Scheme' (The European Money and Finance Forum, 2009).
Buiter, Willem H., 'Lesson from the 2007 Financial Crisis' (2007) Centre for Economic Policy Research Discussion Paper No. 6596.
Campbell, Andrew, 'To Protect or Not to Protect, That is the Question: Statutory Protections for Financial supervisors—How to Promote Financial Stability by Enacting the Right Law', Seminar on Current Developments in Monetary and Financial Law, October 23–27 (IMF, 2006).
Campbell, Andrew and Moffatt, Paula, 'Bank Insolvency: How Can Ring-Fencing Ensure the Continuity of Banking Services in an Insolvent Banking Group' (The INSOL Europe Academic Forum Annual Conference, Berlin, October 2015).

CBRC, '2006 Statistics of Asset Management Companies in China' (2006) http://www.cbrc.gov.cn/chinese/home/docView/2456.html

CBRC, '2017 Annual Report' (China Finance Publishing House 2018)

Council of Economic Advisers, 'The Performance of Community Banks Over Time' (White House, August 2016) https://obamawhitehouse.archives.gov/sites/default/files/page/files/20160810_cea_community_banks.pdf

Crowe, Christopher and Meade, Ellen E., 'Central Bank Independence and Transparency: Evolution and Effectiveness' (May 2008) https://www.imf.org/en/Publications/WP/Issues/2016/12/31/Central-Bank-Independence-and-Transparency-Evolution-and-Effectiveness-21903

Demirgüç-Kunt, Asli, Karacaovali, Baybars and Laeven, Luc, 'Deposit Insurance around the World: A Comprehensive Database' (April 2005) http://siteresources.worldbank.org/INTRES/Resources/DepositInsuranceDatabasePaper_DKL.pdf

Demirgüç-Kunt, Asli and Kane, Edward J., 'Deposit Insurance around the Globe: Where Does It Works?' (2001) National Bureau of Economic Research Working Paper 8493.

Deslandes, Jerome J. P., Magnus, Marcel and Dias, Cristina S. P., 'Liquidation of Banks: Towards an "FDIC" for the Banking Union' (European Parliament, 8 February 2019) http://www.europarl.europa.eu/thinktank/en/document.html?reference=IPOL_IDA(2019)634385

Edmonds, Timothy, 'Banking Services: Reform and Issues' (House of Commons, London, December 2017) https://researchbriefings.parliament.uk/ResearchBriefing/Summary/CBP-7234

Ellis, Diane, 'Deposit Insurance Funding: Assuring Confidence' (FDIC, November 2013) https://www.fdic.gov/deposit/insurance/assuringconfidence.pdf

FCA, 'FCA Mission: Our Approach to Authorisation' (December 2017) https://www.fca.org.uk/publication/corporate/our-approach-authorisation.pdf

FCA, 'Financial Services Compensation Scheme Funding Review Instrument 2018' (2018) https://www.handbook.fca.org.uk/instrument/2018/FCA_2018_29.pdf

FCA, 'Reviewing the Funding of the Financial Services Compensation Scheme' (December 2016) https://www.fca.org.uk/publication/consultation/cp16-42.pdf FCA,

FDIC, '2016 Annual Report' (February 2017) https://www.fdic.gov/about/strategic/report/2016annualreport/2016ar_final.pdf

FDIC, 'FDIC Community Banking Study' (December 2012) https://www.fdic.gov/regulations/resources/cbi/report/cbi-full.pdf

FDIC, 'Managing the Crisis: The FDIC and RTC Experience: 1980–1994', (1998) https://www.fdic.gov/bank/historical/managing/

FDIC, 'Resolutions Handbook' (December 2014) https://www.fdic.gov/about/freedom/drr_handbook.pdf

FDIC, 'Strategic Plan 2015–2019' (2015) https://www.fdic.gov/about/strategic/strategic/strategic_plan_2015_2019.pdf

FDIC, 'The First Fifty years-A History of the FDIC 1933–1983' (FDIC, 1984) https://www.fdic.gov/bank/analytical/firstfifty/

Financial Stability Board, 'Thematic Review on Deposit Insurance Systems Peer Review Report' (8 February 2012) http://www.fsb.org/wp-content/uploads/r_120208.pdf?page_moved=1

Financial Stability Forum, 'A Consultative Process and Background Paper' (June 2000) https://www.iadi.org/en/assets/File/Core%20Principles/Consultation_Paper_English.pdf

Financial Stability Forum, 'Guidance for Developing Effective Deposit Insurance Systems' (September 2001) http://www.fsb.org/wp-content/uploads/r_0109b.pdf

Folkerts-Landau, David and Carl-Johan, Lindgren, 'Word Economic and Financial Survey: Toward a Framework for Financial Stability' (International Monetary Fund, 1998) http://www.imf.org/external/pubs/ft/wefs/toward/pdf/file03.pdf

Ford, Gerald R., 'Public Papers of the Presidents of the United States' (General Services Administration, 1974) https://quod.lib.umich.edu/p/ppotpus/4732025.1974.001?view=toc

Fund, Ben, George, Jason, Hohl, Stefan and Ma, Guonan, 'Public Asset Management Companies in East Asia: Case Studies' (February 2004) https://www.bis.org/fsi/fsipapers03.pdf

FSA, 'Consumer Compensation: A Further Consultation' (June 1999) https://www.fscs.org.uk/uploaded_files/Publications/unknown/Consultation_24.pdf

FSA, 'The Turner Review: A Regulatory Response to the Global Banking Crisis' (2009) http://www.fsa.gov.uk/pubs/other/turner_review.pdf

FSCS, 'Annual Report and Account 2016/17' (FSCS, London, 2017) https://secure.viewer.zmags.com/publication/381260a7#/381260a7/1

FSCS, 'Class Statements 2017/18' (June 2018) https://www.fscs.org.uk/globalassets/annual-reports-and-class-statements/fscs-class-statements-2017-18.pdf

FSCS, 'Vision for A Confident Future' (2015) https://www.fscs.org.uk/uploaded_files/Publications/201219_fscs_5-year_vision_2014_web.pdf

Garcia, Gillian G. H., 'Deposit Insurance Actual and Good Practices: Good Practice for Deposit Insurance' (2000) International Monetary Fund, Occasional Paper No. 197, 4.

Garcia, Gillian G. H., 'A Survey of Deposit Insurance Practices' (1999) International Monetary Fund, Working Paper WP/99/54.

Geithner, Timothy, 'Secretary Geithner Introduces Financial Stability Plan' (US Department of the Treasury Press Center, 2009) https://www.treasury.gov/press-center/press-releases/Pages/tg18.aspx

HM Treasury, FSA and Bank of England, 'Financial Stability and Depositor Protection: Strengthening the Framework' (January 2008) https://assets.publishing.service.gov.uk/government/uploads/system/uploads/attachment_data/file/243413/7308.pdf

Hoelscher, David S., Taylor, Michael W. and Klueh, Ulrich H., 'The Design and Implementation of Deposit Insurance Systems' (2006) International Monetary Fund, Occasional Paper No. 251, 9.

IADI, 'Annual Survey on Deposit Insurance' (2011 and 2018) https://www.iadi.org/en/core-principles-and-research/deposit-insurance-surveys/

IADI, 'Enhanced Guidance for Effective Deposit Insurance Systems: Deposit Insurance Coverage Guidance Paper' (March 2013) http://www.iadi.org/en/assets/File/Papers/Approved%20Guidance%20Papers/IADI_Coverage_Enhanced_Guidance_Paper.pdf

IADI, 'Enhanced Guidance for Effective Deposit Insurance Systems: Ex-Ante Funding Guidance Paper' (International Association of Deposit Insurer, June 2015) http://www.iadi.org/en/assets/File/Papers/Approved%20Guidance%20Papers/IADI_Enhanced_Guidance_on_Ex-Ante_Funding_June_2015.pdf

IADI, 'Funding of Deposit Insurance Systems Guidance Paper' (IADI, May 2009) http://www.iadi.org/en/assets/File/Papers/Approved%20Guidance%20Papers/Funding%20Final%20Guidance%20Paper%206_May_2009.pdf

IADI, 'General Guidance on Early Detection and Timely Intervention for Deposit Insurance Systems' (June 2013) https://www.iadi.org/en/assets/File/Papers/Approved%20Guidance%20Papers/2013-06_Early_Detection_Timely_Intervention-publication_final.pdf

IADI, 'General Guidance for the Resolution of Bank Failures' (Basel, December 2005) http://www.iadi.org/en/assets/File/Papers/Approved%20Guidance%20Papers/Guidance_Bank_Resol.pdf

IADI, 'Governance of Deposit Insurance Systems Guidance Paper' (6 May 2009) http://www.iadi.org/en/assets/File/Papers/Approved%20Guidance%20Papers/Governance%20Final%20Guidance%20Paper%206_May_2009.pdf

IADI, 'Handling of Systemic Crises' (IADI October 2012) http://www.iadi.org/en/assets/File/Papers/Approved%20Research%20-%20Discussion%20Papers/IADI_Research_Paper-Handling_of_Systemic_Crises-Final_201210(2012-12_to_IADI).pdf

IADI, 'Public Awareness of Deposit Insurance System Guidance Paper' (May 2009) <https://www.iadi.org/en/assets/File/Papers/Approved%20Guidance%20Papers/Public%20Awareness%20Final%20Guidance%20Paper%206_May_2009.pdf

IADI, 'Transitioning from a Blanket Guarantee or Extended Coverage to a Limited Coverage System' (IADI March 2012) http://www.iadi.org/en/assets/File/Papers/Approved%20Research%20-%20Discussion%20Papers/Transitioning_Paper_29March2012_Final_for_Publication_1.pdf

ICBC, 'ICBC US Resolution Plan Public Section' (FDIC, December 2018) https://www.fdic.gov/regulations/reform/resplans/plans/icbc-165-1812.pdf

Jickling, Mark and Murphy, Edward V., 'Who Regulates Whom? An Overview of US Financial Supervision' (Congressional Research Service, Washington DC, 2010) https://fas.org/sgp/crs/misc/R40249.pdf

Kahn, Charles M. and Santos, Joao A C., 'Allocating Bank Regulatory Powers: Lender of Last Resort, Deposit Insurance and Supervision' (BIS, August 2001) https://www.bis.org/publ/work102.pdf

Ketcha Jr, Nicholas J., 'Deposit Insurance System Design and Considerations' (1999) Bank for International Settlements (BIS), Policy Paper No. 7, 221.

King, Mervyn, 'Banking from Bagehot to Basel and Back Again' (The Second Bagehot Lecture, New York, October 2010).

Kocherlakota, Narayana and Shim, Ilhyock, 'Forbearance and Prompt Corrective Action' (2005) Bank for International Settlements (BIS) Working Paper No. 177.

Kyei, Alexander, 'Deposit Protection Arrangements: A Comparative Study' (1995) International Monetary Fund Working Paper No. 95, 134.

Laeven, Luc, 'Pricing of Deposit Insurance' (2002) World Bank Policy Research Paper No. 2781, 54.

Liao, Min, Sun, Tao and Zhang, Jinfan, 'IMF Working Paper on China's Financial Interlinkages and Implications for Inter-Agency Coordination' (IMF, August 2016) https://www.imf.org/external/pubs/ft/wp/2016/wp16181.pdf

Liu, Shiyu, 'China's experience in Small and Medium Financial Institution Resolution' (BIS, October 1999) https://www.bis.org/publ/plcy07t.pdf

Ma, Guonan, 'Who Pays China's Bank Restructuring Bill' (February 2007) https://www.bis.org/repofficepubl/arpresearch_fs_200702.01.htm

MacDonald, Ronald, 'Deposit Insurance' (Bank of England 1996) http://www.bankofengland.co.uk/education/Documents/ccbs/handbooks/pdf/ccbshb09.pdf

McCoy, Patricia A., 'The Moral Hazard Implications of Deposit Insurance: Theory and Evidence' Seminar on Current Development in Monetary and Financial Law, October 23–27, 2006 (IMF, Washington, DC).

McGuire, Claire and Lee, Yejin C., 'Deposit Insurance Systems' (World Bank, 2013) <http://siteresources.worldbank.org/EXTFINANCIALSECTOR/Resources/282884-1303327122200/VP340-Deposit-Insurance-Systems.pdf

Mehrez, Gila and Kaufmann, Daniel, 'Transparency, Liberalization, and Financial Crisis' (2000) World Bank Policy Research Working Paper No. 2286.

O' Keefe, John, Olin, Virginia and Richardson, Christopher A., 'Bank Loan-Underwriting Practices: Can Examiners' Risk Assessments Contribute to Early-Warning System?' (2003) Federal Deposit Insurance Corporation Working Paper No.2003-06, 16.

PBOC, 'Basic Knowledge of China's Deposit Insurance' (July 2015) http://www.pbc.gov.cn/jinrongwendingju/146766/2165207/2813774/index.html

PBOC, 'China Financial Stability Report 2005' (September 2005) http://www.pbc.gov.cn/jinrongwendingju/146766/146772/146776/2889089/index.html

PBOC, 'China Financial Stability Report 2006' (December 2006) http://www.pbc.gov.cn/jinrongwendingju/146766/146772/146776/2899533/index.html

PBOC, 'China Financial Stability Report 2009' (2009) http://www.pbc.gov.cn/jinrongwendingju/146766/146772/146776/2898290/index.html

PBOC, 'China Financial Stability Report 2018' (November 2018) http://www.gov.cn/xinwen/2018-11/04/5337137/files/48b31c0c3cec41ac977b18a2b6b9590a.pdf

PBOC, 'Report on Steady Progress in Market-based Interest Rate Reform' (January 2005) http://www.pbc.gov.cn/english/130721/2831321/index.html

PBOC, 'Statistics of Deposit Insurance Fund' (March 2017) http://www.pbc.gov.cn/jinrongwendingju/146766/2165207/3273186/index.html

Powell, Jerome H., 'Ending 'Too Big to Fail' '(Institute of International Bankers 2013 Washington Conference, Washington, DC, March 2013)

PRA, 'Calculating risk-based levies for the Financial Services Compensation Scheme Deposit Class' (2017) https://www.bankofengland.co.uk/-/media/boe/files/prudential-regulation/statement-of-policy/2017/calculating-risk-based-levies-for-the-fscs-deposits-class-sop-update.pdf?la=en&hash=AAA45341CF34A1584C02C425F459CA20FF59BEBE

Schich, Sebastian, 'Financial Crisis: Deposit Insurance and Related Safety Net Aspect' (OECD, December 2008) https://www.oecd.org/finance/financial-markets/41894959.pdf

Talley, Samuel, 'Deposit Protection and the Spread of Deposit Insurance: Some Guidelines for Developing Countries' (World Bank, June 1994) http://documents.worldbank.org/curated/en/190571468781531830/Deposit-protection-and-the-spread-of-deposit-insurance-some-guidelines-for-developing-countries

Treasury Committee, 'Examination of Witness on Mervyn King and Sir John Gieve (HC 2007-08) Questions 1740–1749'

Treasury Committee, 'The Run on the Rock (fifth report)' (HC 2007-08, 56-I) 98–103

US Department of the Treasury, 'Blueprint for a Modern Financial Regulatory Structure' (March 2008) https://www.treasury.gov/press-center/press-releases/Documents/Blueprint.pdf

US General Accounting Office, 'Financial Services Regulators: Better Information Sharing Could Reduce Fraud' (March 2001) http://www.gao.gov/new.items/d01478t.pdf

Wesemann, Andreas, 'The Abolition of Deposit Insurance: A Modest Proposal for Banking Reform' (Centre for Policy Studies, January 2016) https://www.cps.org.uk/files/reports/original/160112130402-TheAbolitionofDepositInsurance.pdf

Xu, Bing, Rixter, Adrian V. and Leuvensteijn, Michiel V., 'Measuring Bank Competition in China: A Comparison of New Versus Conventional Approaches Applied to Loan Markets' (Bank for International Settlements, August 2013) https://www.bis.org/publ/work422.htm

Zhang, Longmei, et al, 'China's High Savings: Drivers, Prospects, and Policies' (IMF, December 2018) https://www.imf.org/en/Publications/WP/Issues/2018/12/11/Chinas-High-Savings-Drivers-Prospects-and-Policies-46437

Zhang, Tao, 'Global Challenge on the Economic Growth and Financial Reform' (Lujiazui Forum, Shanghai, June 2016)

Zhou, Xiaochuan, 'Changing Pro-Cyclicality for Financial and Economic Stability' (G20 Meeting of Financial Ministers and Central Bank Governors, San Paulo, 15 November 2008)

D. Articles

Akerlof, George A. and Romer, Paul M., 'Looting: The Economic Underworld of Bankruptcy for Profit' (1993) 2 *Brookings Paper on Economic Activity*, 70.

Backup, Benjamin R. and Brown, Richard A., 'Community Banks Remain Resilient Amid Industry Consolidation' (2014) 8 *FDIC Quarterly*, 38.

Bair, Sheila C., 'FDIC Chair Describes New Resolution Authority' (2010) 29 *American Bankruptcy Institute Journal*, 10.

Baxter, William R., Sheller, Ryan D. and Storch, Robert F., 'FDIC Loss-Sharing Agreement: A Primer' (2010) 7 *Supervisory insights*, 3.
Bennett, Rosalind L., 'Failure Resolution and Asset Liquidation: Results of an International Survey of Deposit Insurers' (2001) 14 *FDIC Banking Review*, 13.
Benston, George J. and Kaufman, George G., 'Deposit Insurance Reform in the FDIC Improvement Act: The Experience to Date' (1998) 22 *Economic Perspectives*, 2.
Bradley, Christine M., 'A Historical Perspective on Deposit Insurance Coverage' (2000) 13 *FDIC Banking Review*, 14, 18.
Booth, Charles, 'The 2006 PRC Enterprise Bankruptcy Law: The Wait Is Finally Over' (2008) 20 *Singapore Academic of Law Journal* 275, 278.
Bovenzi, John F. and Murton, Authur J., 'Resolution Costs of Bank Failures' (1988) 1 *FDIC Banking Review*, 2.
Brødsgaard, Kjeld E., 'Politics and Business Group Formation in China: The Party in Control' (2012) 211 *The China Quarterly*, 628.
Campbell, Andrew, 'Bank Insolvency and the Interests of Creditors' (2004) 7 *Journal of Banking Regulation*, 133.
Campbell, Andrew, 'Bank Insolvency and the Problem of Nonperforming Loans' (2007) 9 *Journal of Banking Regulation*, 25.
Campbell, Andrew, 'The Run on the Rock and Its Consequences' (2008) 9 *Journal of Banking Regulation*, 62.
Campbell, Andrew and Cartwright, Peter, 'Co-insurance and Moral Hazard: Some Reflections on Deposit Protection in the UK and USA' (2003) 5 *Journal of International Banking Regulation*, 10.
Campbell, Andrew and Moffatt, Paula, 'Protecting Bank Depositors after Cyprus' (2013) 1 *Nottingham Insolvency and Business Law eJournal*, 27–50.
Campbell, Andrew and Moffatt, Paula, 'UK Depositor Protection in the Aftermath of the Banking Crisis' (2010) 25 *Journal of International Banking Law and Regulation*, 488.
Campbell, Andrew, et al., 'A New Standard for Deposit Insurance and Government Guarantees after the Crisis' (2009) 17 *Journal of Financial Regulation and Compliance*, 224.
Carboni, Jessica, et al., 'Deposit Protection in the EU: State of Play and Future Prospects' (2008) 9 *Journal of Banking Regulation*, 92.
Chari, V. V., 'Banking without Deposit Insurance or Bank Panics: Lessons from a Model of the US National Banking System' (1989) 13 *Federal Reserve Bank of Minneapolis Quarterly Review*, 3, 19.
Chari, V. V. and Jagannathan, Ravi, 'Banking Panics, Information, and Rational Expectations Equilibrium' (1988) 43 *Journal of Finance*, 751.
Chin, Gregory T., 'Understanding Currency Policy and Central Banking in China' (2013) 72 *The Journal of Asian Studies*, 528.
Curry, Timothy and Shibut, Lynn, 'The Cost of the Savings and Loan Crisis: Truth and Consequences' (2000) 13 *FDIC Banking Review*, 27.
Demirgüç-Kunt, Asli and Detragiache, Enrica, 'Does Deposit Insurance Increase Banking System Stability? An empirical Investigation' (2002) 49 *Journal of Monetary Economics*, 1378.
Diamond, Douglas W. and Dybvig, Philip H., 'Bank Runs, Deposit Insurance, and Liquidity' (1983) 91 *The Journal of Political Economy*, 401, 416.
Eisenbeis Robert A. and Wall, Larry D., 'Reforming Deposit Insurance and FDICIA' (2002) 87 *Economic Review*, 6, 7.
Fan, Jianjun, 'The Urgency of Establishing Deposit Insurance in China since China's Interest Rate Liberalisation Started' (2013) 2 *Journal of Chongqing University of Technology (Social Science)*, 27.
FDIC, 'The Orderly Liquidation of Lehman Brothers Holding Inc. under the Dodd-Frank Act' (2011) 5 *FDIC Quarterly*, 38.

Flood, Mark D., 'The Great Deposit Insurance Debate' (1992) 74 *Federal Reserve Bank of St. Louis Review*, 51, 77.

Fissel, Gary S., 'Risk Measurement, Actuarially-Fair Deposit Insurance Premiums and the FDIC's Risk-Related Premium System' (1994) 7 *FDIC Banking Review*, 18.

Garcia, Gillian G., 'Failing Prompt Corrective Action' (2010) 11 *Journal of Banking Regulation*, 183

Golembe, Cater H., 'The Deposit Insurance Legislation of 1933: An Examination of Its Antecedents and Its Purposes' (1960) 25 *Political Science Quarterly*, 189.

Goodhart, Charles and Schoenmaker, Dirk, 'Should the Functions of Monetary Policy and Banking Supervision Be Separated?' (1995) 47 *Oxford Economic Papers*, 539–560.

Gray, Joanna, 'Judicial Review of Financial Services Compensation Scheme's Exercise of Power to Impose Compensation Costs Levy' (2011) 19 *Journal of Financial Regulation and Compliance*, 203.

Hall, M. J. B., 'The Deposit Protection Scheme: the Case for Reform' (1987) *National Westminster Bank Quarterly Review*, 45.

Hall, M. J. B., 'The Reform of Federal Deposit Insurance: The Options' (1990) 43 *PSL Quarterly Review*, 445.

Hanten, Mathias and Plaschke, Marion, 'EU Law Impact on Deposit Protection in the Financial Crisis: Icesave (2014) 51 *Common Market Law Review*, 299.

He, Weiping, 'Banking Regulation in China: What, Why, and How?' (2012) 20 *Journal of Financial Regulation and Compliance*, 367, 384.

Heilmann, Sebastian, 'Regulatory Innovation by Leninist Means: Communist Party Supervision in China's Financial Industry' (2005) 181, *The China Quarterly*, 10, 17.

Helfer, Ricki Tigert, 'What Deposit Insurance Can and Cannot Do' (1999) 36 *Finance and Development IMF*, 24.

Huang, Delong, Lu, Fei and Yang, Xiaoguang, 'A Comparative Study of the Risk Rating of Commercial Banks between Watchdogs in USA and China' (2006) 11 *Finance Forum*, 51.

Huang, Hui, 'Institutional Structure of Financial Regulation in China: Lessons from the Global Financial Crisis' (2010) 10 *Journal of Corporate Law Studies*, 230.

Huang, Jianhui, Wang, Yifeng and Ma, Yan, 'A Study and Analysis on Non-performing Loans of China's Commercial Banks (2017) 20 *China Mingsheng Bank Review*, 6.

Jackson, Patricia, 'Deposit Protection and Bank Failures in the United Kingdom (1996) 38 *Financial Stability Review*, 39.

Jackson, William D., 'Glass-Steagall Act: Commercial VS. Investment Banking' (1987) *Congressional Research Service*, 2.

Kaufman, George G., 'Bank Runs: Causes, Benefits, and Costs' (1988) 7 *Cato Journal*, 571.

Kleftouri, Nikoletta, 'Rethink UK and EU Bank Deposit Insurance' (2013) 24 *European Business Law Review*, 105.

Koch, Christoffer, 'Deposit Interest Rate Ceilings as Credit Supply Shifters: Bank Level Evidence on the Effects of Regulation Q' (2015) 61 *Journal of Banking and Finance*, 317.

Kochan, Nick, 'The Fuss over FSCS' (2001) 12 *Operational Risk & Regulation*, 30.

Krawiec, Kimberly D., 'Don't "Screw Joe the Plumber": The Sausage-Making of Financial Reform' (2013) 53 *Arizona Law Review*, 68, 70.

Kushmeider, Rose M., 'The US Federal Financial Regulatory System: Restructuring Federal Bank Regulation' (2005) 17 *FDIC Banking Review*, 8.

LaBrosse, John R., 'Time to Fix the Plumbing: Improving the UK Framework Following the Collapse of Northern Rock' (2008) 9 *Journal of Banking Regulation*, 295.

Lastra, Rosa María, 'Systemic Risk, SIFIs and Financial Stability' (2011) 6 *Capital Markets Law Journal*, 197–213.

Leng, Jing, 'China's Banking Reform in the Context of Globalization and Transition' (2006) 17 *European Business Law Review*, 1281

Li, Jiangfeng, 'Non-performing Loans and Asset Management Companies in China: Legal and Regulatory Challenges for Achieving Effective Debt Resolution and Recovery' (2013) 1 *Peking University Transnational Law Review*, 85, 122.

Li, Keqiang, 'Issues and Thoughts on Deepening Economic Reform' (2014) 9 *QiuShi,* 1.
Lin, Justin Yifu, 'WTO Accession and Financial Reform in China' (2001) 21 *Cato Journal*, 13.
Lin, Justin Yifu and Tan, Guofu, 'Policy Burdens, Accountability, and the Soft Budget Constraint' (1999) 89 *American Economic Review* 426, 429.
Liu, Mingkang, 'Retrospective Review and Prospect of the Banking Industry in China' (2009) 19 *China Finance*, 14.
Lovett, Willam A., 'Moral Hazard, Bank Supervision and Risk-Based Capital Requirements' (1989) 49 *Ohio State Law Journal*, 1365.
Lou, Jianbo, 'China's Bank Non-Performing Loan Problem: Seriousness and Causes' (2000) 34 *The International Lawyer*, 1147, 1192.
Lu, Longjie, 'Bankers' Remuneration and Political Incentives in Chinese State-Owned Commercial Banks: Regulation and Practice' (2019) 19 *Journal of Corporate Law Studies,* 487.
MacNeil, Iain, 'The Trajectory of Regulatory Reform in the UK in the Wake of the Financial Crisis' (2010) 11 *European Business Organization Law Review*, 492.
Mantripragada, Karishna G., 'Depositors as a Source of Market Discipline' (1992) 9 *Yale Journal on Regulation*, 548.
Miller, Geoffery. P., 'Deposit Insurance for Economies in Transition' (1997) 2 *Yearbook of International Financial and Economic Law*, 103.
Ozdemir, Nilufer, 'Implications of the Dual Banking System in the US' (2016) 44 *Atlantic Economic Journal*, 92.
Pan, Yanhong, 'Research on the Core Issues of Deposit Insurance System on the Establishment of Deposit Insurance Corporation' (2010) 11 *Journal of Shanghai Business School*, 18, 22.
Schenk, Catherine R., 'Summer in the City: Banking Failures of 1974 and the Development of International Banking Supervision' (2014) 129 *The English Historical Review*, 1129, 1156.
Schwarcz, Steven L., 'Ring-Fencing' (2014) 69 *Southern California Law Review*, 72.
Sczudlo, Raymond S., 'Consolidation of US banking Regulation Proposed' (1994) 13 *International Financial Law Review*, 20
Shen, Wei, 'Is China's New Deposit Insurance Scheme a Pancea? And Why Now? A Functional Analysis' (2016) 31 *Journal of International Banking Law and Regulation*, 88.
Shull, Bernard, 'How Should Bank Regulatory Agencies Be Organized?' (1993) 11 *Contemporary Economic Policy*, 99.
Shy, Oz., Stenbacka, Rune and Yankov, Vladimir, 'Limited Deposit Insurance Coverage and Bank Competition' (2016) 71 *Journal of Banking & Finance*, 103, 104.
Singh, Dalvinder and LaBrosse, John Raymond, 'Northern Rock, Depositors and Deposit Insurance Coverage: Some Critical Reflections' (2010) 2 *Journal of Business Law*, 56.
Suphap, Wally, 'Toward Effective Risk-adjusted Bank Deposit Insurance: A Transnational Strategy (2004) 42 *Columbia Journal of Transnational Law*, 836.
Taylor, Ann M., 'The FDIC's Enhanced Powers over Savings Associations: Does FIRREA Make It "SAIF"?' (1991) 59 *Fordham Law Review*, 384.
Vives, Xavier, 'Competition Policy in Banking' (2011) 27 *Oxford Review of Economic Policy*, 479–297.
Wang, Lijun and Cai, Xingxu, 'A Study on Exit Mechanism under Implicit Deposit Insurance' (2019) 2 *Social Science Journal*, 119.
Wang, Yiyu and He, Songling, 'Corruption Caused by Financial Regulatory Forbearance: Structural Regime and Structural Reform' (2018) 5 *Modern Law Science*, 117, 129.
Weinberg, John A., 'Competition among Bank Regulators' (2002) 88 *Economic Quarterly*, 19.
Weinstein, Harris, 'Moral Hazard Deposit Insurance and Banking Regulation' (1992) 77 *Cornell Law Review*, 1109, 1104.

White, Eugene, 'Deposit Insurance' (1995) The World Bank, Policy Research Working Paper WPS 1541.

Williamson, R. Mark, 'Regulatory Theory and Deposit Insurance Reform' (1994) 42 *Cleveland State Law Review*, 105, 114.

Wilmarth, Jr, Arthur E., 'Narrow Banking as a Structural Remedy for the Problem of Systemic Risk: A Comment on Professor Schwarcz's Ring-Fencing' (2014) 88 *Southern California Law Review Postscript*, 6.

Wilmarth, Jr, Arthur E., 'The Dodd-Frank Act: A Flawed and Inadequate Response to the Too-Big-to-Fail Problem' (2011) 89 *Oregon Law Review* 1044.

Wilmarth, Jr, Arthur E., 'The Transformation of the U.S. Financial Services Industry, 1975-2000: Competition, Consolidation, and Increased Risks' (2002) 2 *University of Illinois Law Review*, 219.

Xing, Huiqiang, 'Optimal Targets and Functions of the Financial Stability and Development Committee under the State Council' (2018) *3 Law Review*, 88, 98.

Xing, Yan, 'Thoughts on the Establishment of Deposit Insurance Agency in China' (2016) 10 *Wuhan Finance*, 7.

Yan, Haipo, 'Difficulty and Choice of Establishing Deposit Insurance in China' (2004) 11 *Journal of Financial Research*, 30.

Yan, Haipo and Chen, Hucheng, 'Six Important Relationships in the Establishment of Deposit Insurance in China' (2005) 2 *Journal of Henan College of Financial Management Cadres*, 7, 10.

Yan, Haipo and Liu, Qin, 'International Experiences on Deposit Insurance' (2007) 3 *The Chinese Banker*, 28, 33

Yan, Haibo and Huang, Ying, 'Deposit Insurance and Banking Supervision in China: The Agenda Ahead' (2008) 33 *The Geneva Papers on Risk and Insurance. Issues and Practice*, 599.

Yan, Qingming, 'Ideas for Establishing Deposit Insurance in China' (2003) 3 *Economic theory and Business Management*, 27.

Yi, Gang, 'Following the Reform and Opening Up Policy to Pursue New Financial Achievement – To Commemorate the 40th Anniversary of Reform and Opening Up Policy and the 70th Anniversary of the People's Bank of China' (2018) 23 *China Finance*, 15.

Zhou, Xiaochuan, 'Retrospective Review and Expectation for China's Big Bank Reform' (2012) 6 *China Finance*, 10.

Zhou, Yi, 'Establishing A Deposit Insurance System in China: A Long-Awaited Move toward Deepening Financial Reform' (2016) 16 *Chicago-Kent Journal of International and Comparative Law*, 66.

Zhou, Zhongfei and Li, Jingwei, 'Independence and Accountability of the People's Bank of China: A legal Perspective' (2006) 17 *European Business Law Review*, 1313.

E. News

Anderlini, Jamil, 'China Opens Door to Private Banks' *Financial Times* (London 2014) https://www.ft.com/content/7096239e-a8e0-11e3-bf0c-00144feab7de?mhq5j=e2)

Barboza, David, 'China Passes Japan as Second-Largest Economy' *The New York Times* (New York 2010) http://www.nytimes.com/2010/08/16/business/global/16yuan.html ?pagewanted=all&_r=0

Blackden, Richard and Franklin, Katie, 'Government Guarantees Northern Rock Funds' *The Telegraph* (London, 17 September 2007) https://www.telegraph.co.uk/news/uknews /1563321/Government-guarantees-Northern-Rock-funds.html

Caixin Glaobal, 'China's Small Businesses Need Effective Support' *Caixin* (Beijing, 28 August 2018) https://www.caixinglobal.com/2018-08-28/editorial-chinas-small -businesses-need-effective-support-101319746.html

China Business News, 'An Explanation on China's Deposit Insurance from Zhou Xiaochuan' *China Business News* (Shanghai, 28 April 2015) https://www.yicai.com/news/4611472.html

Fleming, Sam, Goff, Sharlene and Arnold, Martin, 'Bank Horse-trade on Ringfence Fine Print' *Financial Times* (London, 14 August 2014) https://www.ft.com/content/dfd4da64-23b2-11e4-8e29-00144feabdc0

Gompertz, Simon, 'Icesave: Icelandic Government Wins Compensation Ruling' *BBC* (London, 28 January 2013) https://www.bbc.co.uk/news/business-21231535

Gough, Neil, 'China Rethinks Safety Net for Its Banking System' *The New York Times* (New York, 30 April 2015) https://www.nytimes.com/2015/05/01/business/dealbook/china-rethinks-safety-net-for-its-banking-system.html

Halime, Farah, et al., 'Financial Regulation: Who Is Watching Whom' *Financial Times* (London, 30 July 2009) http://ig-legacy.ft.com/content/313aeca4-7864-11de-bb06-00144feabdc0#axzz5HTlfzfNy

Larsen, Peter Thal, 'UK Launches £37 Billion Bank Rescue' *Financial Times* (London, 13 October 2008) https://www.ft.com/content/83bc2cea-98ef-11dd-9d48-000077b07658

Liang, Yu, 'China Establishes Financial Stability Committee' *Xinhua News* (Beijing, 08 November 2017) http://www.xinhuanet.com//english/2017-11/08/c_136737901.htm

Masters, Brooke, 'FSA to Give Away to "Twin Peaks" System' *Financial Times* (London, 1 April 2013) https://www.ft.com/content/32ebdd78-97bf-11e2-97e0-00144feabdc0

O'Connell, Dominic, 'The Collapse of Northern Rock: Ten Years On' *BBC* (London, 12 September 2017) https://www.bbc.co.uk/news/business-41229513

People's Daily, 'The PBOC Announce It Remove Cap on Deposit Interest Rates' *People's Daily* (Beijing, 25 October 2015) http://cpc.people.com.cn/n/2015/1025/c64387-27737167.html

Pollock, Ian, 'Keydata: Where Did £450m of Investors Money Go?' *BBC* (London, 16 June 2010) https://www.bbc.co.uk/news/10273314

Qiao, Mai, 'Bank of Zhengzhou was on the Verge of Collapse 20 Years Ago' *China Fund* (Beijing, 19 September 2018) http://stock.jrj.com.cn/2018/09/19193225115717.shtml

Raybould, Alan, 'China to Bring in Bank Deposit Insurance, Step towards Liberalisation' *Reuters* (London, 31 March 2015) https://www.reuters.com/article/china-economy-deposits/china-to-bring-in-bank-deposit-insurance-step-towards-liberalisation-idUSKBN0MR1KL20150331

Roberson, Benjamin, et al., 'China's Central Bank Says Baoshang Takeover Is an Isolated Case' *Bloomberg* (London, 2 June 2019) https://www.bloomberg.com/news/articles/2019-06-02/china-s-central-bank-says-baoshang-takeover-is-an-isolated-case

Sina Finance, 'China Will Establish an Independent Deposit Insurer in the Future to Safeguard Chinese Depositors' *Sina* (Beijing, 15 March 2019) https://finance.sina.com.cn/stock/stockzmt/2019-03-15/doc-ihrfqzkc4180732.shtml

Sina Finance, 'Hainan Development Bank: The First Closure in History' *Sina Finance* (Beijing, 26 June 2013) http://finance.sina.com.cn/money/bank/20130626/072415917875.shtml

Sohu Finance, 'Bank of Zhengzhou is Going to List in Hong Kong Stock Exchange, and Who are the Shareholders' *Sohu Finance* (Beijing, 9 October 2015) http://money.sohu.com/20151009/n422778944.shtml

The Economist, 'Lessons of the Fall: Northern Rock' *The Economist* (London, 18 October 2007) https://www.economist.com/briefing/2007/10/18/lessons-of-the-fall

The Wall Street Journal, 'AgBank Finally Take IPO Crown' *The Wall Street Journal* (New York, 16 August 2010) https://www.wsj.com/articles/SB10001424052748703960004575427192644180132

Thomas, Kenneth H., 'FDIC Premium Plan Is Too Little, Too Late' *American Banker* (New York, 23 June 2015) https://www.americanbanker.com/opinion/fdic-premium-plan-is-too-little-too-late

Tran, Mark, 'RBS Buys Stake in Bank of China' *The Guardian* (London, 18 August 2005) https://www.theguardian.com/business/2005/aug/18/china.internationalnews

Volcker, Paul, 'How to Reform Our Financial System' *New York Times* (New York, 30 January 2010) http://www.nytimes.com/2010/01/31/opinion/31volcker.html

Wines, Michael, 'China Bank IPO Raises $ 19 Billion' *The New York Times* (New York, 6 July 2010) https://www.nytimes.com/2010/07/07/business/global/07ipo.htm

Wu, Yujia, Zhang, Yuzhe and Jia, Denise, 'PBOC Sets Up Deposit Insurance Fund Management Company' *Caixin Global* (Beijing, 29 May 2019) https://www.caixinglobal.com/2019-05-30/pboc-sets-up-deposit-insurance-fund-management-company-101421410.html

Wutkowski, Karey and Dobbyn, Tim, 'Update 2-US FDIC Proposes Large Banks Pay for Their Risk' *Reuters* (London, 13 April 2010) https://www.reuters.com/article/banks-fdic/update-2-us-fdic-proposes-large-banks-pay-for-their-risk-idUSN1321819820100413

Xinhua News, 'Li Keqiang Signed on the Regulation on Deposit \insurance' *Xinhua News* (Beijing, 31 March 2015) http://www.xinhuanet.com/politics/2015-03/31/c_1114827127.htm

Xinhua News, 'Report on the Work of the Government of 2014' *Xinhua News* (Beijing, 14 March 2014) http://www.gov.cn/guowuyuan/2014-03/14/content_2638989.htm

Zhou, Xin, 'China's Super Financial Regulator Headed by Vice Premier More Powerful Than Ministries' *South China Morning Post* (Hong Kong, 8 November 2017) https://www.scmp.com/news/china/economy/article/2119001/chinas-super-financial-regulator-headed-vice-premier-more

Index

Page numbers in *italic* indicate figure and **bold** indicate table respectively

For Product Safety Concerns and Information please contact our EU representative GPSR@taylorandfrancis.com
Taylor & Francis Verlag GmbH, Kaufingerstraße 24, 80331 München, Germany

www.ingramcontent.com/pod-product-compliance
Lightning Source LLC
LaVergne TN
LVHW021126300926
849160LV00010B/882
9781041010364